TEACHERS COLLEGE STUDIES IN EDUCATION
Selected Titles

EDUCATIONAL CHANGE
IN SWEDEN:

Planning and Accepting
the Comprehensive School Reforms

Rolland G. Paulston

TEACHERS COLLEGE PRESS
Teachers College, Columbia University
New York

© 1968 BY ROLLAND GLENN PAULSTON
LIBRARY OF CONGRESS CATALOG CARD NUMBER: 68–29907

MANUFACTURED IN THE UNITED STATES OF AMERICA

FOREWORD

As the author of this monograph points out, no comprehensive study of the development of the Swedish comprehensive school has heretofore been written. To be sure, several inquiries with limited purpose have been published—for instance, a recent study by Gunnar Herrström on the 1927 Education Act, which ended the period Mr. Paulston characterizes as one of "stalemate and compromise," and the National Board of Education report on the tryout of the nine-year comprehensive school during the 1950's (*Försöksverksamhet med nioårig enhetsskola*). But nobody else has made an attempt on a broad front to "disentangle and identify formative factors and forces that came into play in the reorientation of Swedish schooling from dualism to unity, from elitism to egalitarianism" during the decade prior to the 1950 Education Act, which marks the turning point in a change-over to a new school structure.

The particular merit of the present study is the attempt to relate educational change to the larger societal framework. It seems to me to be a professional disease among educators, at least in Europe, to conceive of education as if it were operating in a socio-economic vacuum. It is symptomatic that the rather heated debate in Sweden, on organizational differentiation, between-school or between-class grouping, was among most educators mainly conducted in terms of instruction and its outcomes. Few of them realized that the strong forces pressing for a unified school structure with a broadening of educational opportunities on the secondary level reflected a new social order. The two main forces, which were reinforcing each other, were the demand for equality of opportunity, for "democratization" of the system, and the rapidly increasing need of the labor market for skilled manpower in a rapidly expanding economy with severe labor shortage.

v

No political party in Sweden can take full credit for the school
reforms. The demand for a comprehensive foundation school (*bottenskola*) was first raised by Liberals like P. A. Siljeström and Fridtjuv
Berg. An attempt to implement the program was made during the
"harvest time" after World War I by the Social Democratic Minister
of Education Värner Rydén. The Social Democrats took only a marginal interest in education during their first decade of power during
the 1930's and early 1940's, following the compromise between dualistic and comprehensive forces in 1927. The pursuit of fundamental
social and economic reforms was paramount. During the 1930's the
problem of intellectual unemployment made quite a few radicals
more or less tacitly accept the principle of selective or elitist education, whose inequalities they had so bitterly attacked, on condition
that effective support of lower-class students for entry into the system
could be guaranteed.

What, then, brought the school problems into focus during the
"harvest time" after 1945? The coalition government had in 1940
appointed an expert committee of educators with the extensive
mandate to overhaul the entire pre-university school system in
Sweden. But the committee was deadlocked on the structure of the
compulsory school. Should transfer to academic programs be permitted after either the fourth grade or the sixth, as under the *status
quo*, or should all children have a common schooling through grade
six? The stalemate got a Gordian-knot solution by the Parliamentary
School Commission of 1946, which proposed a unitary nine-year school
for all children. The important period around 1945 has been intensively
studied by Mr. Paulston, who has perused many source materials
previously unutilized. We know, thanks to his study, much better than
before not only what happened in the "inner circles" when the new
policy of comprehensive education was framed. More important, we
learn through his analyses how the societal changes brought about
by the establishment of the welfare state and full employment and
the growth of the economy were reflected in the policy-making process
in political parties and popular movements. The way Mr. Paulston
has succeeded in tracing the forces behind the comprehensive reform
provides us with a fascinating illustration of how education operates
in a given, and changing, socio-economic context. This monograph
will certainly be a standard source for study of the history of the
Swedish school reform.

Torsten Husén

ACKNOWLEDGMENTS

During several extended periods of research in Sweden from 1962 to 1965, numerous Swedes kindly assisted in my search for information and source materials, and I thank them one and all. Special acknowledgment, however, is due to Vice-Director Lars Björkbom of the Swedish Institute; Rector Stellan Arvidson; Directors Lennart Bratt, Folke Haldén, and Mats B. Larsson of the Swedish Employers' Confederation; Dr. Jonas Orring of the Royal Board of Education; Secretary Pierre Schori of the Social Democratic Party; Ombudsman N. Ramsten of the Trade Union Council; and Editor Agneta Hebbe of Tidens Bokförlag.

Heartfelt gratitude is extended to those persistent librarians who assisted in the search for obscure source materials at Statens Psykologisk–Pedagogiska Bibliotek and Kungliga Biblioteket in Stockholm, at the Columbia University libraries (especially at Teachers College), at the New York Public Library, and at the Library of Congress.

My wife, Christina Bratt Paulston, translated the poem on page 24, proofread the manuscript, and in uncountable ways helped the work to progress.

I also gratefully acknowledge several years of financial support from the United States government through a National Defense Education Act Fellowship in Comparative and International Education.

R. G. P.

NOTE ON DOCUMENTATION

In footnotes generally, bracketed numbers identify references with the corresponding numbered items in the Bibliography, which provides additional information on many of the works cited in the notes. (For example, the publication data that appear in the Bibliography identify the particular edition of a book for which page references are given.)

The Bibliography is in two sections: Primary Sources (numbers 1–50) and Secondary Sources (numbers 51–182). Some authors are cited in both sections. Both sections are ordered alphabetically.

Wherever the name of an author (or other issuing agency) appears in a footnote without a title, this means that the work has been cited in full (i.e., with title and date) previously in the chapter. All such references are also completely identified by the bracketed numbers. (Letters appended to these numbers indicate that two or more works by the author or agency are cited. For example, [4c] means the third entry for the fourth author in the Primary Sources.)

CONTENTS

EDUCATIONAL CHANGE

IN SWEDEN:

Planning and Accepting
the Comprehensive School Reforms

INTRODUCTION

This study of Swedish school reform from 1918 to 1950 seeks to isolate the relevant forces and factors which influenced the content of and the controversy over educational change during this period.

The introduction is divided into two sections. The first explains in detail the purpose and organization of the study. The second presents an overview of some significant situational characteristics of Swedish social, political, and economic life as well as of the educational background during the period under discussion and the antecedent century. The purpose of these introductory remarks is to limn a background and to illuminate some major themes in Swedish life, work, and values and thereby clarify the chapters that follow.

PURPOSE AND ORGANIZATION OF THE STUDY

The purpose of this study will be to disentangle and identify the principal formative factors and forces that came into play in the reorientation of Swedish schooling from dualism to unity, from elitism to egalitarianism, in both organizational and pedagogical aspects.

The value of the study, and the need for such a work, derive in part from the relevance of the Swedish comprehensive school reform model and from the fact that—to the writer's knowledge—no comprehensive study of the origins and development of the Swedish comprehensive school has ever been written. This work therefore makes available for the first time a systematic, detailed history of Swedish educational change, an account that suggests how Swedish school reformers through democratic process successfully surmounted obstacles to radical educational reorganization and reorientation and how they were able to formulate and adopt a school reform that has placed Sweden in the very forefront of educational innovation in Europe, if not in the world.

1

There is, however, no intention to impute that Sweden's solution may provide a blueprint for other nations that may wish to follow her lead in moving from early selection to common schooling.[1] But even if, the work delineates no general laws or universal preconditions for revolutionary yet peaceful school reform, it is hoped that a serious void in the progress of one area of European educational change will be filled —at least in part—by this historical study.

A wide variety of both primary and secondary source materials have been drawn upon to document the study and support its basic assumptions. The writer has to his knowledge perused all materials relevant to the work during several years of research in Sweden and a like number of years in the United States. Although a plethora of secondary source materials on the reform has appeared in Sweden since the 1950 school act, sources for the earlier periods of formulation and adoption covered in this study are far more limited and consist in the main of parliamentary documents, articles in newspapers and periodicals, and the various publications of political parties, professional organizations, and various interest groups. The criterion used to determine inclusion or exclusion of any particular item of source material was its pertinence to the purpose of this study: the analysis and identification of forces at, work for and against comprehensive schooling.

Any effort to achieve radical school reform in countries with class-linked schools will always become an emotionally charged issue because of the highly institutionalized nature of education and because of the existence of groups with vested interests in the educational status, quo. This has definitely been the case in Sweden where education remained as the last stronghold of the upper classes after several decades of Social Democratic rule and socio-economic reconstruction. Throughout the work, the writer has made every effort to contain his bias for progressive reform and to utilize the material impartially and objectively. Wherever possible, the protagonists have been left to speak for themselves in the hope that they might have a fair hearing and at the same time impart some conception of the spirit of their times.

To this end, the historical method is employed as a discipline to help

---

[1] Schumpeter has observed with reference to the paradigm of European socialism that Sweden because of her highly developed social institutions and well-balanced social structure has achieved solutions to social and political problems, (and he might well have included educational problems as well) that will not survive exportation *in toto*: "That is why it is so absurd for other nations to try to copy Swedish examples: the only effective way of doing so would be to import the Swedes and to put them in charge." Joseph Schumpeter, *Capitalism, Social-, ism, and Democracy*, 1950, p. 325. [152]

Note: Bracketed numbers refer to the corresponding numbered items in the Bibliography (pages 147–162). See Note on Documentation, page viii.

establish the record of past events as accurately as possible, and to evaluate available sources with the application of external and internal criticism so as to produce synthesis, narrative and, ultimately, generalizations of causality. It might be noted at the outset, however, that the writer does not view forces and factors as determinants of change but rather as possibilities for choice of action. He would, for example, agree with Isaiah Berlin that "the same facts can be arranged in many patterns, seen from many perspectives, displayed in many lights, all of them equally valid, although some will be more suggestive or fertile in one field than another . . . or unify many fields in some illuminating fashion." [2] There is therefore no intent here to trace a structure or pattern of inevitable evolution of comprehensive schooling in Sweden, a pattern into which alone all facts will be found to fit. There is no one unique schema or true framework of Swedish educational reform. There is, however, the record presented here of what did actually happen at clearly specified periods of time, and in the context of what went before and what followed after.

The chronological framework below will be used in the study to organize the major periods of activity, or absence of activity, in the ongoing conflict for dualism or unity in compulsory schooling. [3]

Period I: Pre-1918. Early demands by Liberal idealists and social utopians for educational unity in the era of Conservative dominance.

Period II: 1918–1932. Conflict and compromise on partial reforms with universal suffrage and political stalemate.

Period III: 1932–1946. Priority for social and economic welfare state reforms with Social Democratic predominance.

Period IV: 1946–1950. Reformulation and parliamentary acceptance of comprehensive school reform with continued Social Democratic leadership for socio-political reconstruction.

Although there is only exiguous agreement on what constitutes historical generalizations, all historians must perforce use them to express conclusions from a systematic analysis of the sources studied. [4] A number of generalizations and assumptions are, for instance, implicit

[2] Isaiah Berlin, *Historical Inevitability*, 1954, p. 70. [61]

[3] Croce has stressed the absolute need to introduce such an organizational framework so as better "to divide the mass of historical facts and to regroup them conveniently for mnemonic purposes." He is at pains to stress, however, that the function of such a creation must be *subservient* and not *constitutive*. Quoted in Patrick Gardiner, *The Nature of Historical Explanation*, 1952, p. 57. [88]

[4] See, for example, the provocative .collection of positions on this problem in Louis Gottschalk (ed.), *Generalization in the Writing of History*, 1963. [91]

in the conceptual framework presented: (1) duality has been the central problem in Swedish educational reform; (2) attempts to resolve this problem have in the main been dependent on political conditions; (3) the final acceptance of comprehensive school proposals took place under Social Democratic leadership only after the successful implementation of their priority program for social and economic reconstruction; and (4) when faced by the beginnings of an education explosion after World War I, the Social Democratic government took the lead to reorganize Swedish schooling so that it might better reflect in both form and content the egalitarian values of the welfare state.

Correspondence between the chronological framework and the chapters of the study is not complete but follows closely. Chapter 1, for example, presents a historical overview of the long period before World War I when a few progressive clergymen, schoolmen and, later, politicians, sought to replace class-linked schools with a common citizenship school to facilitate social mobility (ståndscirkulation) and, thus, to achieve "social justice." A wide variety of historical sources have been drawn upon to portray the wide class divisions of this period which arose in part from restricted opportunity for education, lack of economic development, and highly restricted suffrage.

In Chapter 2 the first period of intense political controversy over comprehensive school legislation—a period that fell between World War I and the international depression—is described in the main through the use of parliamentary documents and periodicals of the time.

Chapters 3 and 4 recount the third period, the years of Social Democratic political dominance from 1932 to the end of World War II. This period saw the ruling Social Democrats completely lose interest in achieving their earlier program for a six-year comprehensive school and instead focus their attention and energies first on the economic and social problems of arresting the depression and the gradual building of the welfare state, and then on national survival during the dark years of Hitlerian aggression.

The fourth and final period, presented in Chapters 5 and 6, deals with the return of the Social Democrats, among others, to the idea of comprehensive schooling. At this time a parliamentary school commission successfully reformulated the 1918 common school proposals in an attempt (1) to cope with the beginnings of an education explosion and (2) to bring the highly selective school system into greater harmony with the new egalitarian social norms of a well-established and prosperous social democracy.

Chapter 7 concludes the study with an evaluation of the primary forces and factors that influenced Parliament to reject the traditional,

bifurcated educational system and to adopt in its place a comprehensive citizenship school similar in its essentials to earlier unheeded
proposals from the previous century yet in its essential character designed more to consolidate than to alter a new status quo.

THE SOCIAL, ECONOMIC, POLITICAL, AND
EDUCATIONAL BACKGROUND

The dominant characteristic of the Swedish population of some 7.6
million people is its marked homogeneity so far as matters of language,
ethnic factors, and religious affiliation are concerned.[5] This homogeneity has not eliminated problems of social class conflict, but it has
undoubtedly been a moderating influence to the extent that it has
made compromise possible and desirable.

From viking times, independent farmers constituted well over two-
thirds of the Swedish population stratified into four estates (nobles,
clergy, burghers, and farmers) until 1866. After this time a combination of rapid population increase and economic stagnation resulted in
the growth of an agricultural proletariat that sought relief through
emigration and organization into popular movements. The transformation of Sweden from an impoverished agrarian country to an indus-
trialized community has taken place in the past seventy-five years with
the advent of late (and frequently rural) industrialization and with
intensified demand for Swedish staple goods (wood products, iron ore,
and others) from other advanced industrial nations (Germany, England, France).

Before World War I the Swedish social structure in many ways
resembled that of Germany. The small privileged classes at first fiercely
resisted growing demands for universal adult suffrage, yet ultimately
accepted the worker's right to participate in and ultimately to dominate
the polity. Although much of the earlier elitist quality of Swedish life
has gradually declined under more than thirty years of Social Democratic rule, there remain even today "strong elements of ascription,
elitism, particularism and diffuseness in the Swedish value system."[6]

[5] In 1960 the main minorities in Sweden were (1) the 10,000 Lapps in Norr-
land; (2) the 35,000 Finns living in the northeast; and (3) some 50,000 aliens
who have come either as refugees or as much-needed labor. The monopoly of the
Lutheran State Church has only been slightly dented by the dissenter movement
of free churches (with about 350,000 members). See Anna Lisa Kälvesten, *The
Social Structure of Sweden*, 1961, pp. 3, 53. [113]

[6] Seymour Lipset has hypothesized that although Sweden instinctively looked
to Germany for cultural and intellectual leadership, she has—by escaping wars
and military defeats—avoided the class antagonisms that limit socialism in Germany. See his seminal work, *The First New Nation: The United States in Historical and Comparative Perspective*, 1963, pp. 235–236. [125]

Today Sweden is perhaps better known—and rightfully so—for its progressive social policies than for any other aspect of national life. Since social policy has increasingly come under state rather than municipal jurisdiction, and since social policy considerations have weighed heavily in matters of school reform, one must bear in mind the fundamental social goals of the Social Democrats. Quite apart from the natural and universal desire to enhance the production of goods and services, the basic underlying motive in the formation of Social Democratic social policy (the party has been in power continuously since 1932) has been the principle of "universality," i.e., that the government must guarantee to all citizens their share of a general welfare system as a human legal right.[7] Planning therefore becomes imperative in all spheres of national life: in the economic, to achieve sustained growth and full employment, and to avoid violent fluctuations; in the social, to improve family life and facilitate a more equitable distribution and consumption of goods and services; and in the educational sphere, ultimately, to reflect and inculcate the new social norms.[8] According to the influential Socialist educational planner, Claes-Erik Odhner, only through educational planning and the reform of Swedish education from its present "capitalist-character formation" to a "socialist-character formation, creating a socialist self-consciousness," will Sweden achieve a socialist society.[9]

The outstanding political phenomenon in Sweden's modern history must surely be one hundred and fifty years of continuous peace. Even before this period, Sweden waged her frequent wars mostly on foreign soil. This long period of peace has obviously played a decisive role in the growth of modern Sweden from a standpoint of material well-being, mental life, and attitude formation.

[7] Ernst Michanek, *For and Against the Welfare State: Swedish Experiences,* 1964, p. 7. [128]

[8] The shift of social welfare services from the municipalities, which for centuries had been responsible for "poor relief," to the state may be seen in the increase of government expenditures (as a percentage of the GNP) for social purposes: 1900, 1.3 per cent; 1920, 1.7 per cent; 1930, 3.4 per cent; 1939, 5.2 per cent; 1943, 7.4 per cent; and in 1946, 11.1 per cent. At the same time the central government's share rose from 26 per cent in 1920 and 39 per cent in 1930 to 74 per cent in 1943. Åke Elmér, *Svensk socialpolitik,* 1948, p. 307. [82b] It should be stressed, moreover, that by the 1950's only some 10 per cent of the total social welfare expenditure went for benefits to persons in certain lower income brackets. About 90 per cent was used for benefits payable *irrespective of income.* Thus, everyone was brought in under the social welfare system and the line between those paying for and those receiving benefits was to a great degree erased. Michanek [128], p. 10.

[9] Odhner has helped to draft recent Social Democrat party programs for education and is a leading party intellectual; quoted in the article by Perry Anderson, "Sweden: Mr. Crossland's Dreamland," *New Left Review,* May–June 1961, p. 45. [51]

The *riksdag* or parliament in the Swedish system of parliamentary democracy is an ancient body dating from 1435. With the decline of royal power, the *riksdag* alone has come to control educational policy-making in the gradual transformation of Sweden during the past century from an agrarian-bureaucratic state to an industrial-bureaucratic state. Because educational policy is centrally determined for the entire nation, political control in large measure determines the degree and direction of educational change. Thus, Swedish educational institutions have tended to be "enacted" institutions in contrast to the "crescive" institutions that have evolved in the United States and England with much less conscious planning.[10]

In the past century the Swedish political structure has shifted gradually through a succession of political compromises from the limited democracy of the Estates *riksdag* to parliamentarism under a constitutional monarchy. Popular pressure in 1866 brought about the creation of a new bicameral parliament to replace what had become a feudal atavism, yet suffrage remained highly restricted until after World War I. For example, by 1904 only 17 per cent of rural male adults and 25 per cent in the cities could vote in elections (with eligibility based primarily on income) for the still aristocratic first chamber. As late as 1908 only 8.5 per cent and 12 per cent respectively could vote in elections (with eligibility based primarily on ownership of property) for the agrarian-controlled second chamber.[11]

Founded in 1889, the Social Democrat party moderated its initial Marxian position and joined with the Liberals in their struggle to transform suffrage from a plutocratic privilege to a democratic right. By 1918 the Conservatives could no longer ignore this demand. Demoralized by the fall of the German Empire to which they had previously looked for moral leadership in their resistance to democracy, the Conservatives surrendered, and universal male and female suffrage for both chambers was adopted.[12] The transition from oligarchy to democracy was accomplished peacefully, and the circle of politically active Swedish citizens extended only gradually. Until World War II no one party was able to exercise undivided political power and all were forced to compromise. The Conservatives, for example, even-

[10] It should be pointed out, however, that educational administration is *not* centralized but divided between the autonomous Board of Education and the local communes responsible for most operational aspects of compulsory schooling. See Margaret L. King and George A. Male, *Sweden: Educational Data,* 1965, pp. 3 ff. [116]

[11] Elmér [82b], p. 232.

[12] The Liberal M.P. Nils Edén predicated his tactics on the assumption that Germany's fall had prepared the Conservatives for capitulation. See his own account in his book *Den svenska riksdagen under femhundra år,* 1935, pp. 302 ff. [9]

tually accepted democracy with good grace and the socialist government that it brought to power. And the Social Democrats, during their
first decade in power, were able only with Agrarian support to
pursue the practice of social welfare and security substituted for the
original goal of a planned national economy. Since World War II,
major policy differences between political parties have largely been
removed and the three major parties in opposition to continued Social
Democratic rule (the Conservatives, the Liberals, and the Agrarians)
have in large measure come to accept, if not actively support, the
government's programs for social, economic, and educational reform.[13]

In fine, the basic political developments of the past century might
be summarized as follows: (1) between the 1880's and 1920's the
democratization and industrialization of Sweden took place simultaneously and with progressively greater intensity; (2) the Social
Democratic party was one manifestation of these forces and, together
with the Liberals, championed the interests and demands of the new
industrial class and the agricultural proletariat for universal suffrage
and at times for school reform; (3) during the worldwide depression,
the Social Democrats took power in 1932 with a party program
stressing the need for reforms in unemployment and economic policy,
but with only marginal interest in forcing the reform of the parallel,
class-linked school system.

Sweden's large size, small population, and geographical position
create wide divergencies in climate, land use, and settlement that in
turn have strongly influenced the development of a national system of
education. Stretching over a thousand miles from north to south,
Sweden, the fourth largest European country, presents a wide variety
of landscape from the rich farms of Skåne in the south to the semi-
arctic wilds of the north with the mountains and the great forests in
between.[14]

Although one can drive for miles today through the forests and fields
of central Sweden without seeing another person, this has been so only
since the great internal migration of the past four decades from small
farms and crofts to the cities, accelerated by World War II and still
under way. As a result, over 70 per cent of the population today lives

[13] The writer has heard numerous Swedes of Conservative, Agrarian, or Liberal
political persuasion dispassionately defend Social Democratic programs (such as
the national pension scheme or the comprehensive school reform) when arguing
their merits with foreigners. See, for example, the humorous comments in this
regard by the Liberal M.P. Gunnar Helén, "Present Trends and Political Issues,"
in *Differentiation and Guidance in the Comprehensive School*, 1959, pp. 28–31, 36.
[101]

[14] Swedish Institute, *Facts about Sweden*, 1964, p. 50. [44]

in towns of 500 inhabitants or more.[15] As late as 1900, however, over half the population still worked the soil, and industrial development was just getting under way. Only during the past half century has Sweden changed from a nation of widespread poverty, occasional famine, and general economic stagnation to one characterized by a high standard of living, industrial development, and a heavy de- pendence on international trade.[16]

Today through the rational exploitation of her natural resources, through the application of hard work and highly developed skills, the Swedish economy leads Europe in productivity and in GNP per capita.[17] Rejecting the nationalization of industry, the Social Democrats closely linked their economic and social programs to seek essentially pragmatic rather than doctrinaire ends in economic development.[18] The rationale, undergirding this approach has perhaps been best expressed by Ernst Wigforss, Social Democratic Finance Minister from 1933 to 1949. Wig- forss, known to many in the party as *den stora anden* ("the great spirit") of Social Democratic reforms, held that:

It is both necessary and desirable to point out that one produces in order to consume. This, however, should not be taken to mean that an ever greater production of goods is something desirable in and of itself, and quite independent of the conditions under which such production takes place. . . . The real goal of economic activity is in the final analysis not goods and services but human beings and their lives in all their varied forms and with all their hitherto revealed and perhaps not yet revealed values.[19]

For more than a century the dominant theme in Swedish school reform activities has been the demand to meliorate inequalities in

[15] *Ibid.*

[16] The value of both exports and imports during the postwar decades has con- sistently amounted to about 20 per cent of the GNP. Generally favorable terms of trade have been an important benefit to the Swedish economy over and above a constant increase in production. See the concise and comprehensive study by Erik Westerlind and Runé Beckman, *Sweden's Economy: Structure and Trends*, 1965, pp. 77–81. [179]

[17] *Ibid.*, pp. 92–93.

[18] The public sector in Sweden (i.e., the central and local government sectors) accounts for about 15 per cent of the total national production and falls into three main categories: (1) mining and forestry; (2) transportation, communica- tion, power, and other public utilities; and (3) health, education, and other ser- vices. The major part of the *production* of goods and services in Sweden—80 per cent or more—takes place in private enterprise. See Westerlind and Beckman [179], p. 66.

[19] Ernst Wigforss, *Ekonomisk demokrati*, 1948, p. 9. [50a] Unless otherwise noted, translations from the Swedish are by the author.

educational opportunities and to enhance social mobility through fundamental changes in the organization and content of compulsory schooling. Sweden long shared the traditional Western European pattern of "dual" education in which the school system is to a large extent influenced by divisions in the social class structure. Yet in contrast to most countries with parallel branches of practical schooling for the common folk and elite academic schooling for the middle and upper classes, Sweden has had a long tradition of agitation for comprehensive schooling that sought to give children from all social classes a common school experience with a curriculum that stressed social and political goals over mere academic attainment.

Such a comprehensive or common school—variously called *enhets-skola, bottenskola,* and *grundskola* in Swedish—was fervently sought by isolated progressive clergymen, schoolmen, and politicians throughout the nineteenth century as an act of "social justice." [20] It was not, however, until widespread industrialization—and the concomitant growth of a powerful labor party—created an exigent need to extend and expand the parallel school system that demands for comprehensive compulsory schooling became a major political issue in the post-World War I decade. With the achievement of universal suffrage in 1918, the Social Democrats became the largest if not the dominant political party. Their support for a common *bottenskola,* only in part successful, was insufficient to overcome entrenched resistance to compulsory common schooling emanating from the upper and middle classes. Nor did the Social Democrats' call for common schooling suffice to counteract the widespread lack of aspiration for education in working-class families. Consequently on taking office in 1932 the Social Democrats took scant interest in legislating the extension of common schooling and pursued fundamental social and economic reforms. When possible, they gave strong support to the popular voluntary system of workers' schools, study circles, folk high schools and the like that had grown from the elementary or *folkskola,* in part to compensate for and in part to supplement the state school system. Not until after nearly twenty years of Social Democratic hegemony and the attainment of their program of social welfare reform priorities did the long-standing controversy on common schooling culminate in the *enhetsskola* reform accepted by Parliament in 1950. This master plan called for a revolutionary reconstruction of Swedish schooling with the total abolition of all existing parallel schools (vocational, academic, folk, and girls' schools) and their replacement over an unspecified period of time by a nine-year unstreamed comprehensive school for all Swedish children, irrespective of their social class origins.

20 See Walter E. Hurlock, *Svensk-engelsk ordbok,* 1949, pp. 189, 112, 304. [96]

This new "unitary" school would not only replace qualifying examinations with a system of freely chosen electives and thereby eliminate differentiation and segregation into separate "practical" or "theoretical" schools (to use Swedish terms) but it would, in addition, provide all Swedish children with at least a junior high school education. Besides unifying the educational structure below the tenth grade, the new comprehensive school would, according to the 1950 Act, also seek to revolutionize the inner work of the school with the introduction of individualized teaching methods and a completely altered and expanded curriculum that would emphasize "social" learning for all Swedish children rather than (as was previously the case) "academic" instruction for an examination-selected elite.[21]

Numerous studies in comparative education have pointed out that one of the most serious problems in educational reform since World War II—and especially in Western Europe—has been this very problem resolved by Sweden in the *enhetsskola* reform of 1950; the paradox of rigidly separated class-oriented systems of parallel schools in societies where the majority of citizens belong to political parties that profess democratic or even egalitarian values.[22] In such a situation where early selection by examination into separate and unequal schools prevails, the philosophy underlying dualistic schooling may not only be incongruous with prevailing socio-political norms, but in an age of ever greater acceleration of historical change with all its complex demands on the schools, the practice may well be unduly wasteful of talent and inhumane as well.[23]

[21] Stellan Arvidson, "Education for Democracy," in *Scandinavian Democracy,* 1958, p. 297. [55a]

[22] Area studies that treat in part or in whole with problems of differentiation in European countries include, for instance, W. R. Fraser, *Education and Society in Modern France,* 1963 [85]; Ursula K. Springer, "West German School Reform in Social-Political Context," 1964 [158]; and, among others, Olive Banks, *Parity and Prestige in English Secondary Education: A Study in Educational Sociology,* 1955 [56].

[23] See Torsten Husén, "Loss of Talent in Selective School Systems: The Case of Sweden," *Comparative Education Review,* October 1960, pp. 70–74 [111d]; and Glen H. Elder, Jr., "Life Opportunities and Personality: Some Consequences of Stratified Secondary Education in Great Britain," *Sociology of Education,* Spring 1965, pp. 173–202 [81].

Chapter 1

HISTORICAL ORIGINS OF EDUCATIONAL DUALISM AND EARLY PROPOSALS FOR COMPREHENSIVE SCHOOLS 1842–1918

If it is self-evident that society cannot provide one form of justice for the well-born and another for the common folk, then it is equally self-evident as will be realized soon, that it is not right to provide one sort of education for the children of the well-born and another sort for the children of simple folk.[1]

[1] Fridtjuv Berg, *Folkskolan såsom bottenskola: ett inlägg i en viktig samhällsfråga*, 1883, p. 2. [5b]

The Swedish national school system became increas-
ingly bifurcated as the state elementary school—the *folkskola,* founded
in 1842—grew to maturity. By 1900 two almost entirely separate school
systems—the six-year *folkskola* for the masses and the nine-year *gymnasium* [2] for the "well-born"—comprised a parallel structure of class-
linked schooling that had diminishing relevance to the educational
needs and socio-political conditions in Sweden after World War I.

This problem of educational dualism was not finally resolved until
the passage of the 1950 education act which in theory abolished all
competing and parallel schools, and in their place established a nine-
year comprehensive school for children from all classes of society. But
the problem of dualism had its roots in the historical past, in the growth
of the two systems, and in the early efforts made to retain or resolve
the dualism as Sweden moved from a largely peasant nation of four
estates [3] in 1842 to a nascent democracy in 1918 with the granting of
universal suffrage. This chapter presents an overview of the early
proposals for a comprehensive elementary school which were a recur-
ring and integral aspect of the larger process of social and political
change.

PROBLEMS OF EDUCATION AND SOCIETY BEFORE 1842

In part because of poor communications and isolation from the continental arena of revolutionary turmoil in the post-Napoleonic decade,
liberal influences were slow to appear in Sweden before the 1840's.

[2] *Gymnasium* in this context means the *läroverk* (i.e., school) which was divided in 1904 into two sections: a lower secondary *realskola* and an upper secondary *gymnasium.*

[3] In this work the parliamentary Estates will be distinguished from the national
estates, or social classes, by the use of capital letters.

13

And because Swedish society remained organized in a hierarchical
estate pattern under the firm political control of the nobility and the
clergy, when radical ideas did appear and found expression from dis-
satisfied farmers and intellectuals, they had surprisingly little impact.[4]
Yet the landless peasants, almost one-third of the national population,
were becoming increasingly less resigned to live with little hope and
frequent hunger.[5] With no land, they had no status or political voice in
the *riksdag* and because of the enclosure laws of the 1700's, little new
farm land was available for this rapidly growing group. Industrialism
had yet to make an impact; over 70 per cent of the population lived by
farming and stock-raising. Towns were few and poorly developed and
over 90 per cent of the total population lived in rural areas.[6] The
Scottish Liberal Samuel Laing characterized the country in 1839 as
stagnant and under the dead hand of ascription:

The mass of the nation is in a state of pupillage living like soldiers in a
regiment under classes or oligarchies of privileged bodies—the public
functionaries, clergy, nobility, owners of estates exempt from taxation,
and incorporated traders exempt from competition. The time, labour,
property and industry of the rest of the community are disposed of by
legislation for the benefit of these oligarchies;—they are the law givers
and consider themselves as a nation, and their privileges and interests
as the national interests. It is this false system of legislation, this inter-
ference by positive laws in favor of particular classes . . . that de-
moralizes the Swedish nation.[7]

Since the Middle Ages, education had powerfully served the interests of the "privileged bodies": the nobility, the clergy, the burghers.
Although together they never accounted for more than six per cent of
the total population, the three upper estates effectively used education
to perpetuate their social, cultural and political superiority.[8] It was
not, however, a completely closed society, but restricted access to secondary schooling greatly limited class mobility.[9]

Under the influence of the Reformation the *riksdag* reorganized the
gymnasium or academic secondary school in 1649 and it remained un-
altered for exactly two hundred years. It prepared its students for the

[4] Carl Hallendorf and Adolf Schüch, *History of Sweden*, 1929, pp. 371–372.
[93]
[5] Ernst Höijer, *Sveriges befolkningsutveckling genom tiderna*, 1959, p. 41. [106]
[6] Anna Lisa Kälvesten, *The Social Structure of Sweden*, 1961, pp. 6–7, 69. [113]
[7] Samuel Laing, *A Tour in Sweden in 1838: Comprising Observations on the
Moral, Political and Economic State of the Swedish Nation*, 1839, p. 151. [19]
[8] For a pre-1866 distribution of the population by estate, see Douglas Verney,
Parliamentary Reform in Sweden, 1866–1921, 1957, p. 14. [175]
[9] Sten Carlsson, *Bonde-präst-ämbetsman: svensk ståndscirkulation från 1680 till
våra dagar*, 1962, pp. 70–91. [71a]

professions—primarily the clergy and the bureaucracy—by functioning as the foundation school for the universities. As late as 1840 less than one per cent of an age cohort successfully completed its nine years of study to win the prestigious student cap.[10] The burghers, or third' estate, had long provided town, or apologist, schools for their sons., They varied greatly in quality but all tended to give more practical and less classical offerings than did the *gymnasium*.[11]

The fourth estate, the landed peasantry, had received a small amount' of schooling since as early as the fifteenth century. With the Reformation, Lutheran priests served not only as spiritual ministers but also annually conducted what came to be known as "house examinations", (*husförhör*). Everyone in the parish was then required to demonstrate before the priest that he could read and write and had improved over, the previous year. As there were few schools in rural areas, parents with the help of the lesser clergy were responsible for the education of their children in Christian dogma and literacy. The ecclesiastical' law passed in 1686 made this examination official and compulsory. Although the clergy remained preeminent in education after the Reformation, the state retained control and only delegated responsibility for, public instruction to the church.[12]

SCHOOLING FOR THE MASSES: FOUNDING *FOLKSKOLAN*

The movement to establish compulsory elementary education in' state-supported schools grew out of the influences of pietism and the Enlightenment, and the intensification of rural demands for more than, mere literacy education.

Pietism postulated that the religiously inert masses must be vitalized' through education, especially in schools for children, and that an illiterate population could not be expected to be pious.[13] By the 1830's the literacy law of 1686 had become totally inadequate as a basis for mass education. Because no adequate machinery for enforcement was provided, the law had in many instances become little more than the, expression of an ideal.[14] Landquist cites an inquiry of 1839 showing that of the 2,308 parishes in Sweden, 1,211 or over half, had neither

---

[10] John Landquist, "Sweden's Educational System," in *Scandinavia Past and Present: Five Modern Democracies*, 1959, p. 238. [120]

[11] *Ibid.*, p. 236.

[12] Edvard Rodhe, "Den svenska folkskolans förhistoria särskilt under medeltiden," in *Svenska folkskolans historia*, 1940, pp. 17–19. [146]

[13] Pietistic influences on education in Europe are described and analyzed in Wilhelm Sjöstrand, *Pedagogikens historia, från antiken till första världskriget*, 1954, pp. 147–152. [155]

[14] Albin Warne, *Till folkskolans förhistoria i Sverige*, 1929, pp. 372–373. [178]

established nor mobile schools.[15] He claims, moreover, that because the peasants began to take a more active part in the *riksdag* after the constitutional reform of 1809, their demands and need for improved education grew considerably. Whereas pietism was motivated primarily by religious concerns, the Enlightenment placed first emphasis on earthly life and accepted what pietism had accomplished for elementary education as a good basis for further development. The idea of an organic comprehensive school system it shared fully with pietism.[16]

'Institutionally, the state church and the nobility almost consistently opposed demands of the fourth estate for state-supported elementary schools up to the 1840's, but individual clergymen provided the intellectual and moral leadership for the peasants in their fight.[17] These reformers combined the influences of pietism and the Enlightenment with the more recent liberal ideals of social reform arising from the Napoleonic period. Tegnér, the famous poet and bishop, left the conservative resistance and claimed that "in a country like ours where the multitude takes part in lawmaking and the most important matters of state, crudity is unconstitutional and ignorance is treason." [18] Bishop Johan Olof Wallin made concrete folk-school proposals in his "Basis är folkskolan" (i.e., the folk school is basic) speech on October 21, 1837, in the second Estate.[19] Wallin also championed education for girls. In 1831 he and a fellow clergyman, Anders Fryxell, started Sweden's second *gymnasium* for girls in Stockholm.[20]

K. A. Agardh, friend of Fichte and Pestalozzi, attempted to introduce new psychological and pedagogical concepts into Swedish education. Agardh rose from the third estate by way of an apologist school to become a bishop, a professor of botany, and an outspoken educational reformer.[21] He advocated a national school that would embody Pestalozzian concepts, would have examination-free promotion, and be free, of the grinding homework so common in the secondary school.[22] In

[15] See Landquist [120], p. 238.

[16] Warne [178], pp. 65–79.

[17] For an account of similar earlier efforts of individual clergymen in the eighteenth century, see Nils G. Ohlson, *Det pedagogiska problemet i Sverige under frihetstiden och gustavianska tiden till omkring år 1805*, 1939, *passim*. [138]

[18] Cited in K. A. Hultquist, *Om Tegnér och folkskolan*, 1925, pp. 36–37. [110]

[19] Riksdagen, *Prestestândets protokoller vid riksdagarne, 1837*, II, pp. 181–189. [39h]

[20] Klas Aquilonius, "Det svenska folkundervisningsväsendet 1809–1860," in *Svenska folkskolans historia*, 1942, p. 213. [53]

[21] Landquist [120], p. 237.

[22] K. A. Agardh, *Slutanförande: betänkande af comiten till öfverseendet af rikets allmänna undervisningsverk*, 1829, pp. 7–9, 21–22. [1c]

his unsuccessful demands for greater classroom freedom for natural student interaction and for what has become known today as "activity, methods," Agardh put forth an interesting justification: "Experience shows that persons who are forced to stay together without talking become furious or desperate, but this system is almost completely universal in our schools." [23] In this, Agardh opposed the strong Prussian influence in the *gymnasium,* which saw the school as a place for preparation, recitation and repetition of tasks. His long efforts to encourage the creation of a national elementary school for group work and for social and individual activity, however, accomplished little in his life time.

Dean, clergyman, and historian, Anders Fryxell heartily approved of Agardh's proposals and was to take them several steps further. In 1823 he sounded the battle cry for compulsory schools that would (1) stress political socialization, i.e., be "citizenship schools"; (2) be comprehensive, i.e., be the only elementary school for all children; and (3) be not terminal institutions but, rather, organically related foundation schools for the *gymnasium* that prepared for the universities.[24]

In his pamphlet "Proposal for unity and citizenship training in the public educational structure," Fryxell rebelled against the estate-stamp that had characterized Swedish schooling since the Middle Ages.[25] Private tutoring and the military academies, the academic schools, the apologist or general schools of the towns, and the sexton teaching in rural homes comprised a four-step educational structure corresponding to and perpetuating, he believed, the four estates. Fryxell warned that "Sweden's four estates through four different systems of education will, in time create four rigid castes as in India." [26]

The corrective, which Fryxell proposed for this problem and reiterated in his several works, called for a unified school system of organically articulated successive steps founded on a common elementary school for all classes and free from the pernicious instruction in Latin.[27] This solution would stimulate, according to Fryxell, social cooperation and patriotism; it would equalize educational opportunity; and it would aid and facilitate selection of the most able students for

[23] K. A. Agardh, *Försök till rättfärdigande av det nya skolsystemet,* 1844, p. 38. [1a]

[24] A comprehensive study of Fryxell's seminal work in its close relationship to somewhat similar proposals by the *gymnasium* rectors Broocman and Silverstolpe between 1809 and 1832 is included in Bror R. Hall (ed.), "Tidiga enhetsskole-tankar," *Föreningen för Svensk Undervisningshistoria,* 1926, pp. 3–31. [92]

[25] Anders Fryxell, *Förslag till enhet och medborgerlighet i de allmänna undervisningsverken,* 1823, pp. 7–16. [15]

[26] *Ibid.,* p. 1.

[27] Hall [92], pp. 3–31.

later academic study in the *gymnasium*. Although Fryxell did not live to see his proposals materialize, his theme that "a reorganization of the schools is an act of social justice" and that "all children of the state should go to a common school for all" launched a movement for educational reform that from its inception advanced social reasons for a comprehensive school at the elementary level and for an organically unified system of education.[28]

⸋ Although Agardh, Wallin, Fryxell, and others agitated widely for a "modern" state elementary school, the highly conservative *riksdag* hesitated to legislate a school devoted to the full development of the individual, regardless of his social standing.[29] Rather, in the decades before 1842, these reformers prepared the way for the *folkskola* principally by emphasizing the growing dangers of a lack of adequate public schooling for both the landed and landless rural population. Their intellectual leadership received its strongest but by no means unanimous support from the fourth estate, the land-owning farmers who made up almost two-thirds of the population.[30]

'By the 1840's the farmers—although in the main functionally literate —began a concerned effort for legislation to establish free rural schools.[31] Debates in the peasant chamber illustrate their lack of identification with the idealistic proposals made by intellectual reformers on their behalf. Their needs and proposals were more practical. Many were torn between the desire to give their children the obvious advantages of better education (as they had seen in the apologist schools in the towns) and the fear of what it would cost in money and increased subjugation to the clergy.[32] On all sides they became increasingly exposed to new agencies that tended to support and excite demand for education and moral improvement: public libraries, philanthropic schools, the temperance movement,[33] labor movements, educational circles and societies to promote education—in short, the entire complex

[28] A brief account of the early reform movement for comprehensive or *enhetsskola* may be found in Eve Malmqvist, "Enhetsskoletanken i Sverige: en historisk överblick," *Skola och Samhälle*, 1952, pp. 161–167. [127]

[29] The general resistance of the upper two Estates to any reform with a liberal connotation, and their dominance in lawmaking during the nineteenth century and after, is well documented in Verney [175], pp. 76–77 ff.

[30] Malmqvist [127], p. 163.

[31] Laing noted with discouragement in 1838 that a high degree of public literacy and a low state of morals could co-exist. Laing, [19], p. 275.

[32] Riksdagen, *Bondeståndets protokoller vid riksdagarne, 1828–1830*, II, pp. 397 ff. [39a]

[33] This influence is clearly evident in the enthusiastic battle cry of the temperance societies at that time: "Down with the distilleries, up with the schools! Out with strong drink and in with good books." Quoted in Paul Bergevin, *Adult Education in Sweden: An Introduction*, 1961, p. 26. [58]

of folk movements that accompanied the development of Christian socialism in much of Europe after the 1830's.[34]

Early attempts by the fourth estate to instigate school legislation' at first centered on the pros and cons of the Bell-Lancaster system. A school of this type would, it was argued in 1828, (1) meet rural educational needs; (2) be cheap to operate; and (3) be difficult for the clergy to dominate.[35] However, the bill that each parish establish a monitorial school failed to gain a majority. Yet the notion that schools of some sort were absolutely necessary was, nevertheless, widely held by the farm population. Anders Nilson from Värmland supported the, proposals in a somewhat awkward fashion by claiming that "the other three estates being already enlightened could not fully appreciate what it meant to be deprived of this blessing." [36]

The peasants' class consciousness, moreover, prompted them to stand on certain definite principles. They recognized the right of the state to create and control schools but insisted that as much immediate control as possible be vested in boards of elected communal authorities. They wanted elementary schools to be financed to a large extent—as' were all the state academic secondary schools—by the national treasury. They wanted educational costs spread as widely as possible and would not permit the school system to become a feeding ground of, bureaucrats and clergy.[37]

Economic conditions, as well as social considerations, also influenced' the creation of a Swedish elementary school system. The years from 1807 to 1830 were depressed economically and little money was available. In addition, the disposition in the Estates for the appropriation of funds to popular education was in the main viewed unsympathetically, by the upper three estates.[38] Other considerations influencing the founding of the *folkskola* were social and demographic changes which aggravated the rural need for both qualitative and quantitative increases in compulsory education. For example, a pronounced struc-\ tural change in Swedish society took place in the ninety years between 1750 and 1840. The most marked symptoms were (1) a rapid increase in the total population; and (2) a "proletarization" of the rural lower classes. Following the successful application of the enclosure laws during this period, the number of land-owning farmers increased only

[34] See the chapter "Labor and Poverty" in B. J. Hovde, *The Scandinavian Countries, 1720–1865: The Rise of the Middle Classes,* 1948, pp. 647 ff. [109]

[35] Riksdagen [39a], pp. 521–538.

[36] Quoted in Sven Nylund, *Våra folkskolor,* 1924, p. 7. [137]

[37] Stig Jägerskiöld, *Från prästskola till enhetsskola,* 1959, pp. 35–40. [112]

[38] Arthur Montgomery, *Svensk socialpolitik under 1800-talet,* 1934, pp. 125 ff. [130c]

16 per cent, while the number of landless peasants (and crofters) more than quadrupled and by 1840 they were nearly as numerous as the farmers who had little interest in these rural poor. This development made the Estates system in both a political and social sense totally unrepresentative.[39]

Tegnér believed the causes of increased population to be "peace, potatoes, and vaccination," but the ensuing problems of hunger, unemployment, and child labor he blamed on lack of administrative initiative in stimulating employment and on the long-standing paucity of popular schooling.[40] The urban areas were not greatly affected. They accounted—usually in very small towns—for only 9.77 per cent of the total Swedish population in 1800 and 12.95 per cent in 1870.[41] Until the 1850's, the population increase was almost entirely a rural phenomenon; but even so it was of sufficient magnitude to disrupt the traditional social pattern.

The old communal system that schooled in literacy and protected the weaker social elements with poor relief began to break down under the influence of rural poverty and unemployment on the one hand, and individualistic, profit-seeking agriculture on the other. The farmer (with what might be called the agricultural revolution) began to account for his expenses and income more carefully and in the process frequently reduced his labor needs and also reduced his charity.[42] Consequently, parish schooling deteriorated and the feeble attempts of philanthropy helped only slightly.[43] Reports of the Swedish provincial governors in 1822 showed that there were few parish schools, but also, because of home instruction, few illiterates.[44] In the 1835 riksdag every chamber requested that the government initiate some action for state elementary education to cope with the serious problem of growing folk discontent. They all, however, recommended that the communes should not be forced to establish and maintain schools.[45] Moreover, the fear was prevalent among the upper estates that to permit the fourth and "fifth" estates to share—as they increasingly demanded—the educational ad-

[39] Nils Wohlin, Den jordbruksidkande befolkningen i Sverige 1751–1900, 1909, pp. 1–51. [182a]

[40] Esaias Tegnér, Om fattigvården i Vexiö stift, 1848, p. 327 [46]; Hultqvist, [110], p. 44.

[41] Statistisk årsbok för Sverige, 1930, p. 4. [42]

[42] See Nils Wohlin, Svenska jordstyckningspolitiken, 1936, pp. 716 ff. [182b]

[43] Individual philanthropy between 1820 and 1842 founded some 786 charity schools—mostly urban—attended by over 30,000 pupils. See C. C. Andrews, "Report on the Educational System of Sweden," 1871, p. 7. [3]

[44] Landshöfdinge berättelser, 1822, Kronobergs län, p. 17; Jönköpings län, p. 5. [20]

[45] Simon Nordström, Kort öfversikt öfver det svenska folkskoleväsendets utveckling till år 1842, 1887, pp. 25–26. [136]

vantages of the upper classes would be tantamount to sowing the seeds of revolt.[46] In the very least, it was warned, if schooling were to be provided for children of the rural proletariat (who in the 1840's numbered nearly one million), they would soon demand political, representation as well.

The liberal K. A. Agardh attacked the opponents of the "folk" school idea in an address before the new Society for the Dissemination of Useful Popular Literature in Karlstad Diocese, July 22, 1837.[47] He rejected the upper-class rationale that better education would incite the masses to rebel. Although Agardh stressed the seriousness of the social crises in Sweden and elsewhere in Europe, he insisted that the danger lay not in the granting of compulsory education to the working class but rather "solely in the faulty organization of society, itself." [48] And for Agardh, Fryxell, and the other liberal educational reformers education especially in a comprehensive elementary school would provide a primary lever to reconstruct the faulty organization of society.[49]

Pushed by liberal reform partisans from the three upper estates, peasant demands, and increasingly severe social dislocation, the government circularized the twelve councils of bishops on the practicability of establishing compulsory schools. Replies of the councils, which held responsibility for the operation of all academic *gymnasia*, limned a revealing picture of the intensity of clerical opposition. The bishops replied promptly, and they unanimously opposed any innovation in the field of folk education. Their reasons may be summarized as follows: (1) education is a local responsibility in which the state should not meddle; (2) poverty and lack of appropriate clothing would prevent the attendance of most children; (3) sufficient educational opportunities exist; and (4) the peasantry ought not to receive any further education beyond reading, writing, elementary arithmetic, and "a sufficient knowledge of religion." [50] The Bishop at Lund, the seat of a university, offered his solution to the problem: "The proposed system of public schools cannot be introduced into Sweden, which naturally disposes of the question whether it ought to be introduced. . . . Although by such means," he continued, "we may acquire an intelligent

---

[46] *Ibid.*, p. 30.

[47] K. A. Agardh, *Om de lägre folkklassernas upplysning,* 1837, pp. 28–32. [1b]

[48] *Ibid.*, p. 29. Some three decades later in 1868, the Liberal M.P. and common school champion Adolph Hedin prescribed the same solution even more emphatically: "To those who complain of the dangers of democracy and who are so terrified of these dangers, we can recommend only one means of avoiding them. This means is infallible and its name is Popular Education." See Hall [92], p. 70.

[49] Malmqvist [127], pp. 162–163.

[50] Andrews [3], pp. 9, 10.

folk it does not thereby follow we shall have a good folk." The Bishop concluded that "if Sweden has a folk who fear God and honor their King, they may disregard the learning that is only found in books."[51]

The views and desires of the Bishop of Lund and the forces for the defense of the status quo that he represented did not, however, prevail completely, as becomes clear with subsequent developments. In the same year that the councils replied, Laing remarked on the restless aspirations of the Swedish people, including their demand for schools, which he prophetically believed all the powers of conservatism could not stop:

Society in the present age is on the eve of a mighty change—is in the act of transition from a lower to a higher state; and human powers—a Swedish king, a Russian Emperor, or an alliance, holy or unholy, of all earthly potentates—can no more arrest its progress, than they can prevent the transition of the living generation to another state of being.[52]

THE FOLKSKOLA ACT

In large part through the enlightened interest and leadership of Crown Prince Oscar, the government brought in a bill in 1840 for a nationwide system of elementary schools. The bill was modified in debate and eventually accepted by the Estates in 1841, and was signed by the king in a law of June 18, 1842. For the first time all Swedish children would be required by law to attend school. Every parish—the civil and religious administrative unit in Sweden—would be required to maintain at least one school with at least one seminary-trained teacher.[53] To the consternation of the farmers, both administration and financial support for folkskolan devolved on the parish.

The requirement to build, organize and staff a new school system imposed heavy, indeed almost impossible, educational and financial burdens on the parishes. State subventions were available in small amounts only for the more impoverished parishes and to facilitate the creation of teacher training institutions.[54] The negative consequences of the delegation of nearly all responsibility for the new school to unprepared and frequently impoverished local communities soon became apparent: (1) elementary school quality and development were

[51] Quoted by Andrews, in *ibid.*, p. 11.
[52] Laing [19], p. 431.
[53] Aquilonius [53], pp. 313–317, 318.
[54] The farmers' plan to have *folkskola* teachers trained in the *gymnasium* was defeated by the nobility and clergy who wanted no changes in the secondary school's classical curriculum.

extremely uneven for the following four or five decades; (2) over one-third of all children continued as in the previous century to receive instruction at home or in "ambulatory schools"; [55] (3) in the absence of administrative directives for textbooks or a common curriculum, and with very few formally trained teachers, the clergy to a considerable extent was able to continue its earlier role of putting a religious stamp on supposedly secular compulsory education; [56] and (4) folk schools because of their limited support and unsatisfactory conditions tended to be looked upon by the estates as well as by the working class as a continuation of the charity schools (*fattigskolor*) which they had in many cases replaced in name only.[57]

The *riksdag*'s reaction to the pressures to extend the educational system so as to include the lowest social levels had in reality made no more than a minimal response in the *Folkskola* Act. In the four decades following the Act, however, the school was gradually, if laboriously, improved. Two men, one a liberal educator, the other a conservative politician, took the lead in this work. The educator, Per Adam Siljeström, sought to achieve a *folkskola* strong enough to serve as a comprehensive elementary school and the sole foundation school for the *gymnasium*. The politician, F. F. Carlson, as Minister of Education in the Conservative governments from 1863 to 1870 and from 1875 to 1878, also sought to improve and strengthen the *folkskola*, but primarily through improved external control and supervision in the belief that if the elementary school were better organized and brought under government inspection, it would more efficiently meet the demands of mass compulsory education. Carlson sought to strengthen *folkskolan* so that it could function independently as a segregated terminal school for those who, before the parliamentary reform of 1866, had generally been classed as the rural proletariat or landless "fifth estate." [58]

[55] In ambulatory schools the teacher and pupils met by rotation in the homes of the community. They were quite common in rural areas until after World War I.

[56] Some idea of how the clergy approached *folkskolan* as a new field for missionary endeavor may be gleaned from Fredrik Dahlbom, *Den svenska folkskolans kristendomsundervisning 1842–1919*, 1927, *passim*. [77]

[57] G. Thunander, although he tends to stress the farmer estate's estrangement from the *folkskola*, gives an excellent account of charity school-*folkskola* relationships in urban and rural Sweden in the nineteenth century. See his *Fattigskola-medborgarskola*, 1946, pp. 24–77. [172]

[58] The work of F. F. Carlson to make elementary education in *folkskolan* a self-contained system and separate from the older academic system is described in K. A. Westling, "C. A. Agardh, F. F. Carlson och undervisningsfrihet," in *Till Bengt J. Bergqvist*, 1920, pp. 103–115. [180] Note also Carlson's statement: "One must consult Prussia, which leads in educational theory and practice" (in *Undervisningsplan for rikets folkskolor*, 1851). Carlson's work greatly reinforced the German influence in Swedish education, which remained potent, especially in the *gymnasium* and universities, down to World War II.

Before evaluating the contributions of Siljeström and others to the development of a comprehensive *folkskola,* it may be helpful first to examine some of the basic problems responsible for the slow development of the elementary school up to the 1880's when Sweden began the transition from a rural, pre-industrial society to a modern, industrial democracy.

PROBLEMS OF IMPLEMENTATION

Sweden in the latter half of the nineteenth century was an underdeveloped country rapidly moving toward the point of "take-off" or self-sustaining production in the economic sector.[59] New industries, frequently in rural locations, grew up to exploit the rich resources of timber and iron ore for export to the more advanced industrial nations, of Western Europe.

Agriculture became increasingly rationalized and efficient. The national productive capital—such as electric power networks, railroads, canals, harbors, and highways—increased annually through heavy government and private investment.[60] Internal isolation of the provinces decreased as did Sweden's isolation from Europe and the world at large. Moreover, a combination of crop failures and lack of employment opportunities—plus improved transatlantic transportation and free land in North America—stimulated a heavy flow of emigration among the large number of landless and jobless rural folk.[61]

[59] For a brief description of economic conditions in Sweden during the period of take-off in the 1870's and 1880's, see Walt W. Rostow, *The Stages of Economic Growth: A Non-Communist Manifesto,* 1962, pp. 62 ff. [148]

[60] Modernization of the Swedish economy was most intense and socially disruptive in the period from 1880 to World War I. See the excellent studies by Eli F. Heckscher, *An Economic History of Sweden,* 1954, Chapter 6 [98]; and Arthur Montgomery, *Industrialisms genombrott i Sverige,* 1947, *passim* [130b].

[61] In the period 1851–1910 over one million emigrants left Sweden for the United States. The bitterness and pathos of this latter-day great Swedish folk movement is artfully portrayed in the historical novels of Vilhelm Moberg. See, for example, his *The Emigrants* [129]. For a scholarly treatment of Swedish emigration, its causes and its effects on the social structure and national economy, see Montgomery [130b], or the excellent work in English by John S. Lindberg, *The Background of Swedish Emigration to the United States: An Economic and Sociological Study of the Dynamics of Migration,* 1930 [122].

In a less scholarly vein, the following poem by the worker poet K. J. Gabrielson presents a personal view of the hopelessness of the rural folk during this period.

> And could I forget my childhood home
> and my father's helpless steps
> and forget us children, us hungering five,
> and forget how my mother cried,
>
> . . . . .
>
> And could I forget how I ran away
> from home at eleven years,

During the initial stages of industrialization, the state continued its large investment in the elite-building secondary schools and universities. In 1870, as shown in Table 1, these two state-supported educational institutions together accounted for 43.5 per cent of the budget for cultural expenditures whereas locally financed elementary school instruction for some three-fourths of all Swedish children received only 10.7 per cent. By 1900 government investment in the latter had more than tripled to 34.2 per cent; the former had sunk to 29.3 per cent. Note also the significant decline from 16.8 per cent to 4 per cent of the expenditures for cultural affairs in the allocation of government funds to the state church.

Andrews, writing in the early 1870's, commented on the operation— and what he believed to be the injustice—of the tax structure supporting local elementary and governmental secondary education:

The *folkskola* are principally maintained by local and direct taxation. The higher schools for the middle and upper classes are supported by direct appropriation out of the treasury of the state. And this money is principally derived from import duties on necessities, or articles of common consumption, such as coffee, sugar, molasses, tobacco, and cotton fabrics. (On $380,765 worth of cotton fabrics imported in 1867 the duty was $117,000, or about 30 per cent. On $834,148 worth of wine imported in the same year the duty was $81,152, or about 10 per cent, a rate only ⅓ as high as on cotton fabrics.) It would seem therefore that the great mass of the people, or common class, not only pay in a large degree the expense of the folk schools, but also the principal part of the expense of the higher schools, which, as a general rule, their children do not attend.[62]

In addition to financial matters, numerous other problems prevented the development of the *folkskola* into something more than an institution providing minimal instruction for the lower classes. Two of the most important were in some ways mutually reinforcing: the predominance of religion, and the continuing popular image of the institution as a charity school.

The clergy had for centuries been responsible to the state for the administration of the urban grammar and rural literacy schools. Sim-

---

when one cold spring in consumption
my mother's life ran out!
And could I forget the cuts and blows
that brutality daily served
and forget that a charity case was all I was
however I worked and strove.

Quoted in Åke Elmér, *Från fattigsverige till välfärdsstaten: social förhållanden och socialpolitik i Sverige under 1900-talet*, 1963, pp. 12–13. [82a]
[62] Andrews [3], p. 27.

Table 1. State Grants for Cultural Purposes, 1870–1900 [a]

(In thousands of kronor and percentage of total cultural budget)

	1870		1880		1890		1900	
Receiving Agency	Kr.	Per cent	Kr.	Per cent	Kr.	Per cent	Kr.	Per cent
State Church	834	16.8	828	8.2	839	6.3	661	4.0
Royal academies	243	4.9	396	3.9	433	3.3	472	2.9
Universities	460	9.3	718	7.1	812	6.1	995	6.1
Secondary education	1,694	34.2	2,624	25.9	3,250	24.5	3,805	23.2
Folk instruction	530	10.7	2,802	27.6	4,220	31.8	5,608	34.2
Total	3,761	75.9	7,368	72.7	9,554	72.0	11,541	70.4

[a] Source: Riksdagen, Riksdagens riksstat. [39r]

ilarly, they soon came to exert a powerful influence in the new "secular" public elementary schools.[63] Every parish under the 1842 law constituted a school district, and each school district had a school board of which the local rector was by law president and the local minister the secretary. The school day began with prayers, religious songs and Bible reading. The subjects studied most frequently were writing, Bible history, and catechism. The curriculum as designed by F. F. Carlson and the conservative government he represented had two basic aims: to teach basic literacy and arithmetic, and to prepare for confirmation and instill a Christian concept of life according to the teaching of the Swedish state church.[64]

Erastian liberal elements bitterly criticized the teaching of Scripture and the continued use of the Bible in lieu of reading primers in the supposedly secular elementary school. They considered Scripture an obstacle to the introduction of more useful subjects needed to give information and guidance in social and vocational matters. Scripture—indeed, the entire religious character of the folkskola—was seen by Swedish radicals as an upper-class instrument to keep the lower classes in ignorance and superstition, and to make them humble before the authorities.[65]

[63] See Jägerskiöld [112], pp. 56–70.

[64] Revealing accounts of the religious emphasis in the folkskola at mid-century are included in the collected work of memoirs, När jag gick i skolan: skol och ungdomsminnen från 1800-talets senare hälft, 1934, passim [26]; for an account of Carlson's impact on folkskolan, see Westling [180], pp. 105–110.

[65] Opposition to the religious nature of compulsory elementary school education by liberal and radical elements in Swedish society is described in Chapter 6 of Gunnar Richardson's work, Kulturkamp och klasskamp: ideologiska och sociala motsättningar i svensk skol och kulturpolitik under 1880-talet, 1963, pp. 31, 309–368. [144]

In addition to the emphasis on religious instruction in the *folkskola,* other distinctions were made in the curricula of folk and grammar schools. Military drill played an important role in the *folkskola* where it reflected the influences of nationalism, German militarism, and class differences in school functions. An eyewitness reported:

. . . boys at the *folkskola* are paraded in their uniforms on certain military occasions, which is not the case for those of the same age in the grammar schools, who never appear in organized companies or in any military manner in public. The distinction seems to give the former the appearance of being wards of the public.[66]

Furthermore, many Swedes found the name of the elementary school highly objectionable. It implied, they complained, that *folkskola* was only for the most lowly in society. As such, it stigmatized the school, kept children of the upper classes away, and generally served as "a constant and disagreeable reminder of irregularity." [67]

EARLY DEMANDS FOR COMPULSORY
COMPREHENSIVE SCHOOLS

Individual liberal clergymen had in the main led the fight for the founding of a compulsory school. After 1842, however, liberal educators and politicians came to the fore to work and agitate for the *folkskola's* improvement and to propose its transformation to a compulsory comprehensive school. Three outstanding nineteenth-century champions of educational and social reform were Count Torsten Rudenschöld (1798–1859), Per Adam Siljeström (1815–1892), and Fridtjuv Berg (1851–1916). The reform proposals of these three former *folkskola* teachers had much in common in their basic ideas of legitimate means and goals for a national educational policy. These ideas, in turn, helped to shape and propagate a program for comprehensive school reform that changed little until the 1940's.

Count Torsten Rudenschöld published his famous work "Thoughts on Class Mobility" in 1845 after he had kept a *folkskola* for some eight years in his own castle. In these years of elementary school teaching Rudenschöld evolved a theory of the causes of the contemporary sociopolitical dissatisfaction which was manifest throughout Europe and

[66] Andrews [3], p. 26. See also the illustration in Anna Sorenson, "Det svenska folkundervisningsväsendet, 1860–1900," in *Svenska Folkskolans Historia,* 1942, p. 59. [157a]

[67] Andrews [3], p. 26.

was threatening Sweden. The answer to the problem of intensified class animosity could be found, Rudenschöld believed, in requiring all children to experience a common education that would facilitate "self-realization" and social mobility, or *ståndscirkulation*.[68] This approach would, he predicted, lead to a just selection of natural talent and at the same time provide a basic civic training, including physical activity in order to develop a healthy respect for physical work, and fostering a sense of "Christian brotherly love" and social comradeship.[69]

Rudenschöld opposed the 1842 Act because he believed it aggravated Sweden's social and educational problems in several dangerous ways. First, it created the beginnings of a state-supported parallel system where children of manual laborers and the like attended one school, and all the children—regardless of talent—of the "upper classes" attended the *gymnasium* or private schools.[70] Second, it perpetuated the inferior monitor schools and made no proper provisions to subsidize and thus encourage properly trained teachers. Worst of all, he claimed, it did little to facilitate the development of intellectual talent regardless of social class origins.[71] Rudenschöld believed that this imperative could only be accomplished if the *folkskola* gradually became a comprehensive "*nationell skola*," a basic school for all Swedish children up to the age of fifteen years.[72] Fellow liberal P. A. Siljeström was one of the handful who supported him in the *riskdag* on this demand but cooperation between the two great reformers led only to the acceptance of Rudenschöld's motion in 1858 that *småskolor*, or separate primary schools, should comprise the first three years of the elementary school.[73] In the following year Rudenschöld died of tuberculosis.

One of the first major bills for educational reform presented in the new bicameral *riksdag* (following the parliamentary reform of 1866) proposed that the *folkskola* should be renamed the *kommunalskola*, or community school, and should function as a comprehensive school. The bill failed to gain the support of any political group and was defeated by a very large margin. The author of the bill, Per Adam Siljeström, nevertheless continued—as educator, author, and editor—to

[68] Rudenschöld's utopian social reform thinking about comprehensive elementary education can be found in his works *Tankar om ståndscirkulation*, 1845 [27c]; and *Tankar om ståndscirkulations verkställighet*, 1846 [27d].

Sten Carlsson rates Rudenschöld as an important innovator in sociological concepts still valid and useful today. See his comments, [71a], pp. 9–12, 76–78.

[69] Torsten Rudenschöld, *Tankar om folkskolan*, 1921, pp. 57 ff. [27b]

[70] Torsten Rudenschöld, *Den svenska folkskolans praktiska ordnande*, 1921, p. 145. [27a]

[71] *Ibid.*, p. 147.

[72] Torsten Rudenschöld, *Tankar om vår tids samhällsfrågor*, 1920, p. 26. [27e]

[73] Aquilonius [53], p. 359.

warn the Swedish nation of the dangers of educational dualism in a country that had supposedly abolished all ascriptive privileges in 1866.[74]

Two major themes dominate Siljeström's school reform work. One sought to develop the *folkskola* into the *nya skola* or new school that would lead to progressivism and democracy in contrast to the old *lärda* ("learned") Latin school which encouraged conservatism.[75] During his entire adult life as a teacher of the poor, a grammar school *lektor* in physics, a director of an experimental school and of a teacher training college, as an editor and a Liberal member of the *riksdag*, Siljeström worked to improve the *folkskola* to the point where it might serve as the sole foundation school, or *bottenskola*, for grammar school and university.[76] Considering the rigid social divisions in Swedish society and the severe deficiencies of the elementary school in the 1860's and 1870's, Siljeström's work had marked idealistic and optimistic overtones in the tradition of his mentor, Torsten Rudenschöld. But if Siljeström was a social utopian in terms of his ultimate goals for Swedish compulsory education, he was on the other hand a hardheaded pragmatist, reminiscent of Horace Mann, in his labors to provide improved texts, teachers and ideas for the impoverished new school. In his many concrete contributions to the secularization and improvement of the *folkskola*, Siljeström doggedly and realistically sought to prepare the way for his long-term goal of organic unity in the national school system.

A second theme in his work stressed the need for individual self-realization—he had been much impressed by Bishop Grundtvig's work in Denmark—through the use of activity methods in examination-free comprehensive schools.[77] Siljeström thought of this proposed "ideal"

---

[74] Note his stricture that "the degree to which special privileges are acknowledged in education, in like degree will privileged classes in society appear or disappear," in Per Adam Siljeström, *Handlingar och skrifter rörande undervisningsväsendet*, 1884, p. 947. [29b]

[75] *Ibid.*, p. 521. Bertrand Russell has well described this tendency: "A classical education is almost entirely critical: a boy learns to avoid mistakes and to despite those who commit them. This tends to produce a kind of cold correctness, in which originality is replaced by respect for authority. Correct Latin is fixed once and for all: it is that of Virgil and Cicero. Correct science is continually changing, and an able youth may look forward to helping in this process. Consequently the attitude produced by a scientific education is likely to be more constructive than that produced by the study of dead languages." *Education and the Good Life*, 1926, p. 142. [149]

[76] Siljeström is credited with coining the word *bottenskola*, for comprehensive compulsory school, which stirred heated political debate and legislation in the 1920's. See Torsten Husén, *Fridtjuv Berg och enhetsskolan*, 1948, p. 18. [111c]

[77] Per Adam Siljeström, *Lärjungen—eller om individualitetens betydelse för uppfostran*, 1884, p. 6. [29c]

educational institution as the key to the regeneration of both society and the individual, a goal worthy of a lifelong effort.[78]

Siljeström traveled widely in the United States at a time when "common," or comprehensive, schools were being systematically developed in New England by his acquaintances, Horace Mann and Henry Barnard.[79] Beyond doubt the work of Fryxell, Agardh, and Rudenschöld as well as his own experience teaching in a charity school had already shaped Siljeström's school reform ideas long before his visit to the United States in 1849–1850. Yet it is probable, as evidenced by Siljeström's description of his American experience, that to see a country where his ideals of comprehensive schooling were not talked of as ideal theories but actually put into practice, strengthened his faith that New England's practical solution for public education might well become Sweden's solution if the ground were properly prepared.[80] It is also apparent from Siljeström's writings that those aspects of American education that most powerfully aroused his enthusiasm (the common schools, the normal schools for women, coeducation, the school libraries, the standardization of school buildings and equipment, and secular control and content) were precisely those goals that he strove most actively to attain in Sweden.[81]

Siljeström drew interesting conclusions from his observation of the contrast between what he characterized as the healthy and viable free common schools of New England and the dual system of charity-supported and private schools in the Middle Atlantic states. He likened the American poor schools to the *folkskola* and proclaimed that the only way to convert such a school to the New England model would be to require the attendance of children from all social classes. Then, Siljeström said, parents of the rich and well-born children would become interested in the school and insure its efficiency and support. For this reason he saw private schools as an unmitigated evil. Their existence, he said, was

very detrimental, not only because they contribute to separate the various classes even in childhood, but also because they monopolize

78 Per Adam Siljeström, "Tankar om uppfostran," in *Årsböcker i Svensk Undervisningshistoria*, 1929, pp. 129–133. [29h]

79 A fascinating account of his travels and observations will be found in Per Adam Siljeström, *The Educational Institutions of the United States: Their Character and Organisation*, 1853. [29i]

80 Siljeström's belief in the possibility of successful transfer of educational models is frequently indicated in his book *Resa i Förenta Staterna*, 1852, passim. [29g]

81 For example, cf. Siljeström's later writings: *Folkbildning: något om emigrationen samt ett ord till herrskapsklassen*, 1853 [29a]; "Om utsikterna och hindren för en högre folkskolebildning," *Framtiden*, 1877 [29e]; and *Om skolhusen och skolmaterialen*, 1853 [29d].

the attention and interest of the educated and wealthy classes who are thus chiefly engaged in favor of schools of a different order. The public schools cannot, of course, under such circumstances count upon the same support and supervision on their part as they would be likely to enjoy were the children of these classes educated in them.[82]

In addition to his educational activities, Siljeström was also an active member of the Agrarian party in the reformed *riksdag*. His radical democratic views, however, were as unpalatable to his own party as they were to the dominant Conservative majority in the still aristocratic first chamber. He had, many believed, been dangerously tainted by his interest in American republicanism and the common schools that supported it.

In his later years Siljeström devoted most of his efforts to the problems of teacher training. He joined forces with Anders Berg, a fellow pioneer, who had in earlier years also worked with Torsten Rudenschöld.[83]

Fridtjuv Berg, son of Anders Berg, had grown up with both Rudenschöld and Siljeström as "household gods." Even as a young folk-school teacher he was committed to carry on the educational reform work of his mentors, i.e., to secure a comprehensive *folkskola*.[84] His ultimate reform program, the first to present a logical rationale for common schooling, embodied a freely acknowledged debt to the strong influences of Fryxell, Rudenschöld, and Siljeström. It found expression and force within the context of the new demands put upon education in a rapidly modernizing nation; the political possibilities for school reform advanced with the emergence of political democracy and distinctive political parties. His predecessors had fought as dedicated individuals without organized support. In Berg's day, however, the question of dualism in elementary education had become a strongly contested political party issue: first under his leadership in the Liberal party and following his death in 1916 under the leadership of the Socialist Värner Rydén.[85]

[82] Per Adam Siljeström, "Promemoria av 1858 till folkskolestyrelsen i Göteborg," in *Göteborgs Folkskoleväsen i Gamla Dagar och i våra*, 1923, p. 78. [29f]

[83] Hjalmar Berg, *Anders Berg, en föregångsman i den svenska folkskolan*, 1940, p. 101. [57]

[84] For an outstanding study of the influence of nineteenth-century school and social reformers on Berg, see the dissertation by Klas Broms, *Fridtjuv Bergs pedagogik: med tyngdpunkt på tiden före hans första statsrådsperiod*, 1964, p. 37. [69]

[85] The Liberals and Socialists were not, however, without sharp differences concerning reform priorities, especially in the matter of school reform. For example, after its founding in 1881 and until 1918, the Social Democratic party took a comparatively slight interest in educational problems. This may possibly

During the years between 1883—when Berg wrote his famous manifesto "The Folkskola as a Comprehensive School: A Contribution to an Important Social Question"—and World War I, the elementary school had been vastly improved to the point where it stood as a fully developed and segregated school system with its own curriculum, administration, and standards.[86] The *folkskola* teachers, with the beginnings of professional awareness and ambition, organized into a professional body in 1879. A few years later, through their several new publications, this group lent its full organizational support to Berg's program for an eight-year *folkskola* as the one and only foundation school.[87] In 1894 the beginnings of sympathetic political support for this reform, primarily from the more progressive Liberals and the Socialists, succeeded for the first time in gaining a concession from the conservative first chamber advantageous to the *folkskola* vis-à-vis the *gymnasium*. The 1894 Act provided for three years of elementary schooling as a prerequisite to admittance in the state grammar school.[88] With this common three-year primary school, the first small link had thus been forged between the two separate educational structures. Exactly ten years later, however, protests dating back a half-century from the urban middle class persuaded the *riksdag* to divide the nine-year *gymnasium* into a lower Latin-free six-year *realskola* with a leaving examination (the *realskola* examination), and a three- or four-year upper secondary *gymnasium* with a matriculation examination which was an admission to the universities.

The *folkskola* supporters viewed this reform of secondary education as a disaster. They feared, and with good reasons, that the elementary

---

have been the result of its initially Marxian social outlook. The Socialists maintained that educational problems were subordinate to economic and social problems, which, when solved, would automatically solve the former. The "hunger problem" had to be solved first. The Liberals, the Socialists believed, erroneously began with the consequences instead of the causes. See Herbert Tingsten, *Den svenska socialdemokratiens idéutveckling*, 1941, pp. 88–89. [174]

[86] Fridtjuv Berg, *Folkskolan såsom bottenskola: nutidsfrågor på uppfostrans område*, 1911. [5c] This is a later revised and expanded version of the original 1883 work; Berg's 1892 proposal for four-year municipal middle schools to be added to the elementary school was accepted in 1909. These schools were instrumental in enabling students from the working class or rural areas to obtain secondary education of an academic type. Transfer to the *gymnasium* was very rare but possible. See Torsten Husén, *Problems of Differentiation in Swedish Compulsory Schooling*, 1962, pp. 5–6. [111e]

[87] In Swedish, the organization is called *Sveriges Allmänna Folkskollärarförening* (SAF). Its principal publication, *Svensk Lärartidning*, began pubilcation in 1882.

[88] Riksdagen, *Andra Kammaren, Motioner No. 87, 88, 1894*. [39f] The act placed no restrictions, however, on the numerous private elementary schools which prepared upper-class children for private *läroverk*, the combined *realskola* and *gymnasium*.

school would now lose all possibility of attracting middle-class children for more than the required three years of attendance and, consequently, that the *folkskola* might very possibly sink back to its previous charity-type school function. Creation of the *realskola* had, said Berg in a committee minority report on the legislation, "put aside the hopes for an elementary school for children of all social classes in a more decisive way than anything that has occurred in a generation." [89]

Berg has been called the father of the 1950 Comprehensive School Act by Husén and other students and participants of that reform. This act of symbolic allegiance, however, tells us more of the modern reformers seeking antecedents than it does of Berg. Nevertheless, there is little doubt that his influence on subsequent reform policy, even after World War II, was considerable and formative.[90] Berg served as Minister of Education in Karl Staaff's Liberal governments from 1905 to 1906 and from 1911 to 1914. He had as early as 1883 formulated in his manifesto a concrete program for an eight-year comprehensive school to provide *inter alia* for "the individual's right and freedom to develop his talents and personality." There Berg for the first time developed a logical and comprehensive program and proposal for the *nya skola* and buttressed it with powerful psychological, social, economic, and pedagogical arguments.[91]

Despite his long tenure as Minister of Education, Berg was unable singlehandedly to override the still dominant conservative forces in the *riksdag*. He had little doubt, nevertheless, that the wave of dissatisfaction sweeping Sweden would eventually bring democratic reform to both the political and social systems and recognition of the necessity to train children in a progressive and democratic *bottenskola* such as he had long proposed.[92] He saw his role as one who prepares the seedbed, as one who points the way. Berg gave evidence of this belief in a speech before Sveriges Folkskollärarförbundet (the Folk School Teachers Association) in 1902. He said that it devolved upon the new generation of *folkskola* teachers to consummate the reform

[89] Quoted in *Arbetet*, July 5, 1904, p. 5. [54]

[90] Berg's impact and the continued influence of his thought on Swedish schooling are evaluated in the following works: Ecklesiastikdepartementet, *1946 års Skolkommissionens betänkande med förslag till riktlinjer för det svenska skolväsendets utveckling* [38a]; Oskar Olsson, *Skolreformen: tal och uppsatser*, 1945 [140b]; Sune Björklöf, "Fridtjuv Berg, pedagog och provokatör," *Lärartidningen*, 1965, pp. 22–23 [63]; B. Salqvist, "Torsten Rudenschöld och Fridtjuv Berg," *Skola och Samhälle*, 1942 [151]; and in two books by Torsten Husén, *Fridtjuv Berg, folkskollärarkåren och stavningsreformerna*, 1946 [111b], and *Fridtjuv Berg och enhetsskolan* [111c].

[91] Berg [5c], pp. 5 ff.

[92] Fridtjuv Berg, "Hur tankar mogna" (i.e., "how thoughts ripen"), *Svensk Lärartidning*, 1894, pp. 259 ff. [5d]

program for an eight-year comprehensive school for which his own generation had fought, but with little success.[93]

Berg's death in 1916 and the appointment of Värner Rydén as Minister of Education in the 1918 Liberal-Socialist coalition government began a new era in the politics of Swedish educational reform. Profound socio-economic changes gave the old demands for comprehensive schooling and a unified system a new functional justification that had been notably lacking in the idealistic and visionary work of men like Fryxell, Rudenschöld and, to a lesser extent, Siljeström and Berg. And with the voting reform of 1918, which granted universal suffrage, proposals for comprehensive compulsory schooling became less utopian and increasingly more realistic because of the new possibilities of bringing popular support to bear on the reform of public education through democratic procedures.

In summary, there are several themes common in nineteenth-century school reform proposals, and they are tightly woven into the fabric of Berg's 1883 manifesto on the elementary school as a comprehensive foundation school. Whereas the conservative opposition opposed this plan on the grounds of educational inefficiency, i.e., that the *folkskola* lacked the quality or "carrying power" to support the *gymnasium*, Berg and his gentlemanly predecessors essentially justified their demands on grounds of "social justice." The opposition believed that, because the *folkskola* and the grammar school had different origins and aims, no close collaboration should be sought; the reformers advocated the structural unification of a bifurcated school system so as to achieve and further pedagogical and social unity.

Ellen Key, the great Swedish feminist, pedagogue, and champion of "a common school for all children of the country until reaching the age of, say, fifteen" also railed against the "class badge" stamped upon lower-class children in the inferior *folkskola*. Key, in 1914, acknowledged "the magnitude, indeed, hopelessness of securing a new school of this kind [comprehensive school]" and therefore counseled the young Socialists who shared her anger to "continue their work of self-education that they have so well begun, and continue it above all within their own class, in their own meetings, in their own lectures." [94]

---

[93] Cited in Torsten Husén's informative booklet on Berg (published in 1948, at a time when Swedish politicians and others were formulating the 1950 Comprehensive School Act): *Fridtjuv Berg och enhetsskolan*, p. 88. [111c] Husén's concluding remark on Berg's influence was: "The harvest time for his plan has arrived at last."

[94] See her prophetic book (dedicated to the two Socialist leaders, Hjalmar Branting and Carl Lindhagen), *The Younger Generation*, 1914, p. 126. [115]

Chapter 2

STALEMATE AND COMPROMISE IN THE LIMITED
REFORMS AFTER WORLD WAR I
1918–1927

*Over the years a vociferous protest has been set up
against the whole idea of a common foundation
school and surely the coming months will see the
most fanatical efforts to hinder every reform along
this line. Will they succeed? It would be strange
if the* riksdag *of universal suffrage should let itself
be confounded regarding right and justice on this
matter. The program for the comprehensive foundation school has mustered everything that is honest
democracy in this country for more than a generation. Is democracy to fail in this critical moment?* [1]

[1] Värner Rydén, "Grundläggande synpunkter på enhetsskoleproblemet," *Tiden,* May 1927, p. 9. [28]

In Sweden as across much of Europe after the war, intensified demands for equality and unity in national systems of education arose as a consequence of the allied victory "to make the world safe for democracy," and as an integral part of resurgent working-class demands for long postponed political and social reforms.[2] A case in point may be seen in the exhortation of the Socialist Minister of Education Värner Rydén quoted above. His reference to the new *"riksdag* of universal suffrage" and its implied solidarity of interests with the comprehensive school program is illuminating and illustrative of a new and essentially political phase in the Swedish school reform movement during and after 1918. This chapter deals with some of the postwar conditions and changes in Sweden that collectively influenced the tempo and content of an on-going movement for comprehensive school reform.

[2] In Germany and Austria socialists and others unsuccessfully agitated for an *Einheitsschule* (corresponding to the Swedish *enhetsskola*), a comprehensive school undifferentiated up to the fifteenth year. In France the Compagnons de l'Université Nouvelle in like manner demanded an *école unique* (a term meaning "single" school or "one school for all"; or comprehensive school). All French children should receive, they believed, free and common education to the age of fourteen if the demands of "social justice," educational efficiency, and economic evolution were to be adequately met. Various attempts were made during the 1920's to adopt these proposals, but without success. See Ernst Papenek, "Political and Educational Interaction within the Austrian School," 1960, pp. 10–11 [142]; and W. R. Fraser, *Education and Society in Modern France*, 1963, pp. 6, 53–54 [85]. A comprehensive account of the influence of World War I on European socio-political thought and action is given in Volume I of Carl Landauer's epic study, *European Socialism: A History of Ideas and Movements from the Industrial Revolution to Hitler's Seizure of Power*, 1959, pp. 663–864. [119]

THE POLITICAL CRISIS OF 1918

Neutral Sweden suffered little more than acute food shortages and loss of trade and shipping in World War I. Nevertheless, in the postwar period she fully shared the wave of revolutionary upheavals that toppled monarchies in a number of Eastern and Central European nations. The political crisis in Sweden reached menacing proportions in November of 1918.[3] The king, anxious for the monarchy and fearful of revolution, supported the demands of the new Liberal-Socialist coalition government for universal suffrage in elections to both houses of parliament. Members of the first chamber—a house that since its creation in 1866 had remained profoundly conservative and protected by rigorous voting restrictions—opposed all attempts to reduce their privileged bastion.[4] Its long practice of arbitrary rejection of suffrage and other liberal reforms was no longer tolerated by the nonenfranchised in the explosive milieu of 1918. On November 11, after numerous governmental appeals to the first chamber—and a like number of rejections—the Left Socialists seized the initiative from the government and issued a communiqué to their members and the Swedish people.[5] In threatening terms it called for (1) workers' and soldiers' soviets; (2) the overthrow of the monarchy and the hated first chamber; (3) a constituent National Assembly; (4) the division of large land holdings; (5) worker control of industry; and (6) preparations for a general strike.[6] That same day the Chief of Police in Stockholm reported that the Royal Horse Guards were unreliable. On November 12 the two defense ministers reported pronounced revolutionary sympathies in the Army and Navy and bolts were ordered removed from army rifles.[7] Finally, reacting to the importunate advice of the monarch and to the threats of the crowd, the first chamber capitulated and the government's suffrage bill passed both houses to extend the franchise to some 3,200,000 Swedish adults.[8] In November 1918 there

---

[3] An excellent account of this period is given in Verney's *Parliamentary Reform in Sweden 1866–1921*, 1957, pp. 202–214. [175]

[4] For the respective party strengths in the first and second chambers of the *riksdag* from 1905 to 1952, see Appendix C.

[5] Cf. the Liberal Prime Minister Nils Edén's own account in his book *Den svenska riksdagen under femhundra år*, 1935, pp. 302 ff. [9]; and Gunnar Gerdner, *Det svenska regeringsproblemet 1917–1920*, 1946, *passim* [89].

[6] Karl Hildebrand, *Gustav V som människa och regent*, Vol. 2, 1948, p. 290. [104] The Left Socialists were a radical Marxian splinter group from the Social Democratic Party led by Hjalmar Branting. In 1918, they had 15 members in the *riksdag* and some 20,000 mostly young members as compared to the Social Democratic party's 120,000. See Verney [175], p. 210.

[7] Hildebrand [104], Vol. 2, p. 290.

[8] See Ragnar Svanström and C. Fredrik Palmstierna, *A Short History of Sweden*, 1934, p. 419 [164]; and Verney [175], p. 213.

were political riots and disturbances in Denmark, Germany, Switzerland, and Holland but there were none in Sweden.[9] The aristocratic defenders of privilege and the proletarian champions of revolution, socialism and egalitarianism had met on a middle ground of liberal constitutionalism and compromised their differences.[10]

SCHOOLS FOR INDUSTRY

The question of a general remodeling of the Swedish educational system had been raised as early as 1913 but it was not until the political reform in 1918 that the *riksdag* took definite action in the matter. Under the leadership of Rydén the movement for school reform for the first time enjoyed the advantage of support by the government in power and the dedicated interest of the Minister of Education. Rydén had earlier, as a disciple of Berg, sought a comprehensive *bottenskola* and other reforms within the small radical-populist section of the Liberal party. Prior to the great war, Rydén had left the increasingly more moderate Liberals and had gone over to the Social Democratic party where he attempted almost singlehandedly to make the *folkskola-bottenskola* program a more actively sought-after goal in that party's program.[11] The first important legislative act which he piloted to acceptance as Minister of Education attacked the universally recognized problem of inadequacy in training students for industry and commerce; the second approved the formation of a royal commission to prepare legislation for a thorough overhaul of the Swedish educational system. Both acts sought answers to problems arising from social,

[9] John Lindgren, *Per Albin Hansson i svensk demokrati, 1885–1920*, Vol. 1, 1950, p. 396. [124a] Lindgren, a Social Democratic historian, claims that the threat of revolution in November 1918 was a bluff on the part of the Socialists who at no time were prepared to use unparliamentary means of obtaining political power. See his chapter "Den Stora Bluffen" ("The Great Bluff").

[10] John Lindgren credits Branting, leader of the Social Democrats, as being the strong man in the crisis who rejected the possibility of becoming president of a Swedish republic because he sought more than governmental reorganization alone. He needed, Lindgren claims, Liberal party support to gain further social and economic reform through similar compromise in a constitutional manner. See his very interesting—if somewhat polemical—little work *Varför Sverige icke är republik*, 1955, pp. 49–50 ff. [124b]

[11] Rydén's initiative achieved the inclusion of a school reform program in the Social Democratic program for the first time at the party's congress meeting in 1920. It included under Point V the following goals: (1) free schooling in public schools; (2) a comprehensive *folkskola* as a foundation for common civic education; (3) continuation trade schools for industry, agriculture, and commerce; (4) assured admittance of able students to secondary and higher education with state subsidies when necessary; (5) an end to confirmation-oriented teaching, and creation of truly secular public schools; and (6) the promotion and encouragement of unfettered educational research. See *Protokoll, Sveriges Socialdemokratiska Arbetarepartis tionde kongress*, 1920, p. 51. [35b]

political and economic dysfunctions in the rigidly dualistic educational system, and both stood high on the list of priorities for educational reforms in the Social Democratic party program.

The founding in 1918 of *praktiska ungdomsskolor*, or practical trade schools, meant that a superstructure had been built on the *folkskola*— and that the *folkskola* would become a type of *bottenskola* for advanced training even if it remained rigorously separated from the academic system.[12] The new trade schools provided a two-year continuation vocational course for terminal male students who had completed the *folkskola*.[13] In this way the track of "general" elementary education for the Swedish masses was linked up for the first time with training of a purely vocational character.

Swedish industry had expanded at a remarkable rate in the decades prior to World War I, and the suddenness of this activity caused serious difficulties for the two-track system of education, a system that in neither branch provided any real vocational training at all.[14] Director General of the Royal Board of Education Bergqvist, a Liberal, described the problem succinctly shortly before the reform became law in 1918:

Big industry, with all the good and less good economic and social aspects of modern industrialism, has during the past generation swept down with the speed of a hurricane upon our country and it appears likely to gather increasing momentum the more we develop the natural wealth of our country.[15]

After describing the far-reaching effects of mechanization on agriculture and industry, Bergqvist pointed out that Sweden's growing dependence on export markets would demand a far more intensive kind of training than had ever been required before. "Everything," he said, "has cooperated to make it more difficult, as well as more important, for the nation and for individuals to acquire technical knowledge and to practice economy. The influence of these changes has

---

[12] For a study of the effect of superstructures built onto the *folkskola* in aggravating the problems of transfer and parallelism, see Wilhelm Björck's book *Skolreformen: en orienterande redogörelse för Skolkommissionens förslag till enhetsskoleorganisation*, 1922, pp. 11–49. [62]

[13] The 1918 Act required attendance for two years (with a minimum of 360 hours instruction). If pupils failed to obtain the trade school certificate at the end of the two years, they could be compelled to continue in attendance until they were eighteen. See B. J. Bergqvist, *De nya praktiska ungdomsskolorna*, 1918, pp. 37–38. [6]

[14] Before 1918 vocational training could only be obtained in an apprenticeship situation.

[15] Riksdagen, *Kommittee berättelse 1918*, Vol. 3, No. 50, pp. 391–392. [39b]

permeated every class of society, but very naturally has been most felt by that section of the community which, through extraordinary short-sightedness at an earlier stage, was left least equipped to meet the new difficulties and the new demands." [16]

Bergqvist further pointed out the urgent need for the elementary school branch to (1) train girls as well as boys for the labor market; (2) "foster a love for and an appreciation of agricultural employment" by teaching new farming techniques; and (3) provide the moral and social training that the old apprenticeship system and the home had once supplied but which with a fast growing industrial work force, was increasingly becoming a school function and thus, ultimately, a state responsibility.[17]

Rydén regarded the new vocational school as a nonpolitical impera-tive to meet the expanding economy's urgent functional demands on education. And in light of the widening of the franchise, such schools, he believed, might serve to extend compulsory education for two years after the *folkskola* and thereby hopefully increase the general educa-tional level of future voters.[18] There is little doubt, however, that Rydén's major concern and interest lay in the so-called Great School Commission of 1918, the crowning achievement of his ministry and the handmaiden of his program for a comprehensive foundation school.[19]

THE GREAT SCHOOL COMMISSION OF 1918

Appointed by the king on December 31, 1918, on the initiative and at the request of the Socialist Minister of Education Rydén, the Com-mission began its work a month after the suffrage reform and in the same spirit of buoyant optimism about thoroughgoing and funda-mental changes in the old order. Rydén left no doubt as to what he expected the Commission to accomplish when he enumerated several concrete goals to guide the investigation: [20]

1. The coming school system must above all be organized to form an organic whole with only one foundation school, supported by the state. The practical superstructures, created in 1918, should

[16] *Ibid.*, p. 393.

[17] *Ibid.*; see also Riksdagen, *Protokoll vid lagtima riksmötet 1918, Andra Kam-maren*, Vol. 6, No. 4, 1919, pp. 213–217 [39i], for a discussion of the extent of new state responsibilities in compulsory education.

[18] *Tiden*, December 6, 1918, p. 6. [173]

[19] See Rydén's comments on this matter quoted in Eve Malmqvist, "Enhets-skoletanken i Sverige," *Skola och Samhälle*, 1952, pp. 167–168. [127]

[20] Rydén's controversial strictures to the 1918 School Commission are included in *Skolkommissionens betänkande, 1:1 Grunder för en ny läroverksorganisation*, 1922, pp. x ff. [40a]

have corresponding academic superstructures built directly on
the public common school. Gifted students, from whatever social
level, must be more effectively cared for.

2. The state must assume responsibility for the education of girls
in the same degree as for boys. Private girls' schools should
gradually be converted to state or communal schools. The change-
over should not, however, aim at simply reproducing a previous
pattern but should be flexible enough to leave room for experimental schools conducted under specially prominent pedagogical
guidance.

3. The upper secondary *gymnasium* must be qualitatively improved
and made academically more selective in light of a growing overproduction of graduates.

4. The transition to the new system should not be delayed, but
caution was necessary with regard to the means and forms of
transition.

Rydén made effective use of his influential position as Minister of Education to define concrete final aims for a group that had been created
as an exploratory commission of some fifteen educators. He made no
mention of the earlier liberal justifications for the comprehensive school
(i.e., to facilitate social justice, democratic attitudes, self-realization,
or class solidarity and mobility) but rather stressed the need to rationalize, to make education more efficient and productive so as better to
serve the national demands for trained manpower in the economic
sector.

Some three years later on April 28, 1922, the Commission presented
its findings in four sizable volumes for the consideration of Parliament.[21] This report, the first official blueprint calling for a thoroughgoing reorganization of the Swedish educational structure, closely
followed the guidelines formulated by Rydén in 1918. As such, it
reflected to a high degree both the earlier reform aspirations of Berg
and others for a comprehensive *enhetsskola* and the school reform
program of the Social Democratic party. In its frontal attack on the
problem of educational dualism, the report excited widespread public
debate and effectively polarized the forces for and against the *folkskola*
as a comprehensive school into alignments that for decades altered
little. The following section examines the main points of the Commission's blueprint, and explains why—despite a Liberal-Socialist majority
in both houses—it became a victim of political and economic circumstances and was not even brought to a vote.

---

[21] The four volumes were published in 1922. See [40a]. A fifth volume, dealing with organizational and economic matters, appeared in 1923.

To summarize, the Commission's chief proposals called for the following changes:

1. The school system must be structured to meet individual and state needs in education. This can only be accomplished in a "ladder series" of schools built end-on. More specifically, a six-year elementary school free of foreign languages and terminal exams must be the only public foundation school. No private schools paralleling this common school should receive subventions from the state or municipalities. (See Figure 1, part B.)
2. A four-year coeducational *realskola* built on the common school will supply all higher general education and terminate with an examination (*realskola* exam) when the student is sixteen or seventeen.
3. A three-year coeducational *gymnasium* built on the *realskola* will administer its own special entrance exam (formerly entrance followed a fifth year of *realskola* completed with passing grades) to insure proper selection. The curriculum in the *gymnasium* must be modernized and reorganized in terms of subjects for examination; electives will be introduced.
4. Six-year special state secondary schools for girls should be built on the comprehensive school to accommodate girls' interest in education.
5. A new seven-year school, the *lyceum*, should be built on the foundation school. It would be parallel to the *realskola* and *gymnasium*, accomplishing in seven years, through concentrated studies, the same as the two schools in an eight-year course.
6. Years of attendance for the various school forms should be:
   For the *real* exam: ten years—six in the elementary school and four in the *realskola*.
   For the *studentexamen:* thirteen years—six in the common public elementary school and either four in the *realskola* plus three in the *gymnasium*, or seven in the *lyceum*.
7. Some experimental schools outside the organization of state schools may operate with state approval.
8. The school's curriculum should be reformed and brought into line with the modern ideals and practices of the *Arbeitsschule*, or activity school. More time should be allotted to practical work, laboratory activities, and games and sports.
9. Changes in teacher training and support are necessary properly to implement these proposals.

Public reaction to the Commission's plan was immediate, widespread and intense. Opposition centered primarily on the means proposed to

Figure 1 A. Structural Organization of the Swedish School System: The System before 1927. (*Source:* Ecklesiastikdepartementet, *Sammanfattning av allmän organisationsplan,* 1945, pp. 40–47. [38c] Adapted; normal schools not shown.)

Grade		Age
	Studentexamen	
12		19
11	*Latin gymnasium* / *Real-gymnasium* — *Real-examen*	18
10	*Real-examen*	17
9	Private girls' schools / Municipal middle schools / Continuation schools (compulsory after 1921) / Higher elementary and vocational schools	16
8		15
7		14
6	*Realskola*	13
5		12
4		11
3	Private prep. schools / *Folkskola* / Compulsory schooling	10
2	Primary school	9
1		8
		7

break down the existing barrier between the elementary school and the secondary school through the creation of a six-year comprehensive school and, to a lesser degree, on the possibility of compulsory co-education. There existed, it should be noted, a rather general consensus about the desirability of the principles involved in the proposals. It was about the realization of these principles that controversy raged.[22] The proposed postponement for three additional years of foreign language study and its transfer to the *realskola* was seen by many as an attack on the academic school and an unnecessary penalization of prospective secondary school students.[23] Despite the cautiously apolitical phrasing of the Minister's reform rationale, the Social Democrats in general, and Rydén specifically, were widely accused of attempting

[22] For the division of public opinion on the matter of *bottenskolan* by social class and political identification, see Eva Nordland, *Verdier i gammel og ny skole,* 1958, pp. 19–27. [134]

[23] See for example the article entitled "Enhetsskolan: ett bristfälligt och helt illusorisk förslag" (Comprehensive Schools: A Defective and Deceptive Proposal), *Nya Dagligt Allehanda,* May 13, 1922, p. 4. [84]

Figure 1 B. Structural Organization of the Swedish School System: The System Proposed by the 1918 School Commission (Not Adopted). (*Source:* Ecklesiastikdepartementet [38c], pp. 40–47. Normal schools not shown.)

to capture the nation's schools to further Socialist policies of "social leveling" and "ideological manipulation."[24]

In keeping with traditional Swedish legislative practices, the government sent copies of the report to over eight hundred public and private bodies to elicit reaction and opinion on the suitability of the proposals. Faculties of every kind of educational institution, school inspectors and school officials, as well as city councils, county councils and other holders of political offices offered criticism, approval, or counter propositions.[25]

From the replies later published by the government and from the record left in the popular press and journals of professional organizations, it is possible to sense something of the magnitude and intensity

[24] The conservative newspaper *Svenska Dagbladet* led the popular opposition to Rydén's work and ideas.

[25] See *Sammanfattning av utlåtanden och yttranden i anledning av Skolkommissionens betänkande avgivna den 28 April 1922, I & II*, 1923. [36d]

Figure 1 C. Structural Organization of the Swedish School System: The Compromise of 1927 for a "Double Connection" to Secondary Schooling. (*Source:* Ecklesiastikdepartementet [38c], pp. 40–47. Normal schools not shown.)

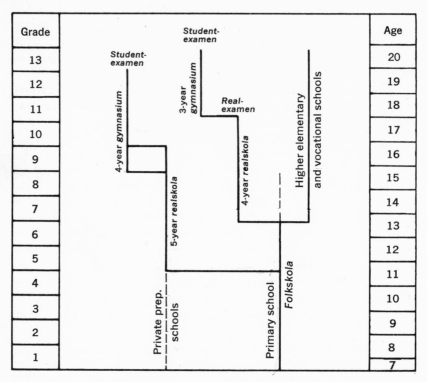

of the controversy provoked by the Commission's work.[26] The record also indicates that the most outspoken forces supporting or opposing the reform fell into two distinct camps that identified themselves either with the elementary or the secondary branch of the national school system. Those who would be most directly involved—in terms of perceived interests, status, and the like—in any change to a comprehensive school led in the controversy. For example, the following, in the main, staunchly supported the proposed six-year comprehensive school: the elementary school teachers and inspectors, the normal school teachers, the boards of municipal middle schools, the municipal councils, and most of the locally elected public school boards. The majority of the Royal Board of Education also supported the proposals, although Director Bergqvist favored a mixed system of three-, four-,

[26] Nordland [134], pp. 19–27.

and six-year elementary schools in an attempt to satisfy all demands.[27]

Opponents of the *bottenskola* included all the faculties and organizations of the *gymnasium* and the *realskola,* private coeducational schools, private girls' schools, commercial and technical *gymnasia,* all university authorities and county councils, higher teachers colleges, diocese chapters, and a minority of the Board of Education, consisting mainly of the members of the secondary education division.[28]

One important consequence of the public and political controversy over the proposed reform was that it placed Branting, as a minority prime minister, in a tenuous political position. By playing down their socialization propaganda in the 1921 elections for the first chamber, the Social Democrats had been able to form a minority "Swedish National Popular" government. Its continued existence depended on support from the Liberal party which held the balance of power and the majority of whose members had become disenchanted with Rydén and his school reform efforts.[29] Branting therefore, it would seem, was willing to accept defeat on school reform—the proposals were never even brought to a vote—rather than further antagonize the Liberals and lose their possible support for what he believed to be more significant reforms in the nation's tax, unemployment and agricultural policies.[30] Furthermore, in addition to Branting's shift of interest, the general conservative reaction to the ferment and reforms of 1918, and

[27] For Bergqvist's report on his activities as the 1918 Commission chairman, and recommendations for a compromise solution to the impasse, see his interesting and reasonable book, *Våra skolor: en granskning i anledning av Skolkommissionens reformförslag,* 1923. [59b]

[28] See Wilhelm Cederschiöld, *Skolfrågan ur samhällets synpunkt,* 1927, pp. 34–40 [73], for the rationale of the conservative opposition which changed little in later decades of common school controversy. This view held that democracy and social mobility would be best served not by a restrictive common school but by an educational system "with many branches so that every child will have the best possibility to develop his unique talents in a competitive situation." *Ibid.,* p. 39.

[29] Chagrin over what many Liberals claimed was the pirating and radicalization of their school reform program by Rydén and the Socialists is evident from an editorial in the liberal press of the time: "The common citizen school was a liberal idea long before social democracy was born in Sweden. The present program was first formulated fifty years ago by a liberal schoolman [P. A. Siljeström] who first enlisted the public school teachers and liberal-minded public in its cause." *Dagens Nyheter,* July 27, 1927, p. 2. [76] The liberal press, as well as the Liberal party, was divided in support for the reform. Cf. Gunnar Herrström, *1927 års skolreform,* 1967 (Stockholm: Scandinavian University Press), *passim.*

[30] Branting's maneuvering during the 1921–1922 period of minority governments, and the emergence of a mature four-party system is discussed by Dankwart A. Rustow in his book *The Politics of Compromise: A Study of Parties and Cabinet Government in Sweden,* 1955, pp. 91–101. [150]

the Socialists' failure to achieve a parliamentary majority, a fourth factor had, by 1922, made school reform appear less crucial and desirable to the Socialists than in the heat and excitement of 1918. This new element, the first Swedish postwar depression, reached its apex of severity in 1921–1922 and put one-third of the trade union membership out of work.[31] Consequently the major energies and attention of the Social Democratic Party turned to the more immediate economic concerns of its working-class members. Rydén was consequently left with his hard-won program for *enhetsskolan* but without active party support or allies in the *"riksdag* of universal suffrage." Because Rydén had to a large extent lost his political support and because opposition to the Commission's proposals had been highly effective in casting doubts on the pedagogical and social desirability of a six-year foundation school, a new, Conservative Minister of Education, S. A. Clason, was able with impunity to reject the Commission's report in 1924. The new minister claimed, and the Socialists did not put it to the test of a vote, that "the 1918 Commission's proposals could not form a basis for the future organization of the school system without extensive modification." [32] Clason thereupon appointed a new Expert Committee of five educators to devise such modifications as they might judge appropriate, all the while guided by his directives which called for studies of (1) *folkskolan's* qualitative ability to support alone all secondary education; (2) means of preventing an extension of elementary schooling; (3) need for foreign languages; (4) possibilities of grants to rural students for secondary schooling; and (5) extending the freedom of private schools.[33]

Although Rydén, the *folkskola* groups, and others supporting the comprehensive school received a bitter setback with the work set in motion by Clason, their unsuccessful efforts had nevertheless been instructive and had made school reform a major public concern. The public came to appreciate—although they might differ on a solution— some of the incongruity of a dualistic educational system and the pressing need for unity or at least for some manner of connective links between the rigorously separated elementary and secondary structures. The politicians were also instructed by the Commission's findings and the heated polemics; on all sides they began to accept the political necessity to compromise on attempts to find solutions for educational problems too long ignored or postponed.

[31] See Åke Holmberg, *Sverige efter 1809: politisk historia under 150 år*, 1961, pp. 103–104. [108]

[32] *Svenska statsrådets protokoll, juni 1924*, p. 3. [43]

[33] Ecklesiastikdepartementet, *Tillkallade sakkunniga: utredning angående det svenska skolväsendets organisation*, 1926, p. xi. [38d]

FOLKSKOLAN–BOTTENSKOLAN: THE COMPROMISE OF 1927

From time to time, after the founding of the compulsory elementary school in 1842, Parliament had separately legislated numerous internal modifications in the elementary and secondary school structures. Pressure from the political left and from various *folkskola* groups forced the first small step toward structural unification in 1894 with the enactment of a law requiring three years of attendance in the elementary school before entrance to the state secondary school. Thirty-three years later, in 1927, all political parties in the *riksdag* agreed on the need to modernize the two separate parts of Swedish schooling in order to achieve closer articulation.[34] But during the first decade following the parliamentary reform none of the four major political parties had a clear majority, although the Socialists followed by the Conservatives comprised the two largest political parties. (See Appendix C.) No one party—as the Socialists especially learned—and no single reform program could be sure of a majority, and the pragmatic necessity of compromise tempered all legislation. This situation did much to modify the original demands of Rydén and the Socialists for the uncompromising adoption of a six-year comprehensive school. It was not only in their demands for school reform that a similar moderating process was taking place—though in a more formative way—as the need and inclination to compromise slowly changed the Social Democrats from a revolutionary Marxist party in the 1880's to a nonrevolutionary socialist party which, during the 1920's, willingly cooperated and compromised with a number of minority governments.[35] Before turning to the substance and importance of the 1927 Act, we might first look at the political situation which influenced this first step in bridging the two separate branches of Swedish education.

The parliamentary constellation prevailing in Sweden from the early 1920's until 1932 largely explains the successive government defeats and government crises that ruled out the possibility of securing controversial legislation whether it originated in either the political Right or

[34] See the very thorough study of the problem of intrastructural linkage in Ecklesiastikdepartementet [38d], pp. 9–46 ff. Sweden of course shared the general European problems of dual systems of schools (i.e., the proliferation of higher elementary continuation, trade and technical schools, the difficulties of transfer, and the need for relevant curricula and methods in light of progressive industrial development) during the interwar period. For a cogent summary of similar continental experience, see I. L. Kandel, "The End of an Era," in *Educational Yearbook of the International Institute of Teachers College, Columbia University, 1941, passim.* [114]

[35] Frans Severin, *The Ideological Development of Swedish Social Democracy,* 1956, pp. 9–12. [154]

Left.[36] For the relative strengths of the four parties were such that the Liberals held the balance between the Socialists on the one side and the Conservatives and Agrarians (who generally followed the Conservative program during this period) on the other. With the increasing prosperity and expansion of trade and industry in the late 1920's, the interests of the political parties to a considerable extent turned away from unemployment problems and back to special interests. The Conservatives worked to strengthen national defense and the Swedish military establishment; the Socialists sought increased and improved social services—not the least of which was the six-year comprehensive foundation school. The Liberal program may be described as the seeking of economies in both of these areas.[37] By swinging their votes to the Conservatives on questions of tax reform and unemployment policy, the Liberals brought down Socialist governments in 1920, 1923, and again in 1926. By joining with the Socialists on the defense issue they brought about a Conservative defeat in 1924.[38] Thus, the coolness of the Liberals to the 1918 Commission's school reform proposal of 1922 might well have insured its ultimate defeat if it had ever been brought to a vote.

Although the Liberals accounted for only 14 per cent of the second chamber and 23 per cent of the first chamber, a Liberal government held office when the 1924 School Committee (appointed by S. A. Clason) reported its findings and when the *riksdag* eventually passed the 1927 school reform bill. In addition to sustained Socialist support and leadership the Liberal theory of "gravitational parliamentarianism" and the process of compromise that it entailed must be seen as a basic contribution factor in Parliament's passage of the 1927 school reform. This compromise legislation incorporated the demands of both political extremes and might well symbolize the political stalemate of the 1920's following on the political revolution of 1918.[39]

The main problems dealt with in the school reform bill presented by the Liberal government in 1927 fall into two major sections: (1) those that relate to articulating and linking up the system's two branches; and (2) those that are of a pedagogical character and bear upon the curriculum, methods of work, and instruction in the various

---

[36] See Ake Elmér, *Svensk socialpolitik*, 1948, pp. 47–49 ff. [82b], for a discussion of the interaction between the political balance and the pace of reform legislation during this period.

[37] See Edvard Thermenius, *Sveriges politiska partier*, 1933, pp. 29, 30. [171]

[38] Rustow [150], p. 97.

[39] "Gravitational parliamentarianism," according to the Liberals, meant that the party at the "center of gravity" should take over the government in the absence of a majority party. See the historical study of Swedish liberalism in Hans-Krister Rönnblom, *Frisinnade landsföreningen, 1902–1927*, 1929, pp. 41–42. [147]

schools.[40] Liberal Minister of Education N. J. F. Almqvist stressed the intimate connection between these two types of problems in his statement of why the Liberals proposed and supported the bill: "The school is not an end in itself; it only fulfills its function when it serves as a handmaid of the community and helps to promote its cultural development. What determines both its organization and development, therefore, is the development of the community as a whole." With this guiding principle established, the minister summed up the major defects in the existing public elementary school system and in the resources and organization of secondary education: [41]

It is admitted that with rapid development in every branch of community life in the past decades, the need for a system of secondary schools better adapted to this development is coming to be increasingly recognized. From the point of view of the general development of the community the present organization of secondary education shows serious shortcomings which in the opinion of the *riksdag* it should be a matter of importance to the community to remedy by all possible means. The *riksdag* considers these shortcomings, broadly speaking, to be the following:

1) The present system of schools places children from economically less well-to-do homes in a less favorable position as regards the possibility of receiving secondary schooling than children from better homes.[42]

2) The present school system does not provide for the education of girls in a way which can be considered as meeting the claims of social justice.[43]

3) The present school system is organized with special reference to the circumstances of towns and the larger communities but to a great extent penalizes the population of the countryside.[44]

The item provoking the greatest disagreement revolved around the length of elementary schooling and the age of transfer to the lower

40 See Riksdagen, *Kungl. Maj:ts Proposition, No. 116: bihang till Riksdagens protokoll*, Vol. 1, 1927, pp. 121 ff. [39d]

41 Riksdagen, *Riksdagens Skrivelse*, No. 262, 1927, pp. 146 ff. [39s]

42 This argument was greatly weakened by the fact that until the 1930's no valid documentation could be presented to support the assumption. Sweden lagged in empirical studies of all kinds, and such statements could only be supported by subjective opinions.

43 Cf. Statens Offentliga Utredningar (SOU) 1927:27 and 1929:33 for findings and proposals of the Expert Committee on the provision of secondary education for girls equal to that provided for boys. Prior to 1927 girls could only obtain secondary schooling in elite private institutions at considerable expense.

44 The difficulties of rural students moving from the rural *folkskola* to the urban *realskola* is described by G. J. Fredlund in *Konturer till en enhällig skolorganisation: huvudsakligen i vad den rör anknytningen mellan barna och ungdomsskolan,* 1926, pp. 44–49. [86]

secondary *realskola*. On this particular point the parties divided in the following manner:

	Folkskola	Realskola	Total
1. Conservative and Agrarian Parties	4 years	5 years	9
2. Pre-1927 system. Also advocated by the above	3 years	6 years	9
3. Social Democrats	6 years	4 years	10

4. The Liberal Party favored a combination of No. 1 and No. 3 as parallel systems. (This is what finally passed.)

When the Liberal Minister of Education brought in a bill on February 18, opposition to the possibility of even a quasi-six-year comprehensive school system emerged once more. Popular sentiment ran high, but many saw only narrow professional interests at work in a battle between the university-trained teachers defending the secondary system against the normal-school-trained *folkskola* teachers. Others saw the comprehensive school plan as an attempt of the Swedish Socialists to do peacefully to the middle class what the Bolsheviks had done with violence in the USSR.[45] The Liberal Prime Minister Ekman, who defended the bill, was maligned as a "voice out of the barbaric woods" by the Conservative press for his statement that the "last constitutional and socially organized privileged stronghold of the moneyed class would fall if the Committee's proposal were accepted." [46] The Liberals —despite Ekman's leadership—and the Agrarians, in the middle, were divided in their support of the six-year comprehensive school.

The basic arguments presented by supporters of the reform held that (1) democracy demands equal opportunity for all; and (2) a system that separates students into two distinct and unequal branches at the age of ten after only three years of school is unjust to children from working-class homes and partial to children of the upper and middle classes.

Speaking in support of the bill, Olof Olsson, a former Social Democratic cabinet minister, rhetorically asked the following rather typical question: "The school shall reflect society. By far the largest percentage of our population consists of working men; is this also the case of the parents of students in the secondary schools?" [47] To answer his question, Olsson cited a study of parental occupational backgrounds of students attending the combined lower secondary *realskola* and upper secondary *gymnasium*—the *läroverk*.[48] It should prove beyond a

[45] Cederschiöld [73], p. 25.
[46] See *Svenska Dagbladet*, May 20, 1927; and Riksdagen, *Riksdagens protokoll, Andra Kammaren*, No. 33–34, 1927, p. 19. [39n]
[47] Riksdagen, *Riksdagens protokoll, Andra Kammaren*, No. 32, 1927, p. 57. [39o]
[48] *Ibid.*, p. 58.

doubt, he claimed, the glaring injustice in early selection for secondary schooling:

Occupation of parent	Number of students per 1000
1. Manual and industrial laborers	2
2. Farmers, farm hands, gardeners	5
3. Trades, craftsmen	27
4. Commercial owners and managers	154
5. Clergymen	174
6. Teachers in secondary and higher education	177
7. Physicians, dentists, veterinarians, and pharmacists	188

Nils Helger further pointed out that girls from working-class families were even more dramatically underrepresented in private girls' schools.[49] Corresponding figures for girls with parents in the first occupational group were 0.6; in the second, 2; in the third group, 9; and in the seventh, 114.

Conservative opponents of the reform rejected Helger's study as statistically unsound, asserting that for social reasons the pupils had given misleading information about their parents' occupations. They cited studies by eugenicists to support their contention that since "Sweden has long experienced a pronounced social class mobility, . . . natural selection has already brought about intellectual predominance in the professional classes."[50] Furthermore, since this social mobility had taken place within the past decade under a parallel school system there was therefore no valid reason for reform because the school system was demonstrably democratic in character. Although the supporters of comprehensive schooling could not accept these arguments, they did, however, acknowledge that Swedish secondary schools had for generations been accessible to a limited number of needy gifted boys, perhaps in a higher degree than in any other European country.[51]

Those who championed the secondary school against the encroachments of the elementary school realized that some extension of the latter was inevitable and they mustered all possible arguments for differentiation into secondary schooling after four years rather than after six years as proposed by the progressive elements.[52] They had also

[49] Nils Helger, *Barnens rätt, några synpunkter i ett par aktuella skolfrågor,* 1927, pp. 45–46. [102]
[50] *Svenska Dagbladet,* May 20, 1927. [167]
[51] Riksdagen [39d], p. 78.
[52] *Svenska Dagbladet,* April 4, 1927, p. 2. [167]

been led to believe by the minister's remarks that in selected places the old arrangement of transfer after three years in the *folkskola* would be retained in order to determine if that system could hold its own against any new arrangement.[53] Thus both the longer and the shorter foundation schools would be able to prove their merits. This, however, was not to be the case. Because of the controversy generated by the proposal, Parliament appointed its own Special Committee on Schools to clarify the government's bill, which had already been amended many times. To the surprise of many, the Committee chairman turned out to be Värner Rydén, the most outspoken partisan for the *enhetsskola*, who in 1918 had originally begun the legislative process for a six-year common school. Through manipulation and dealing, Rydén was eventually able to radicalize Minister Almquist's proposal so that not only would the six-year school be privileged in various ways, but the three-year foundation school—to the great dismay of the Conservatives—was abolished altogether.[54]

Parliament passed the modified bill on May 19, 1927, with a vote in the first chamber of 84 for, and 62 against; and in the second chamber of 152 for, and 64 against.[55] After Rydén had effected a compromise with Bondeförbundet (the Agrarian Party), the voting had followed almost exclusively along party lines.[56]

In summary, the final Act provided for the following changes:

1. Transfer to the secondary school would be postponed by at least one year. It would henceforth take place after four or, preferably, after six years (see Figure 1, part C). In many specifically named localities the classes of the shorter (i.e., nonparallel) four-year *realskola* must be entirely filled before the longer five-year lower secondary school (and transfer after four years in the *folkskola*) would be permitted. The aim of the law is "to keep children together in a foundation comprehensive school for as long as possible; consequently, the six-year *folkskola* is favored over all other forms." [57] Permission to make any changes could come only from the *riksdag*, not, as usual, from the Royal Board under the Ministry of Education.[58]

Further evidence that the 1927 Act favored the six-year school is found in the fact that private and semi-private schools—although not banned as the more outspoken reformers desired—would no longer receive state aid for any grades paralleling the six-year comprehensive

53 Riksdagen [39o], p. 25.
54 Riksdagen [39d], p. 23.
55 *Dagens Nyheter*, May 20, 1927. [76]
56 Riksdagen, [39d], p. 92.
57 *Ibid.*, p. 25.
58 *Ibid.*, p. 28.

school. Moreover, school teachers in any such private schools lost all state contributions to their salaries and pension plans.

2. No foreign languages were to be taught in the six-year elementary school. German would continue to be the first and English the second language studied in the *realskola;* French would be an elective.

3. The length of total schooling was increased by one year when the six-year foundation school was attended, although secondary schooling had been shortened with the introduction of the four-year *realskola* and the new three-year *gymnasium.*

4. The Act introduced the principle of coeducation in all public education—at least in theory. The *folkskola* had from its inception been the only public school open to both boys and girls. Although a number of *realskolor* and *gymnasier* were opened to girls after 1927, the more common practice was for the government to provide separate but equal state-supported secondary schools for girls only.[59]

Because the discussion in the *riksdag* had been almost entirely focused on the basic principle of one comprehensive foundation school for all children the problem of school curricula had received scant attention. The *riksdag* agreed therefore to have the Ministry of Education develop detailed courses of study in the spirit of Minister Almquist's proposals to "establish the secondary school along the lines of the Activity School." [60] However, because of political and parliamentary changes after 1927 the *riksdag* committee charged with responsibility for this program was dissolved. Nor was the serious problem of injustice to rural youth (because of their educational isolation from all but the *folkskola*) specifically dealt with—except for the provision for an alternate six-year *bottenskola*—to any extent in the 1927 Act. Postponement of differentiation would conceivably allow rural children going on to the *realskola* to remain at home for an additional year before moving to the city where the great majority of secondary schools were located. Prior to 1927, rural children were of necessity required to board away from home at the age of nine or lose the opportunity to transfer at an early age. They would therefore, if electing later transfer, lose several years of lower secondary work and would usually need extensive tutoring.[61] Official statistics illustrate the educational disadvantages of rural youth that were only partly meliorated

[59] *Ibid.,* pp. 36, 38, 40–41. Swedish male aversion to coeducation stemmed primarily from fears of economic competition in the restricted job market, as well as from long-standing traditions and prejudices. See Gösta Börjeson, *Folkskollärareröverflödet,* 1926, pp. 20–22. [67]

[60] See Rydén's criticism in *Tiden,* Vol. 12 (1929), p. 30.

[61] Ecklesiastikdepartementet, *Vissa frågor rörande tillämpning av 1927 års skolorganisation,* 1929, p. 15. [38j]

by the 1927 structural changes. For example, in 1922 about 30 per cent of the Swedish population lived in towns with secondary schools of some type. Yet in 1923 over 80 per cent of the students in *realskolor* came from urban homes. On the other hand—although they represented 70 per cent of the total population—only 19.5 per cent of secondary pupils came from the total rural population. Of these 9.8 per cent commuted and 9.7 per cent boarded. Figures for the *gymnasium* show a slightly more favorable ratio for rural youth.[62]

The supporters of the movement to transform the *folkskola* into a comprehensive school for all children and a foundation school for all types of secondary education viewed the 1927 Act as a mildly satisfying compromise if not a stunning victory. The opponents of the foundation school reform, essentially a structural reorganization to unify the lower sections of the parallel system at the expense of the *realskola*, accepted their limited defeat gracefully and thereafter concentrated their energies on defending, where possible, the academic system during the six-year period assigned to implement the bill's provisions. During this time Conservative members were able, through their strong position on an Expert Committee in 1931, to modify some of the Act's provisions concerning electives and the rights of private schools.

By 1932, however, the *folkskola-bottenskola* with double connections to the *realskola* was in operation throughout Sweden, signifying a trend, if not a victory, in the reduction of structural dualism.

But popular interest in the question of comprehensive schools had greatly subsided, and the national mood had come around essentially to agree with Bergqvist's observation that reform should be implemented in an apolitical milieu because "as poison in unsuitable proportions harms an organism so also can too much politics—especially in the form of school political dogmas and doctrines—be malignant. It may lead to a limitation and rigidity of perception. A person may stare himself blind on one aspect of a case and overemphasize the importance of one form of organization to the harm of others equally justified." [63]

---

[62] *Ibid.*, p. 38.
[63] B. J. Bergqvist, *Sveriges ungdomsskolor,* 1931, p. 12 [59a]

Chapter 3

EDUCATION AND THE WELFARE STATE: REFORM PROBLEMS AND PRIORITIES 1927–1940

*Judging both from what has been achieved in Sweden
and from what is still on our waiting list of imperfec-
tions to repair, I sincerely believe this to be one of
the most pressing of all things . . . to campaign
for, . . . namely, to fill the still existing gaps in the
elementary school system, to obliterate regional and
rural backwardness. Let us at least have no illusions
about the perfection of our educational systems or
of our democracies if we achieve a few, however
prominent, top-institutions but tolerate the fact that
huge areas are not a part of our twentieth century
civilization.*[1]

[1] From the speech, "Education for Democracy in
Sweden," by Alva Myrdal, Swedish educator and Social
Democratic intellectual spokesman, in *Education for
Democracy*, 1939, p. 173. [24a]

As the year 1918 marked the final breakthrough of
democratic rule in Sweden, the year 1932 witnessed a sharp acceleration in this political movement with the beginning of a long period of
Social Democratic leadership that culminated in what has come to be
known as the Swedish "welfare state." [2] And, as is apparent from the
foregoing quotation, the government's new emphasis on equalization
of opportunity was neither absent nor insignificant in Social Democratic
policy and priorities for educational reform. The principle of egalitarianism did in fact provide the ultimate rationale for the new phase of
school reform that began in 1932 and culminated in the Education Act
of 1950. [3]

The year 1932 is a watershed for other important changes in Swedish
life as well. The economic depression had by then reached its nadir
and in the process had helped to bring the Socialists to power. They
in turn with their Agrarian allies immediately embarked on a pragmatic program of thoroughgoing policy reforms. The success of Social
Democratic political leadership and programs may in part be seen in
Sweden's rapid recovery from the depression with advances in her
national economy, especially during the 1935–1936 "boom," and in the
progressive implementation of a centrally planned and administered
program of social services and social welfare. [4]

Partly because the compromise of 1927 had exhausted public and
governmental interest in matters of school reform and partly because
of contingencies arising from the depression, reform activities in educa-

[2] The best over-all popular study of this development, if a bit overly enthusiastic,
is the work by Marquis W. Childs, *Sweden: The Middle Way,* rev. ed., 1947. [74]
[3] Cf. Childs [74] with Alva Myrdal and Gunnar Myrdal, *Kris i befolkningsfrågan,*
1934, Chap. 20, *passim.* [24c]
[4] G. Arthur Montgomery, *How Sweden Overcame the Depression, 1930–1933,*
1938, pp. 78–80. [130a]

tion after 1932 and up until World War II were in the main limited to the consolidation and full implementation of earlier legislation.[5] Although the Socialists—especially after their gains in the 1936 elections—were certainly in a vastly improved position to attempt a diminution of dualism in the educational system, they showed no interest in the problem, in marked contrast to their earlier attacks on class-stratified education. Rather, the Social Democrats' central legislative concerns, efforts, and activities revolved around the adoption of a theory of national planning to alter Swedish life through, for example, major distributional reforms. This new development in which the state began more and more to assume responsibility for the well-being and equality of opportunity for all the Swedish people did, however, lay the ideological foundation for the radical reformation of Swedish education after World War II when the dual educational system—tolerated in the first two decades of the welfare state—was completely abolished.

This chapter presents a survey of the forces and factors that came into play in the gradual evolution of the Swedish welfare state and in its primary concerns with (1) problems of economic recovery; (2) the population problem; and (3) the movement toward greater equalization in the consumption of goods and services as an integral component of manifest democratization.

DEPRESSION, REFORM, AND EDUCATION

The international economic crisis that began in 1929 had by 1932 severely depressed the Swedish economy. Although unemployment did not reach the extent of the 1922 depression, over 14 per cent of all trade union members were out of work throughout the decade of the 1930's. The peak was reached in 1932 when nearly 23 per cent of the unionized work force was unemployed.[6] But if the economic situation was seriously distressed in Sweden, it did not result in political disturbances against the established democratic political order. For several reasons, the depression, even at its most extreme, was less severe in Sweden than in most other countries. The industrial revolution came late to Sweden, and the 1920's had seen an unprecedented economic expansion and increase in capital investment and real wages.[7] In

[5] Cf. the quantity and contents of official committee reports (Statens Offentliga Utredningar) for the three periods (1) 1922–1931, (2) 1932–1940, and (3) 1941–1950.

[6] See Figure 6, "Arbetslösheten inom fackföreningarna i procent av medlemsantalet, i medeltal per år, 1914–1957," in Åke Elmér, *Från fattigsverige till Välfärdsstaten*, 1963, p. 64. [82a]

[7] *Ibid.*, p. 83. See also G. Arthur Montgomery, *The Rise of Modern Industry in Sweden*, 1939, pp. 232–240 [130d], for an excellent account of post-World War I

addition to a relatively high average standard of living at the depression's outset, foreign demand for wood products, iron ore and other exports remained sufficiently high to provide the government with adequate resources to stimulate artificially the home market and to institute relief programs and thoroughgoing reforms in unemployment policy.[8]

Direct depression influences on Swedish education shifted the emphasis of school reforms already under way. The Social Democrats, and the trade unions, were losing interest in further organizational changes and in the modernization of methods of instruction in *folkskolan*.[9] Instead, the government sought to bring all education up to legislative minimal standards and to use the schools—through the introduction of various student welfare services—as an adjunct to support high priority social welfare reform programs.

Indirectly the depression undermined support in the Elementary School Teachers Association (Sveriges Allmänna Folkskollärarförening) for a continued fight to secure a common six-year elementary school. Since its founding and early leadership by Fridtjuv Berg in the 1880's, the organization had, along with other related elementary school professional groups, single-mindedly and vociferously propagandized for the common school.[10] As a professional body the association had also waged a related campaign to modernize content and methods of instruction and this was intensified in the 1930's. Efforts along these lines had for a number of decades been gaining momentum under the stimulus of advances in educational psychology and under the press of changing social and economic demands on the elementary school.[11]

With the advent of the depression, however, the unity of the organization began to weaken and two separate factions appeared. One

---

economic growth in Sweden, and how "forced saving" during the war enabled Sweden to pay off most of its earlier foreign borrowing for industrialization. After World War I Sweden changed from a capital-borrowing to a capital-exporting nation.

[8] See Montgomery [130a], pp. 83 ff., and Ernst Wigforss, "The Financial Policy during Depression and Boom," *Annals of the American Academy of Political and Social Science*, May 1938, pp. 27 ff. [50b].

[9] The Social Democrats' lack of interest in the compromise comprehensive school reform—in contrast to the 1920's—is evident in the complete absence of discussion on the matter at the 1932 and 1936 party congresses. See *Kongressmotioner* for those years. [35a]

[10] See, for example, the various issues of the organization's newspaper, *Svensk Lärartidning*, for the years of comprehensive school reform conflict in 1918, 1922, and 1927. [165]

[11] The association's generally progressive position on school reform is described in Anna Sörenson, *Pedagoger och pedagogiska problem: Pedagogiska Sällskapet i Stockholm 1892–1942*, 1942, pp. 146–155. [157b]

group, representing the majority of the new teachers, saw the primary purpose of the organization as one of furthering the economic and professional interests of its members.[12] The older group claimed that even if this were true, the interests of the group as a whole could only be advanced in a meaningful way to the extent that the *folkskola* continued to grow as a comprehensive school at the expense of the lower secondary *realskola*.[13]

In working-class and Social Democratic circles, what little concern and support had existed for extended comprehensive compulsory education in the 1920's was in the 1930's largely dissipated by the depression and a number of other factors. Aspiration for secondary education in working-class families had never been marked even in the boom period of the late 1920's. Because working-class children had of necessity to begin earning wages at the earliest possible age and because of the fees and snobbery involved in academic schooling, the secondary schools were generally seen by working-class parents and pupils alike as an exclusive and somewhat forbidding private domain of the middle and upper classes.[14]

The Social Democrats, it would seem, tacitly accepted this view of a social-class-stratified school system. In view of the severe problem of professional unemployment, they concurred that secondary education should remain highly selective, but with the qualification that it was the duty of the state to insure equality of opportunity in so far as possible within the existing system.[15] Overproduction of graduates from the *gymnasium* and universities during the 1920's and 1930's did pose a powerful argument against a liberalization of entrance requirements to secondary education and, in a sense, against the proposed longer common school. And, of course, the danger of an intellectual proletariat grew worse under the influence of the depression and may

[12] See in this regard the policy statement by Secretary Edvin Stålfelt, *Vår förening och dess program*, 1931 [32], reflecting the new emphasis on economic concerns.

[13] Stålfelt and the majority of the organization supporting his views received a trenchant critique from Frida Härner and other supporters of the *folkskola* as a more extensive comprehensive school. See her letter in Ruben Wagnsson, *ABC: vår folkundervisning från medeltid till enhetsskola*, 1955, p. 383. [176]

[14] Interview with Swedish trade union officials, Stockholm, August 14, 1965. K. Svalastoga has noted similar attitudes before 1946 in Denmark where, as in Sweden, it was considered "deviant behavior" for even bright children from working-class homes to aspire to a secondary education in the *realskola* or in the prestigious *gymnasium*: ". . . among my comrades it was not usual to go to school longer . . . it was not done." See his study *Prestige, Class and Mobility*, 1959, pp. 162–163. [163]

[15] See Point 4, Educational Program, of the Social Democratic congress reports for 1928, 1932, and 1936: *Protokoll*. [35b]

well be another reason why once in power the Socialists made little effort to force the educational stalemate with the still powerful supporters of an elitist system of secondary and higher education.[16]

With the death of Värner Rydén in 1930, the Social Democrats lost their only true spokesman for comprehensive school reform and not until after World War II did this cause once again become a priority item in the Socialist reform program.[17] Reflecting its Marxian origins, the Social Democratic party had always given highest priorities to economic and political reforms, and the deterioration of economic conditions after 1929 undoubtedly reinforced this ideological imperative.

During the early depression years, the Social Democrats through a fiscal policy of budgetary expansion sought to quicken activities in the public sector to increase aggregate national purchasing power and the use of unutilized resources.[18] After 1935, however, the government's primary interest shifted and the initial remedial stage of social reconstruction was given primary budgetary consideration. For reasons to be mentioned in a following section, this new policy of social welfare services was principally directed toward problems concerning families and children. It called for an "investment" in the personal capital of the country and was defensible, according to the renowned Social Democratic economist and spokesman Gunnar Myrdal, "not only on grounds of charity and justice, like the older type of social policy, but also by reason of national economy with human capital." [19] Similarly, the primary motive of the Socialist government's investment in educational reforms was to equalize and rationalize the educational base to create a truly uniform elementary school system for all children. Alva Myrdal explained her party's lack of interest in expanded secondary education:

[16] For the conservative point of view on this danger, see the article "Bottenskolelogik" by Erik Wellander in *Svenska Dagbladet*, May 6, 1927 [49]; and *Göteborgs Handelstidning*, November 23, 1935. The trade unions sought relief through (1) better possibilities and facilities for vocational training; (2) unionization as a means to end the exploitation of working youth; and (3) concrete measures to counteract youth unemployment through state grants for leadership training in folk high schools and the like. See Landsorganisationen, *Protokoll elfte ordinarie kongress 9–27 oktober, 1936*, pp. 434–442. [21b]

[17] Rydén's position in the Social Democratic party (i.e., his isolation as a champion of the *folkskola* as a comprehensive school) is critically evaluated by Erik Wellander in *Svenska Dagbladet*, August 30, 1940.

[18] For an excellent summary of Swedish practice in this respect see "Part III, Stabilization Planning in Sweden 1929–1939" in Lewis Lorwin, *National Planning in Selected Countries*, 1941, pp. 93–120. [126]

[19] Gunnar Myrdal, "Population Problems and Policies," *Annals of the American Academy of Political and Social Science*, May 1938, pp. 208–209. [25]

Typical of the Swedish idea of democracy, the desire is to build from the bottom, to raise the minimum standards of education, and to enforce them all over the country. This predilection . . . makes all educational reforms expensive in Sweden. There can be no appropriation which is not aimed to lift the standard of all districts, to extend improved educational facilities to economically disadvantaged regions and groups.[20]

An application of this educational strategy may be seen in the action of the *riksdag* on July 1, 1936, when the Socialists with outspoken Agrarian support carried their proposal to extend compulsory schooling from six to seven years over a ten-year period. As several of the larger urban school districts had for decades required seven and even eight years of elementary school attendance, the bill should be seen as a direct attempt to raise rural school attendance to *de facto* minimal national norms. For example, Socialist Minister of Education Arthur Engberg shocked Parliament with the statement that "only 16 per cent of rural children complete the full six years of compulsory elementary schooling in contrast with a corresponding figure of 72 per cent in the towns." It was his belief that "this is a question of rural ambition for the same demand made in the *riksdag* of 1840, the demand for education equal to that provided for urban children, for are not all Swedish youth equal?" [21]

In the same manner, and in order to effect an equalization of school district expenditures and to provide the additional funds made necessary by the change, the *riksdag* had a year earlier, in 1935, transferred to the state certain expenses for buildings, maintenance and teachers' salaries which had hitherto fallen on the local school districts.[22] Thus, as the Swedish economy in a planned, rational way moved toward autarky in a manner characteristic of the pre-World War II decade in Western Europe so too did the educational system come under stronger centralized control and financial support.

THE POPULATION PROBLEM

When the *riksdag* convened in January 1935, all four major Swedish political parties agreed that legislative action should be taken to arrest,

---

[20] Riksdagen, *Riksdagens protokoll. Andra Kammaren 1936*, No. 2, pp. 84–85. [39k]

[21] *Ibid.*, p. 61.

[22] Nils Hänninger and Dagn Falk, "Sweden," in *Education Yearbook of the International Institute of Teachers College, Columbia University, 1936*, p. 506. [94b]

if possible, an alarming decline in the net reproduction rate.[23] With the rate at less than three-fourths of that necessary to maintain a stationary population balance, the future of the Swedish people stood in peril.[24] The Socialists seized upon the population problem to justify a program of economic redistribution in favor of lower-class children and families in much the same way that the economic crisis arising from the depression was successfully used to gain parliamentary acceptance of a series of economic reforms and the passage of several long-contested unemployment measures.[25]

In the years following 1935 a comprehensive series of new laws came into being in an attempt to increase the birth rate through a reform of the social basis of the family, and through the equalization of the economic costs of childbearing, health services, and education.[26] Beginning at first with measures closely related to maximizing the conditions favorable for a population increase, the program expanded in time to include the entire welfare state rationale that ultimately sought "the people's own welfare and happiness." Under this broad rubric the state under Social Democrat leadership progressively assumed responsibility for sex education at the family, school and adult education levels; family planning; loans for homemaking, housing, and higher education; programs for dietary education and a wide range of health services; social security and social care for the variously handicapped; recreation facilities for students and economically deprived families; state subsidized vacations for housewives and the independently employed; and a wide range of social services for students.[27] The collective result of these and later efforts produced what has come to be called the Swedish welfare state. It should be recognized, however, that its original justification lay in the attempted practical solutions to profound social and economic problems and not in the arbitrary imposition of ideological imperatives.[28] With the continued parliamentary dominance by the Social Democrats after 1936, however, their program of social reform increasingly aimed at the redistribution of production and consumption in keeping with the party's long-standing priorities for the fundamental reconstruction of Swedish

[23] Riksdagen, *Riksdagens protokoll. Andra Kammaren 1935*, No. 1, pp. 35–36. [39j]

[24] See Karl Arvid Edin and Edward P. Hutchinson, *Studies of Differential Fertility in Sweden*, 1935, p. 21. [80]

[25] Gunnar Myrdal, *Population: A Problem for Democracy*, 1962, pp. 208–209. [133b]

[26] *Ibid.*, pp. 210–211.

[27] *Ibid.*, pp. 302–305.

[28] For a discussion of the historical background of state participation in the public sector—especially in matters of social concern such as poor laws, elementary education, pension and insurance laws—see Montgomery [130d], pp. 250–252.

society. Myrdal, revealingly, even went so far as to make the prophecy that "this development [i.e., the decline in the fertility rate to a point far below the rate necessary for population maintenance] must sooner or later unleash in Western society an ideological crisis in popular attitudes towards the welfare question." [29]

ASCENDANCY OF THE SOCIAL DEMOCRATIC PARTY

Swedish Social Democrats initially sought a "new society," a new social system, and a new organization of economic life based on the Marxian conception of the classless millennium which would supposedly follow the violent overthrow of the capitalist system. [30] At the first Social Democratic party congress in 1899, however, the vast majority of the delegates rather effortlessly abandoned "classical" Marxist ideology by forswearing violent revolution and resolving to cooperate with, for example, the Liberal party in a common struggle for suffrage reforms. [31] Hjalmar Branting, the first Socialist *riksdag* member and an important early party leader, effectively oriented Social Democratic party policy in the direction of moderation and compromise in the matter of public ownership, while at the same time the party continued doggedly to fight for social reform, the leveling of incomes, and various state regulatory controls. [32]

In the decades after 1899, the trend toward revisionism became ever more pronounced when the Social Democrats attempted to replace the Liberals as the party of the "small folk." The Marxian "iron law of wages" theory and even the demand for nationalization of industry were dropped from the party program. A further decisive move toward popular acceptance occurred in the 1920's when the Social Democrats patiently accepted the inevitability of cooperation with opposition minority governments and the need to compromise on controversial legislation such as the school reform act of 1927. [33]

The Social Democrats first entered the cabinet in 1917 and during the 1920's formed three short-lived minority governments. It was not until 1932, however, that they first achieved stable rule. In exchange for a pledge of farm price supports, the Social Democrats negotiated

[29] G. Myrdal [133b], p. 65.

[30] Frans Severin, *The Ideological Development of Swedish Social Democracy*, 1956, p. 6. [154]

[31] Nils Andrén, *Modern Swedish Government*, 1961, p. 24. [52]

[32] Branting's success in emphasizing the democratic side of the Swedish Social Democratic party's development is analyzed by Ragnar Edenman in "Brantings första riksdagar (1897–1902)," *Statsvetenskapliga studier*, 1944, pp. 179–213. [79]

[33] Herbert Tingsten, *Den svenska socialdemokratiens idéutveckling*, 1941, Vol. 2, pp. 107–110. [174]

an informal alliance with the back-bench Agrarian deputies to gain a working majority for their antidepression program that had been the cause of such heated controversy in the 1920's. It is perhaps not surprising that these two political parties, representing the two segments of the Swedish work force most severely affected by the depression, joined forces to gain the first stable majority in the *riksdag* since 1917.[34]

Continued electoral gains by the Social Democrats from 1933 to 1939 in both national and municipal elections may be seen in the main as a popular affirmation of the government's expansionistic economic policy in stabilizing farm prices, in reducing unemployment, and in providing desired new social services. At no time, however, did the Social Democrats place a priority on the abolition, or even the diminution, of dualism in the school system. Nor did they make any effort to use their new political power to rectify the compromise made for a "double connection" to the *realskola* in 1927. Their initial reform interests lay elsewhere in fundamental social and economic problems.

EDUCATION AND SOCIAL WELFARE

For a number of reasons, the Socialists—and their allies the Agrarians—largely bypassed the formal educational structure in building a welfare program to provide for the health and well-being of all Swedish citizens. The schools played no substantive part but, rather, on the order of dispensaries, were primarily used—aside, of course, from formal instruction—to provide an increasing number of social services. Reflecting the same pragmatic and ideological considerations that undergirded the national program of social welfare, school social services received a high priority for rapid adoption and implementation.[35] Although hampered by lack of funds and problems of providing social services and facilities for rural pupils equal to those available to urban pupils, Swedish schools gradually provided a comprehensive nationwide program of services in one way or another related to the nurture of children. Among these might be mentioned the introduction of free school lunches, free medical and dental services, clothing allowances, bathing facilities, and free days for outdoor sports and activities. Some of these services, it should be mentioned, had been previously provided on a limited scale—usually in the larger cities—, since the late 1800's. After 1932, however, the government began to

[34] The role of the Socialist-Agrarian alliance in creating what came to be called the "Swedish New Deal" and in preventing the creation of a bourgeois front is discussed in detail by Bjarne Braatöy in *The New Sweden: A Vindication of Democracy*, 1939, Chap. 1. [68]

[35] Socialstyrelsen, *Social Sweden*, 1952, p. 352. [41a]

assume an ever greater responsibility for the nationwide availability of a comprehensive and uniform program of social services in the schools.[36]

Why the Social Democrats—who before 1932 had bitterly attacked inequalities in the dualistic system of education—accepted the status quo in the class-oriented elementary and secondary systems when once firmly in power is a paradox of considerable interest. A review of some of the underlying causes—touching on aspects of ideology, leadership, and expediency—for such a *volte-face* may therefore be helpful in clarifying some basic considerations influencing the government's position on school reform in the creation of the Swedish welfare state.

The ideological origins of the Swedish Social Democratic party in some measure explain the low priority assigned to problems of educational reform once the party took office and possessed the possibility of developing a program of social, economic and political reform.[37] In marked contrast to the earlier liberal-progressive reformers who viewed the school as a fundamental lever for social reconstruction, the Swedish Socialists from the inception of the party in 1881 saw school reform as an end product of, rather than a prelude to, political and economic reform.[38] For only by winning suffrage reforms could radical economic and social reforms be gained through democratic processes. Furthermore, the fact that Liberals and Socialists cooperated in a joint effort to win a universal franchise played a formative role in fostering a moderate and pragmatic spirit within the Swedish Social Democratic movement.[39]

The death of Värner Rydén in September 1930 removed the only

[36] Problems of expanding and equalizing school social services in the late 1930's are discussed by I. M. Bolton, "Social Services," in *Democratic Sweden: A Volume of Studies Prepared by Members of the New Fabian Research Bureau*, 1939, pp. 272–273. [66] See also pp. 305–306 in the same work for observations by M. Cole on shortages and inequalities of services.

[37] Karl Marx's lack of faith in the utility of educational reform to bring about social reform is implicit in his statement: "It is not the consciousness of men that determines their being, but rather, their social being that determines their consciousness." Quoted in George C. Counts, *The Challenge of Soviet Education*, 1957, p. 12. [75]

[38] See p. 31, footnote 84, and G. Hilding Nordström, *Sveriges socialdemokratiska arbetareparti under genombrottsåren, 1889–1894*, 1938, p. 96. [135]

[39] Rustow concludes that the Social Democrats' continued threat of a revolution served only as a reserve weapon and that their pragmatic cooperation with the Liberals saved the Swedish Social Democrats from the "revisionist-radical" dilemma. Sturmthal characterized this as "the basic weakness of European labor . . . the lack of real political participation and constructive thinking on basic social problems" in the pre-World War II decades and before. See Dankwart A. Rustow, *The Politics of Compromise: A Study of Parties and Cabinet Government in Sweden*, 1955, p. 53 [150]; and Adolf Sturmthal, *The Tragedy of European Labor*, 1943, p. 4 [162].

leader in the Social Democratic party's ranks who had a total commitment to the old movement to make the *folkskola* an unequivocal comprehensive *enhetsskola*. Rydén had been very much aware of his role in continuing the movement begun by Fryxell, Siljeström, Berg and others; he had clearly been the armature of Socialist activity in the matter of school reform from 1917 to 1930. Rydén's early years as a *folkskola* teacher and official in the *folkskola* teachers' organization helped to give him an understanding of and dedication to the movement for comprehensive school reform unequaled in the ranks of his party.[40]

Furthermore, a constellation of pragmatic considerations restrained Social Democratic initiative to force the *détente* between *folkskola* and *realskolan*. The resistance of the highly institutionalized secondary school had become starkly evident in the contested reforms of the 1920's. More than likely, therefore, any gains made in the direction of a longer comprehensive school would have entailed increased resistance to what the Socialists considered more expedient socioeconomic reforms.[41] Furthermore, the national economy, although back to pre-depression levels of production after 1935, would very probably not have been able to support fundamental educational reforms on top of the government's high priority measures for (1) unemployment relief; (2) programs related to the problem of population decline; and (3) higher living standards and conditions of work.[42] After the successful enactment into law of most of these programs during the years from 1937 to 1939, the deteriorating international situation began to preoccupy all Swedish legislators and the Socialist Prime Minister P. A. Hansson formed a coalition government of the four major political parties in December 1939, following the Soviet Union's attack on neighboring Finland.[43]

PROBLEMS OF EQUALIZING EDUCATIONAL OPPORTUNITY

By 1939 the Social Democrats had with considerable success secured the essential legislation and public support necesary for the acceptance

---

[40] For tributes and appraisals of Rydén's role as an innovator for school reform programs in the Social Democratic party, see *Arbetet, Dagens Nyheter,* and *Stockholms Tidningen* for September 15, 1930. For a collection of appreciations by the *folkskola* teachers' organization, the Socialist Prime Minister Per Albin Hansson, and others, see Wagnsson [176], pp. 378–381.

[41] For an interesting discussion of this quandary see *Göteborgs Handelstidning,* November 23, 1935, p. 3. The Socialists did not obtain absolute majorities in both chambers until the election of 1940, when, although the majority party, they were politically circumscribed in a wartime coalition government.

[42] See the article by then Minister of Finance Ernst Wigforss, "The Financial Policy during Depression and Boom," pp. 25–39. [50b]

[43] Elis Håstad, *Sveriges historia under 1900-talet,* 1958, pp. 122–123. [97c]

and implementation of their program for the reconstruction of Swedish social and economic life.[44] In this program for a greater equalization of access to goods and services, for the social and economic improvement of families and the lower social level, and for the continued democratization of Swedish life, the Social Democratic leadership could not altogether disregard the traditional disparities in educational opportunities that were inherent in the class-linked system of bipartite schooling. As previously noted the Social Democrats had accepted the *de facto* compromise of 1927 and bypassed dualism in education as a problem too rigidly entrenched to eradicate at that time. But the national school system retained perhaps the most flagrant examples of geographical and class-determined inequalities, especially in selection for post-elementary education.[45] Traditional disparities in the availability of education for rural and urban youth and for children of different social classes, and in the neglect of education for girls, all took on new significance with the gradual extension of social democratic egalitarian philosophy to many central aspects and institutions of Swedish life. More and more the basic concerns of the Social Democrats in matters of educational reform became, first, to use the school— as in the case of supplying social services for children—as an agency to channel the material rewards of reform and second, to eradicate as far as possible all inequalities of opportunity for selection and admission within the entire existing school system.[46] In other words, the Social Democrats attempted to build an educational policy around the democratic belief that "if a country wants to be one country and a democratic country, the general school system must be of but one standard for all the people. There can be tolerated no great regional differences, no backward districts. Education must be used as a basis

[44] Perhaps the best account of this development is found in Karl J. Höijer, *Svensk socialpolitisk historia*, 1952. [107b] See particularly Chapter 6.

[45] Alva Myrdal comments that "*realskolan* is the weak point in the Swedish school system" but makes no specific charges or suggestions for reform in her monumental study *Nation and Family: The Swedish Experiment in Democratic Family and Population Policy*, 1941, p. 373. [132]

[46] The Swedish economist and a leader in formulating the Social Democrats' reform program, Gunnar Myrdal, has given the following three basic reasons for the government's preference "to redistribute incomes through measures *in natura* instead of in cash": (1) economy, i.e., "by organizing public health inspection of school children we get much more 'health consumption' than individual families could ever purchase"; (2) "with the *natura* line, social policy can be integrated rationally in the general economic policy"; and (3) "only in this way is it possible to guarantee that the allowances are used for the good of children. In order to get the maximum qualitative effect, allowances must be attached to specific consumption deemed to be essential for improving the milieu of the children." See Gunnar Myrdal, "Kontant eller *in natura* i socialpolitiken," *Nationalekonomisk Tidskrift*, April 1938, pp. 30–32 [133a]; SOU 1938:7, *Betänkande angående barnbeklädnadsbidrag*, pp. 91–93 [36b].

for social and cultural amalgamation and not for segregation within a nation."[47]

Still cautious after the severe problem of professional unemployment in the 1920's and early 1930's and hostile to the marked social class connotations of secondary and higher education, the Social Democrats made no appreciable efforts to expand recruitment to the academic branch of schooling. Rather, they sought as far as possible to equalize opportunities of all children for acceptance to the existing *realskolan*. Their chief educational concern sought "to provide 100 per cent of the citizens with a solid public school education and an increasing number of good trade school opportunities" rather than to provide secondary education—elitist by tradition, form, and content—for all.[48]

Efforts to consolidate rural education and bring it up to urban standards in both duration, content, and quality characterized this move to achieve a foundation of minimal educational standards. Assisted by the strong support of the Socialist-Agrarian government, local school districts in cooperation with the Royal Board of Education began a program of consolidation that reduced the total number of elementary schools from 14,741 in 1930 to 13,891 in 1939,[49] and long daily bus rides became a fact of life for many rural children. In a similar vein, application of the results of a rapidly developing national industrial technology also began to enrich the curriculum of rural *folkskolor* with the introduction of a school film program and school radio network by the Royal Board of Education.[50] Mobile libraries, and further improvements in educational facilities for the nomadic Lapps, helped to equalize educational offerings even in the most remote reaches of the land.[51]

The problem of the rural elementary school's geographical isolation and lack of communication with the urban secondary school, or for that matter with higher elementary and vocational schooling as well, grew worse during the 1930's with the beginnings of large-scale migration to urban areas and with the government's continued budgetary emphasis on social welfare programs. Few secondary schools could provide for the needs of rural boarders, nor was the economic burden of secondary schooling for rural families, despite extended debate in the *riksdag*, lessened by government subventions to any significant extent. Rural educational standards had, moreover, always been notoriously below those in urban elementary schools. Even as late as 1920, almost one-third of all rural children attended the *folkskola* for less than one-half the

---

[47] A. Myrdal [24a], p. 171.
[48] *Ibid.*, p. 174.
[49] *Statistisk årsbok 1940*, p. 285. [42]
[50] Beginning in the 1920's, Sweden pioneered the use of school radio and film techniques in Europe. See Wagnsson [176], p. 379.
[51] Ecklesiastikdepartementet, *Skolan i samhällets tjänst*, 1944, p. 135. [38f]

yearly term.[52] In 1938 about 6 per cent of all rural pupils were in half-time session and, as previously noted, the majority failed to complete even the minimum of six years: a situation intolerable to a government bent on equalization. A 1938 survey of the home localities of university students gives some indication of the problem of rural underrepresentation in higher education, a problem with obvious roots in the long-standing deficiencies and isolation of rural elementary education. The survey revealed that for each 100,000 urban dwellers, 247 attended universities or other institutions of higher education; the corresponding figure for small towns without secondary schools was 137; while in the country, only 47.[53]

Another serious problem of inequality in prewar Swedish education concerned the limited availability of facilities for secondary education open to girls. It may be recalled that prior to the 1927 Education Act any girl seeking an academic secondary education could find it only in expensive private *gymnasia*. Although these institutions usually provided a few scholarships—a condition necessary to obtain state subsidies—ordinarily only girls from well-to-do families attended secondary schools.[54] After 1927 the state assumed full responsibility for the provision of various kinds of postelementary and secondary education for all girls. In many cities, the state *realskolor* and *gymnasia* were made coeducational and many of the private girls' *gymnasia* were forced to close with the withdrawal of state subventions. Numerous state secondary schools, nevertheless, remained closed to girls for lack of space or, perhaps, because of a certain lack of interest in and low opinion of women's intellectual capabilities that had been a persistent theme in Swedish life.[55] The *riksdag* (in what might be seen as a partial reflection of the aforementioned attitude) created a new six- or seven-year tuition-free municipal girls' school to provide "a higher training for girls in household arts." Yet despite the creation of these practical schools and the state's move to expand coeducational instruction in many existing *realskolor* and *gymnasia*, educational opportunities beyond the *folkskola* for many Swedish girls continued to a great extent to be circumscribed by limited facilities.

[52] See *Ibid.*, pp. 104–109, for a summary of problems in upgrading rural education.

[53] These figures from Alva Myrdal's *Nation and Family*, p. 373, at best merely serve to indicate the general situation. [132]

[54] Riksdagen, *Riksdagens skrivelse angående inrättande av kommunala flickskolor den 5 juni 1928*, No. 356, 1928, p. 13. [39t]

[55] See the interesting comments on this attitude of masculine superiority in *Democratic Sweden: A Volume of Studies Prepared by Members of the New Fabian Research Bureau*, 1939, p. 296 [66]; and B. J. Bergqvist, "Sweden," in *Educational Yearbook of the International Institute of Teachers College, Columbia University: The Expansion of Secondary Education*, 1931, pp. 495–496. [59c]

Although movement across the parallel system of schools into the academic branch had always been possible (if severely restricted) for children of all social classes and definitely served as a means for social mobility, children of agricultural and industrial workers had nevertheless been traditionally underrepresented in the secondary and higher education student population.[56] As late as the mid-1940's children from working-class homes still comprised not more than six per cent of all university students and a somewhat higher percentage of pupils in secondary schools.[57] The Social Democrats sought especially to improve the economic situation of the working-class group through the social welfare program. Through a more proletarian conception of the arts, they attempted to draw the working class into the center of the national cultural life. The Social Democrats did not, however, succeed in providing the financial support necessary for an increased working-class representation in the secondary school. Fees for secondary schools were not prohibitive in the 1930's, but when combined with the need for working-class children to earn wages, and the general expense and foregone earnings involved in prolonged postelementary school study, they did represent a barrier to increased working-class recruitment to *realskolan*.[58] Moreover, the rigorously theoretical and class-linked nature of secondary and higher education—as well as frequently inferior *folkskola* preparation—further served to limit the aspirations of working-class children to the academic branch that led on to the university and the professions.[59]

One result of the remoteness and perceived inadequacy of formal secondary schooling in the eyes of the Swedish working class was the impressive development of popular education in the nineteenth and twentieth centuries. During the 1800's folk high schools, temperance societies and other agencies for adult education came into widespread favor largely among the rural working class to provide leadership for folk movements and to supplement the minimal schooling provided by six years or less of exposure to the *folkskola*. With the growth of a large urban working class in the 1900's the workers themselves took

[56] A study by Sten Carlsson of social mobility in Sweden since the seventeenth century reveals that sons of landowning farmers were surprisingly well represented in higher education during the nineteenth century. They constituted about 15 per cent of university students in the first half of that century and about 20 per cent in the second half. See *Bonde-präst-ämbetsman*, 1962, pp. 81, 100. [71a] Gunnar Richardson has concluded from his study of social recruitment to secondary education in the 1880's that upward of 15 per cent of the students were sons of farmers. *Kulturkamp och klasskamp*, 1963, pp. 288–308. [144]

[57] SOU 1963:53, p. 56. [36e]

[58] Sten Carlsson, "From the Estates to the Educational Society," in *The Intellectual Face of Sweden*, 1964, pp. 12–13. [71b]

[59] Interview with Folke Haldén. Stockholm, August 26, 1965.

the initiative to adapt earlier types and to create appropriate new forms of adult education.[60] With success at the polls it had become increasingly necessary for union leaders and members to contribute and participate in complex negotiations, in legislation and policy-making that involved national as well as trade union interests. Rejecting secondary education as offered in the *realskola* and *gymnasium* and seeing little hope that the elementary school would in a reasonable period be changed to provide the requisite education workers needed to cope effectively with problems of modern life, the trade union organization (Landsorganisationen) bypassed the formal educational system to found the Workers Educational Association (Arbetarnas Bildningsförbund, or ABF) in 1912.[61] This important program sought to provide workers with the practical and theoretical instruction necessary for participation in a democratic and industrial society as a citizen or, if need be, even as a prime minister. Through the use of some 70,000 study circles and classes, hundreds of thousands of workers had by 1940 participated in what had become a viable, efficient workers' "high school" in the "folk branch" of the bipartite educational structure. Courses and studies—largely at the student's own expense—in order of frequency of instruction included: (1) organization technique and problems; (2) general culture and foreign languages; (3) political science and local government; and (4) the arts, trade unionism, and arithmetic.[62] Moreover, by 1939 over 1,500 ABF libraries were in use, many in Swedish communities without other library facilities.[63] In the creation of their own educational system the trade unions abjured political affiliation with any group and thereby gained financial support from both the national and municipal governments. Understandably, state grants for this private educational activity received warm support from even the Conservative element in Parliament.[64]

[60] For an illuminating study of the compensatory role of the popular education movement in Sweden, see Per G. Stensland, "Adult Education," in *Scandinavia between East and West*, 1950, pp. 225–231 [159]; and Gunnar Hirdman, *Adult Education in Sweden*, 1947, pp. 12–18. [105]

[61] The ABF originally also served to "retool" union leadership after their disastrously unsuccessful general strike of 1909. ABF has roots in the earlier *folkhögskola* (rural folk high school) movement, and strong ties with the powerful cooperative movements. For a description of ABF and other reform-linked sections of the large and effective adult education movement in Sweden before World War II, see Ivar Andrén, *Det fria och frivilliga bildningsarbetet i Sverige 1944*, 1944, *passim*. [2]

[62] A. Myrdal [24a], p. 177.

[63] Paul Bergevin, *Adult Education in Sweden: An Introduction*, 1961, p. 22. [58]

[64] In the post-World War II decade governmental support had been increased to pay for some 40 per cent of all expenses. The balance was met by contributions from affiliated unions (15 per cent) and from participant fees (40 per cent). See *ibid*.

In light of the foregoing, it may be concluded that despite concerted efforts by the state, many groups of Swedish children—especially girls and those from working-class and rural backgrounds—continued to have in one way or another a disadvantaged educational situation in a nation whose ruling majority sought the goal of equality of opportunity in education as in all other areas of national life. Nevertheless, the literature of the immediate prewar period describing and evaluating the Swedish educational situation and the possibility of further corrective measures conveys a general impression that on the whole there existed close to a national consensus that the segregated educational system, for the time being at least, needed no further major alterations or major reform—that, granted a continual improvement of the elementary *folkskola* and the effective system of adult education in the "folk" secondary school for the masses, the dual system could adequately continue to function to educate a community with old and resistant class distinctions, but with increasingly smaller economic differences.[65]

[65] Gunnar Helén, a Liberal spokesman for comprehensive schooling in the 1950's, has summed up the prevalent attitude of many Swedish parents just prior to World War II as follows: "Give teachers and headmasters time and peace to work and everything will be all right by itself." Gunnar Helén, "Present Trends and Political Issues," in *Differentiation and Guidance in the Comprehensive School*, 1958, p. 30. [101]

Chapter 4

EDUCATION AND DEMOCRACY: REVIVAL OF THE COMPREHENSIVE SCHOOL CONTROVERSY 1940–1946

The current discussion of school problems in Sweden, as abroad, has become increasingly concerned with disparities between the practical and theoretical branches of the compulsory school system, between the folkskola and the realskola and how they must be equalized.[1]

[1] Nils Wikström, "Anmälan," *Svensk Skoltidning*, January 8, 1944, p. 3. [181]

The march of events following Hitler's invasion of Poland in September 1939 eventually found Sweden isolated from the democratic world and provoked a searching reexamination of her own democratic values and institutions. Sweden alone of the three Scandinavian countries escaped the totalitarian onslaught that saw both Denmark and Norway fall to the invading forces of Nazi Germany in March 1940. Through an arrangement with Germany to provide Swedish iron ore and transit rights for German troops to Norway and in return to receive essential supplies of fuel and strategic goods, Sweden was able to eke out a precarious "neutral" status.[2] With invasion imminent, the wartime cabinet closed ranks and agreed that "one of the preconditions for the work of the national coalition government is that internal differences of political opinion be set aside," and the Swedish people and their leaders united for the common defense of their democratic heritage.[3]

If the war brought a hiatus to the controversial program of social reformation, it also led to the reemergence of the still unresolved school reform controversy of 1927. Turning inward in a period of international crisis, the Swedes began to question the role of their schools in developing and strengthening the democratic values that then seemed so fragile and valuable. Questions arose concerning the ability of the parallel school system to educate all children for social and national unity, to meet existent and future needs for expanded secondary schooling, and to offer equal educational opportunities for all students

---

[2] Sweden's tenuous "neutrality" in the early years of World War II is documented in the compilation of official communications and parliamentary debates in Utrikespolitiska Institut, *Svensk utrikespolitik under andra världskriget,* 1946. [48]

[3] Riksdagen, *Riksdagens protokoll. Första Kammaren 1940,* No. 3, pp. 33–35. [39p] The "nondemocratic" national socialist parties of the right and the Marxian party of the left were excluded from the wartime coalition government.

77

regardless of social class background, location of domicile, or sex.[4]
Earlier cautions about the elitist and authoritarian nature of Swedish
education found new justifications in the threatening example of Nazi
Germany. Might not the secondary *läroverk*, the Social Democrats and
others asked, because of its pronounced Germanic heritage (as in its
rigorously academic emphasis, and elitist nature) conceivably fail to
arrest antidemocratic tendencies in Swedish education, as had happened in the German *gymnasia* and universities?[5]

For the foregoing pragmatic and ideological reasons Gösta Bagge,
the Conservative party leader and Minister of Education in the coalition
cabinet, appointed a committee of educational experts on November
22, 1940, to make a full-scale survey of deficiencies in the entire public
educational system. Professor Düring has observed that the investigation might be seen as a "cultural rearmament," simultaneous with the
move to concentrate the bulk of Sweden's physical resources in military
rearmament. In his directive to the committee, Bagge stressed that a
small nation like Sweden could only hope to offset qualitative deficiencies with the careful nurture of national intellectual assets, and that
"the nearest means at hand to this goal is the improvement of the
mental and physical education of our youth by the improvement of our
educational system."[6]

A further intimation of the rational frame of reference prevailing
in Sweden at that time of imminent invasion, and of the role that the
school would be called on to perform is found in the minister's statement of general principles underlying the investigation:

The ultimate aim of the school should not be the imparting of knowledge but education in the widest and deepest meaning of the word.
The purpose of the school is to develop the capabilities of the young
people in a harmonic way, not only intellectually but also physically
and morally. Our time demands well trained adolescents who can
stand comparison with the young people of their own age in other
nations [i.e., democratic nations], but it also needs young people who
combine quickness in decision and action with a calm judgment. The
whole activity of the school should be directed toward the service of
character development.[7]

[4] See, for instance, the article "Demokratiens skola och democratiens ungdom"
(democracy's school and democracy's youth), which reviews the influence of the
war in stimulating new interest in what were perceived to be antidemocratic
aspects of Swedish schooling, especially in the *läroverk*. Socialdemokratiska Ungdomsförbund, *Skolan och folket*, 1941, pp. 30–40. [31]

[5] Ecklesiastikdepartementet, *Skolan i samhällets tjänst*, 1944, p. 146. [38f]

[6] Ingemar Düring (ed.), *The Swedish School Reform: A Summary of the
Government Bill at the Request of the 1946 School Commission*, 1951, p. 30. [8]

[7] Ecklesiastikdepartementet [38f], p. 28.

THE 1940 EXPERT SCHOOL COMMITTEE

The fifteen members of the committee represented a broad cross section of Swedish education, with the majority drawn from the ranks of the academic secondary schools.[8] The Conservative Minister of Education, Professor Bagge, chaired the committee with Bishop Andrae as vice chairman. Over a period of more than six years, the committee produced a total of twenty reports that in profuse detail examined six critical problem areas of Swedish education singled out for attention by the minister: (1) elementary school curriculum and methods; (2) goals and organization of higher elementary schools; (3) connections between the *folkskola* and the *realskola* (i.e., conditions for selection to secondary schooling); (4) organization of the *gymnasium*; (5) the problem of examinations; and (6) regional variations in the supply of and demand for various types of schooling.[9]

For the purposes of the present investigation point three and the controversy it generated are of primary importance. For within the comprehensive study assigned to the committee, the constant problem of articulation between *folkskola* and *realskola* came to dominate the attention of the experts and eventually polarized the committee into partisan groups with vested interests for and against an extension of the elementary school as a comprehensive school.[10] This impasse of the experts in turn led to the reemergence of popular and political interest, debate, and controversy in the long-dormant issue of school reform, especially in the extension of compulsory education in a context of comprehensive schooling.[11]

The highly controversial issue that divided the committee concerned the most "advantageous" age for transfer from the elementary to the secondary school. In addition to the historical background of conflict surrounding the question, it had marked political implications and revealed powerful group interests. One group in the committee identified with the interests of the *folkskola* and sought to eliminate early transfer to *realskolan* and to secure the 1918 School Commission's plan for the nationwide implementation of the six-year comprehensive

---

[8] Members associated with the elementary school were six in number. See *ibid.*, pp. 8 and 294.

[9] *Ibid.*, p. 34.

[10] For the alignment of committee members, see *ibid.*, pp. 294–305.

[11] See, for example, the record of the Social Democratic Youth Congress, held in Stockholm September 26–27, 1941, which contains an interesting admonition to the party's leaders: "It is a fact that we have been appallingly tame especially among the Social Democrats in the *riksdag* when it comes to mastering our school problems. We have done nothing to harness the power of the school to help us accomplish our goals." Socialdemokratiska Ungdomsförbund [31], p. 135.

school as the common school upon which all higher types of schooling should be built.[12] The experts supporting the interests of the secondary schools or *läroverk* (combined *realskola* and *gymnasium*) urged the continuation of the educational status quo—with some modifications— by continuing the "double connection" legislated in 1927.[13]

The committee attempted an "educational" solution to this problem by seeking to establish objective proof of the "effectiveness" of the two types of lower secondary school: the five-year *realskola*, entered after four years of elementary school and the four-year *realskola*, entered after six years. Through a study of some 10,000 children who had attended both types of *realskolor*, the members endeavored to establish certain objective criteria for determining the relative efficiency of each type. Promotion, grade repeating, marks, examination performance and age distribution at the *realskola* leaving examination were all analyzed in great detail.[14]

Thus, for the first time in the long history of agitation for common schooling, various objective measurements and research studies replaced subjective individual opinions in official investigations to determine national educational policy.[15] This nascent development proceeded along two distinct lines. The first was concerned with the accurate collection of data on all aspects of attendance, recruitment, selection, and wastage in the two kinds of *realskola* and for each of the various types of schools that had burgeoned in the elementary school branch. The second was concerned with evaluation of these data by experts who, they hoped, would be able to counsel the committee as to the desirability and consequences of possible lines of action. This would conceivably give Parliament a sound basis on which to formulate new legislation for both organizational and internal changes in the schools. In retrospect, however, it can be seen that although the committee succeeded brilliantly in documenting inadequacies and inequalities in Swedish education, they were at a loss on how the data should be interpreted and, particularly, on what action should be initiated.

The results of the central investigation of conditions in the *realskola* revealed, for example, that although the two types created by the 1927

12 Ecklesiastikdepartementet [38f], p. 113.
13 Ecklesiastikdepartementet, *Sambandet mellan folkskola och högre skola*, 1944, pp. 214–215. [38e]
14 Ecklesiastikdepartementet, *Den psykologiska forskningens nuvarande ståndpunkt i fråga om den psykiska utvecklingen hos barn och ungdom*, 1943. [38b]
15 The reluctance of Swedish educators and politicians to use psychological testing or controlled investigations in shaping educational reform during the 1920's and early 1930's is contrasted with the American experience in this respect by Christina S. von H. Bogoslovsky, *The Educational Crisis in Sweden in the Light of American Experience*, 1932, pp. 229–230. [64]

Act did not, according to the criteria used, "differ greatly in efficiency," they were nevertheless strikingly disparate in the social recruitment of their students, as may be seen in Table 2.

It may be seen in Table 2 that children from working-class families were seriously underrepresented in academic secondary schools on the whole and especially in the five-year *realskola*. Because of its more pronounced academic character, this longer form of the lower secondary school clearly retained a strong attraction for pupils with an upper-class background. Moreover, students in this five-year school reached, on the average, the terminal *realskola* examination one year earlier than students in the four-year school. The second report of the committee, "The Connection between the Elementary and Higher Schools," published in 1944, contains further information and discussion as well as various interpretations of the findings in terms of social, pedagogical, and psychological considerations by the factions for and against early and late differentiation.

Supporters of early selection (at the end of the fourth grade) offered three main arguments:

1. Transfer after grade four permitted students to take the terminal *realskola* examination a year earlier; it provided able students with an extra year of secondary schooling; and it allowed the beginning of foreign language study a full two years earlier than would be the case with transfer after six years of *folkskola*.[16]

2. Early transfer at the age of eleven was entirely consistent with modern psychological theory. At this age a change in intellectual development was thought to take place and the child was ready for more "abstract elements" in the curriculum.

3. It was also stressed by some that early transfer of students into different schools (i.e., the "theoretical" and "practical" branches) would create more homogeneous classes and institutions. This would, it was claimed, greatly facilitate teaching and act as a stimulus and motivation for the homogeneously grouped able students. Because it was thought to be self-evident that differentiation had to take place in any case, early selection could be justified by unassailable pedagogical and psychological arguments.[17]

Those members of the committee who supported a six-year elementary school for all children and the shorter four-year form of the lower secondary school emphasized the supposedly greater social value of postponing selection for practical or theoretical schooling until thirteen years of age. They claimed that: [18]

---

[16] Ecklesiastikdepartementet [38e], pp. 198–204, 214–216.
[17] Ecklesiastikdepartementet [38b], pp. 62–72.
[18] See Ecklesiastikdepartementet [38e], pp. 225–226, and [38f], pp. 96 f.

Table 2. Parental Social Class of Pupils in Swedish Academic Secondary Schools in 1940 [a]

	I (Upper)		II (Middle)		III (Lower)		Total	
	Per cent	Number	Per cent	Number	Per cent	Number	Per cent	Number
Social class distribution of 1940 electorate: [b]								
	5		37		57		100	
Social class distributions of school populations:								
Upper secondary (*gymnasium*)	27.5	(3,438)	61.0	(7,632)	11.5	(1,442)	100	(12,512)
Realskola (attached to *gymnasium*)								
Boys' *realskola*								
5-year line	21.7	(1,555)	61.1	(4,388)	17.2	(1,236)	100	(7,279)
4-year line	9.2	(70)	61.5	(468)	29.3	(223)	100	(761)
Girl's *realskola*								
4-year line	13.7	(188)	59.3	(812)	27.0	(369)	100	(1,369)
Coeducational *realskola*								
5-year line	18.0	(1,605)	57.1	(5,091)	24.9	(2,221)	100	(8,917)
4-year-line	11.4	(394)	60.0	(2,069)	28.6	(987)	100	(3,450)

Realskola (unattached)

Boys' *realskola*							
5-year line	14.6	(296)	59.6	(1,212)	25.8	(524)	100	(2,032)
4-year line	8.0	(22)	51.3	(141)	40.7	(112)	100	(275)
Coeducational *realskola*							
5-year line	12.4	(406)	54.6	(1,782)	33.0	(1,077)	100	(3,265)
4-year line	9.2	(911)	57.6	(5,703)	33.2	(3,288)	100	(9,902)
Municipal middle school							
4-year	6.7	(651)	50.0	(4,863)	43.3	(4,215)	100	(9,729)
All *realskola* and municipal middle schools combined:							
5-year line	18.1	(3,862)	58.3	(12,473)	23.6	(5,058)	100	(21,393)
4-year line	8.8	(2,236)	55.1	(14,056)	36.1	(9,194)	100	(25,486)
All (4- and 5-year lines)	13	(6,098)	56.6	(26,529)	30.4	(14,252)	100	(46,879)

[a] Source: Ecklesiastikdepartementet, *Sambandet mellan folkskola och högre skola*, 1944, pp. 320–321. [38e]

[b] All Swedish voters are classified into occupational groups by the Central Bureau of Statistics and placed in one of the three official "social groups" (*socialgrupper*) as used in this table: i.e., group I, upper class (*högre klassen*); group II, middle class (*medelklassen*); and group III, lower class (*kroppsarbetarnas klass*). See Anna-Lisa Kälvesten, *The Social Structure of Sweden*, 1961, pp. 39–40. [113]

1. Early selection is too frequently influenced by irrelevant economic and social class factors.

2. Despite the presence or absence of ability for "theoretical study," children at the age of eleven are not sufficiently mature to be selected for academic or nonacademic schools. Neither their aptitudes—especially practical aptitudes—nor their real interests can be sufficiently determined at such an early age. Postponement of differentiation for all pupils to the age of thirteen after six years of comprehensive schooling would therefore help to make the differentiation process more accurate, more humane, and by equalizing some of the basic factors, more just.

3. The strongest justification for a common six-year school is social. Such a school would give all Swedish children an equal period of compulsory schooling with a common curriculum and with teachers having the same amount and kind of training. Moreover, they further claimed that the six-year common school would, in contrast to the existing arrangement for double connection, be "a source of national unity, social cooperation and better mutual understanding."

The conflict between the committee members for and against the longer common school did not elicit the earlier polemics of the corresponding teacher organizations representing elementary and secondary schools. The aggressive attacks of the former on the lower *realskola* forms running parallel to the *folkskola*—and the trenchant defense by the latter group—were at the heart of the acrid comprehensive school reform controversies of the 1920's. The restraint of both groups at this time can be explained partially by the fact that the committee worked in closed session, and partially by the need for consensus and national unity in light of the very serious wartime situation. Even more influential was the desire of both parties for a situation conducive to an objective evaluation by pedagogical "experts" of precisely what reforms were most urgently needed and why.

It might be noted here, however, that the various elementary school teacher organizations had not been inactive while awaiting the publication of the committee's findings. On February 11, 1943, they sent a delegation to the king with a petition for spelling reform. The proposal—to simplify spelling by making it more phonetic—aimed at the creation of "a new mother tongue" closer to the vernacular speech of the folk. Because of its social and pedagogical implications, the reform, its supporters claimed, would (1) simplify teaching; (2) facilitate learning; (3) reduce the influence of language as a social handicap; and (4) enhance national unity. The proposal succeeded only in stirring up a storm of disdainful scorn from high-culture groups who supported the sentiments of author Frans Bengtsson that "such matters are not the proper concern of school teachers and should be left to authors and experts." [19]

Modern psychological theory as interpreted by the psychology experts in the matter of differentiation almost entirely corroborated the secondary school group's pedagogical rationale for early selection. Professor Anderberg approved of early transfer because "in our common undifferentiated classes the able student does not meet the competition which will motivate him. . . ." [20] Citing German studies, he further stated that "practical ability" can only be accurately determined at the end of adolescence, and assignment to secondary schools should only take place according to "scholastic ability." [21] Professor Katz stated categorically that "according to modern research in the matter of intelligence, no really serious arguments can be presented in favor of a postponement of selection." [22] Professor Landquist also subscribed to his colleagues' statements and indicated that pedagogical reasons also pointed in the direction of selection of able students after four years: "I cannot recall a single psychologist who has advocated the suitability of a six-year or eight-year common school." [23] Professor Elmgren, although concurring with the possibility of early selection for the more gifted pupils, alone recommended that differentiation be delayed until the age of about 13 or 14 "when specific abilities are more clearly discernible." [24]

Encouraged by the psychology experts, a majority of the committee recommended experimentation on grouping within the elementary school in the fifth or sixth year. The introduction of foreign language study, ability grouping in certain subjects, and the homogeneous group-

[19] Quoted in Ruben Wagnsson, *ABC, vår folkundervisning från medeltiden till enhetsskolan*, 1955, p. 389. [176]

[20] Ecklesiastikdepartementet [38b], p. 8.

[21] In this connection Anderberg speculates that because there are marked differences in scholastic ability between social classes, one alternative might be to differentiate pupils by social class. He rejects the idea, however, because of overlap between the groups and the imprecise categories involved. See *ibid.*, p. 9. It is interesting to note that beginning in 1922 and continuing up to the early 1930's the Swedish State Institute for Race Biology, located in the ancient university town of Uppsala, published several works implying positive correlations between physical characteristics and social class in the Swedish population. Among the Institute's financial supporters were the government, former Conservative Prime Minister C. Swartz, and a number of influential leaders in the university and business world. See, for example, pp. 48–49 and plates, Swedish State Institute for Race Biology, *The Racial Characteristics of the Swedish Nation*, 1926. [45] It might be noted in this regard that supporters of eugenics have not infrequently attempted to obstruct social change by claiming that social ills follow from "bad" heredity and cannot be corrected by changes in the environment.

[22] Ecklesiastikdepartementet [38b], p. 62.

[23] *Ibid.*, p. 71.

[24] *Ibid.*, p. 28.

ing and channeling of students preparing for the *realskola* were steps suggested by the secondary school group to provide a measure of internal differentiation within the *folkskola*.[25] (See Appendix D.) They pointed out that the *folkskola* might with these changes become a truly efficient foundation school for secondary education. The suggestions, however, were strongly opposed by the majority of the *folkskola* supporters as being detrimental to the whole concept of a common school. If two years of differentiated schooling became imbedded in the elementary school, it would mean the beginning of a "multilateral" elementary school with distinct theoretical and practical curricula merely brought together under one roof. Such a school would not bring an end to early selection into different studies but would for the *folkskola* bring an end to the common curriculum and teaching for all the children in the elementary school.[26]

After years of waiting, the interested public and all parties concerned welcomed the committee's first three reports in 1944. A wealth of factual documentation underscored the long recognized fact that serious deficiencies existed in Swedish education. Most of these deficiencies in one way or another revolved around the problem of parallelism in the educational structure and its ramifications for rural and working-class children, and for girls. All conceivable facets of the differentiation problem were examined in monumental detail. But because of an inability to suggest possible lines of development and the lack of unanimity, the committee's final joint recommendations to the *riksdag* were exceedingly circumspect and limited.[27] For example, the committee agreed on the extension of compulsory schooling to eight years. But so had all the major political parties, and a law had been passed in May 1941 that permitted certain school districts to adopt the eight-year period as a voluntary option.[28]

Another basic proposal suggested experimentation with various configurations of partially combined elementary and lower secondary schools with possibilities for parallel courses and foreign language study within a multilateral *folkskola*.[29] Since both factions, however, overqualified their positions and had vastly different interpretations as to what they believed the terms used and the actual proposal meant, the results were confused, ill-defined, and unimaginative.

[25] Ecklesiastikdepartementet [38e], pp. 303–305.

[26] *Ibid.*, pp. 225–226. For further discussion of the pros and cons of streaming in the elementary school, see Ecklesiastikdepartementet, *Sammanfattning av allmän organisationsplan*, 1945, *passim*. [38c]

[27] Ecklesiastikdepartementet [38e], pp. 291–293.

[28] The problem of youth unemployment, an especially serious situation in the 1930's, was a basic consideration in proposals to extend compulsory schooling. See the articles and comments on this problem in Wagnsson [176], p. 385.

[29] Ecklesiastikdepartementet [38e], p. 385. Graphic representation of these various proposals is presented in Appendix D.

The committee also produced a vast body of evidence on the need to upgrade rural schooling and to make post-elementary schooling more equitably available to rural students as well as to girls. Remedial proposals for these problems, in essence, suggested more of the same compensatory measures already to some degree in operation: that is to say, larger government grants to deserving students for study away from home, more boarding facilities, and expanded programs for instruction by radio and correspondence.[30]

The blandness of the committee's suggestions did not, understandably, go unnoticed by the elementary school teachers. Their press, in commenting on the long wait and the deadlock of the two factions, observed that "the recommendations concerning transfer are truly a sad story and in their entirety make a disheartening impression. The School Committee has stuck fast in the old arguments and no new fresh ideas have been put forth to dominate the lengthy discussions."[31] Although other groups, reawakened to the controversy and advocating comprehensive school reform, by and large concurred with this negative evaluation of the 1940 committee's conclusions, the report nevertheless did represent a move toward greater consensus on desirable reform goals with the Conservatives' acceptance of at least a partial *enhetsskola*. Under Bagge's leadership the party began to espouse what they called an *enhetsskola*, which in fact would be a multilateral school with distinct practical and theoretical curricula brought together in one school. This new Conservative position on school reform—although rejected by those who sought a six-year comprehensive foundation school —did however represent (1) the basic anti-obstructionist attitude of the opposition parties and (2) the willingness of the Conservatives to rethink and moderate their earlier positions opposing educational change.

NEW INITIATIVES FOR EDUCATIONAL REFORM

Because of the inability of the experts most intimately concerned with education to formulate suitable concrete proposals for attacking disparities and dysfunctional aspects of the school system, a number of political and folk movement elements began to agitate for school reform in general and for the six-year comprehensive school in particular. We shall first examine this new development at the political level in the Social Democratic, Liberal, and other political parties and then describe the extent to which various popular organizations rallied around the cause of an extended *folkskola*, a cause still closely identified with the

[30] Ecklesiastikdepartementet, *Utredning och förslag angående vidgade möjligheter till högre undervisning för landsbygdens ungdom*, 1944, pp. 96–104. [38i]
[31] *Svensk Lärartidning*, Vol. 9, No. 11 (May 22, 1944), p. 9.

numerous folk organizations supporting the cooperative, temperance, and popular education movements.

As the threat of the Nazi invasion diminished in the last two years of the war, disagreements within the coalition cabinet began to emerge. During the early years of the war, many prominent members of all the political parties had favored a peacetime continuation of a national coalition government. This desire, however, disintegrated soon after a Communist challenge to the Social Democrats in the 1944 elections. Free to pursue partisan interests, the Communists had scored a resounding victory by agitating against the government's wartime wage ceiling with the result that the total Communist vote rose from 3.5 per cent of the 1940 electorate to 10.3 per cent in 1944.[32] The Social Democrats were consequently forced to veer sharply left in their postwar program and the non-Socialists rejected further cooperation unless the Socialists ceased their "propaganda for socialization." Continuous disagreements on internal policy finally led to the dissolution of the coalition government at the end of the wartime emergency. In July 1945 Premier Per Albin Hansson formed a purely Social Democratic government and set in motion a bold new legislative program.

Political Parties

The Socialists' initial postwar program took form at the 1944 party congress when, for the first time, the subject of school reform held a position of fundamental importance. Basically the party's new program was designed to extend the Social Democratic policy of the previous twelve years that sought the "progressive democratization of society, politically, economically, and socially." [33] The program called for the expansion and consolidation of the prewar social welfare program and revised progressive income and inheritance taxes to meet the additional costs. The method for bringing the dual educational system into harmony with the party's program goals for progressive democratization was not, however, as easily agreed upon as were the proposals for new welfare benefits and new taxes.[34]

On May 20, 1944, the participants at the tenth Social Democratic congress began debate in the Stockholm concert hall on point four of the party program: the statement of party policy on school reform. In the give and take of open discussion, party leaders began the difficult

---

[32] Excluded from the coalition government, the Communists felt no compunction in playing party politics with such issues. See Dankwart A. Rustow, *The Politics of Compromise: A Study of Parties and Cabinet Government in Sweden*, 1955, p. 113. [15o]

[33] Socialdemokratiska partistyrelsen, *Berättelse för år 1945*, 1946, p. 45. [30]

[34] *Ibid.*, pp. 58–60 ff.

task of formulating a program and establishing reform priorities to meet the problem of a parallel class-oriented educational system, and how it might be changed to conform more closely with Socialist goals for a democratic and egalitarian society. Or, as delegate Oskar Hallbeck stated the central question, "how to solve the problem of school organization . . . and clarify precisely what we hope to attain through education."[35]

With interruptions for the reading of congratulatory telegrams from exiled Czechoslovakian and German Social Democrats, the party in heated debate forged a six-point program that in somewhat imprecise and general terms proposed: (1) the elimination of all fees in public schools;[36] (2) a common *folkskola* to give basic citizenship education to all children; (3) improved continuation schools to prepare for industrial, commercial and agricultural occupations; (4) guaranteed admission of all qualified students to secondary and higher education with state economic support when justified by need; (5) elimination of instruction in the *folkskola* for confirmation in the state Lutheran Church; and (6) government support and initiative in technological and scientific research.[37]

Although evaluating the suitability of this reform program to the party's ideological commitments, the record contains no mention of the controversy generated in the 1940 School Committee on the pedagogical problems of differentiation. Rather, the delegates tended to interpret the need for school reforms solely in terms of (1) enlarging educational opportunities for children from the working class; and (2) reorganizing the structure and content of schooling to conform more closely to the democratic requirements of equalized opportunity for all. The problems of rural education, as, for example, the need for better vocational education, and the unfortunate economic need of rural and urban working-class families to push their children into the labor market at the earliest possible time, dominated the discussion.[38] In the context of the party's new slogan, "the progressive democratization of education," another question was raised: "Which sections of the educational system should be given priority?"[39] Delegate Stellan Arvidson emphasized that "the most pressing problem for Swedish democracy in terms of education is to extend and develop vocational education and not to push for a program of secondary education for all." Some-

---

[35] Sveriges Socialdemokratiska Arbetareparti, *Protokoll från tionde kongressen,* 1944, p. 140. [35b]
[36] The program cautioned in this respect that "the school should not become a place for private investment." *Ibid.,* p. 134.
[37] *Ibid.,* pp. 131–132.
[38] *Ibid.,* pp. 133–148.
[39] *Ibid.,* p. 131.

what apologetically he explained that "the sparsity of settlement in
many rural areas makes the formulation of a precise demand for a
unified school almost impossible." [40] In reply, S. A. Stahre charged that
vocational education was a one-sided specialization which, without
longer common schooling for citizenship training, would tend to under-
mine democratic gains already won at great effort.[41] Because technical
developments and rationalization have produced new conditions and
hours of work, he claimed, extension of the common school to provide
an adequate basic education and postponement of entry of students
into the labor market should be attempted.[42]

Delegate Malmsjö called attention to the serious deterioriation that
existed in the rural schools as the result of the emphasis that had for
many years been given, successively, to the depression, the population
problem and, finally, wartime national defense needs. This situation
demanded immediate attention if the Social Democrats were to achieve
even minimal nationwide educational standards. This could only be
accomplished, he claimed, through a massive investment in post-
elementary schools with cost-free boarding for students through government stipends, correspondence courses, and other arrangements.[43]
More conservative recommendations included top priority for adult
education, because "It is desirable that all youth who do not continue
their education beyond the elementary school should attend the folk
high school." [44]

Despite vigorous disagreements, the party finally settled for a six-
point program, if not on a hierarchy of priorities for school reform.
After a hiatus of nearly two decades, the Social Democrats had once
again become acutely aware of and concerned with pedagogical problems.[45] No less a party intellectual leader than the former teacher and
then-Minister of Finance Ernst Wigforss boldly stated at the congress
that "One of the most vital means to the realization of democracy and
the implementation of socialism will be to reorganize the school system." But the party had no clearly formulated plans for a school
reorganization and only ill-defined goals and objectives to be sought

---

[40] Arvidson claimed that the results of his study of success and failure of
realskola students disproved the popular contention that any child "with normal
ability" could successfully complete the lower secondary school. Because "only
⅓ of all folkskola students had the ability to pass the realexamen, and ⅛ the gymnasium leaving exam," Arvidson concluded that an expansion of facilities for vocational education would be necessary to cope with steeply rising enrollments. See
ibid., pp. 137 and 144.
[41] Ibid., p. 146.
[42] Ibid., p. 132.
[43] Ibid., pp. 137–138.
[44] Ibid., p. 132.
[45] Ibid., p. 142.

by a "reorganized school system." The need for the Social Democrats to formulate a concise blueprint for educational reform had become apparent and pressing.

In theory the Social Democrats agreed to seek a school system that would represent and reinforce the same democratic objectives sought in other areas of national life, a school system that would help to create the "cooperative man." [46] In the more practical matters of steps to be taken to reshape the content, structure and organization of public education to conform to the democratic goals being pursued, the party arrived at no concrete conclusions or formulations. Moreover, when it was proposed that the new goal of "democratic education" should be included in the party program, Conrad Jonsson, of the party's central committee, counseled against such a move because "the program is sufficiently radical for the future needs of the Swedish people" and since "it is self-evident what all Socialists desire, there is no need to include a plank on making education more democratic in form and content." [47] The congress accepted his advice.

Another objective agreed upon by the congress delegates but not included in the party program should be noted. Although the congress took only slight notice of the fact that academic secondary education primarily served the interests of the "better situated" classes—and made no mention whatsover concerning the possibility or desirability of the elimination of structural parallelism between the theoretical and practical branches of the compulsory school, a somewhat optimistic proposal was accepted to the effect that a greater effort should be made to achieve parity of prestige between the two post-elementary branches of the parallel system.[48] Precisely how this might have been accomplished within the existing bipartite system of scarce and high-prestige academic secondary schooling on the one side, and practical higher elementary, continuation, and vocational schools on the other, no one ventured to say. It was, moreover, hopefully suggested that if the perstigious and time-honored *realskola* and *gymnasium* leaving examinations could in some way be eliminated, then academic secondary education might lose some of its attraction and more realistic aspirations for schooling and careers might be developed.

The lack of unanimity on a school reform program provides interesting insights into what the congress delegates perceived to be the most salient problems in Swedish education and the diversity of

---

[46] The congress delegates, however, were unable to clarify just what they believed to be the means to this end. See, for example, the criticism of delegate Oskar Hallbeck in this respect, in *ibid.*, pp. 139–140.

[47] *Ibid.*, p. 141.

[48] *Ibid.*, p. 132.

opinions about the educational objectives that should receive party support. It was contended, for example, that point two of the program lacked clarity, i.e., should the common school be six, or eight, or nine years in length? Questions were also asked as to how the curriculum of the elementary school might be reformed to provide a democratic citizenship education to meet the requirements of modern society. Moreover, how could the *folkskola* be made more uniform in content and length when school districts retained the privilege of local modification in these matters? To the contention that the *folkskola* should be the common foundation school for all higher academic and practical studies and that comprehensive instruction for all pupils should continue as long as practicably possible, some delegates replied that "to the extent that the *folkskola* is extended with more classes and differentiated instruction, the entire *folkskola* cannot be the basis for all continued education." [49] It was further pointed out that even if the elementary school were extended, at least a decade of herculean efforts would be required to change the school's curriculum—new teacher training, texts, and activity methods—to remake the *folkskola* into a "real school for life." The traditional formal approach to teaching in the *folkskola*, where children are "stuffed with facts like sausages," would invalidate any mere extension simply to keep all Swedish children together longer in a *bottenskola*. The school program would therefore demand prompt attention if the proposed common school was to reflect the democratic values of society and, in turn, serve as an agency to develop and spread these values. [50]

Members of the congress also disagreed on how far to carry the secularization of elementary education. Should the elementary school continue to instruct in the Christian religion (even if not as a preparation for confirmation) or limit itself to "factual and objective" concerns within a framework of general religious history? Those who supported the former position claimed that Christianity would foster democratic attitudes; delegates who preferred the latter alternative warned that instruction in state Lutheranism had long been one of *folkskolan's* greatest liabilities. They further objected to the tendency of the *småskola* teachers in the first three years of the *folkskola* to emphasize religious instruction at the expense of more practical subjects.

Although the Social Democrats accomplished little in the way of formulating a concise or comprehensive party program for school reform at their 1944 party congress, the meeting did serve as a point of departure. Because of earlier social reform priorities that had all but ignored educational problems—and the success of this program, which

49 *Ibid.*, p. 137.
50 *Ibid.*, p. 134.

made educational inequalities more flagrant and distasteful—the Social Democrats welcomed the enforced wartime respite that permitted program revisions on these problems. In a new move the party leadership in 1944 proclaimed top priority for educational reform. A program of minimal objectives, stressing the need for a "democratization" of schooling, for the equalization of educational opportunity, and for the creation of "cooperative man" found uniformly strong support in theory —if not in answers to the kind of organizational and internal reforms that were necessary to realize these new educational objectives.

The Social Democrats' failure during the previous decade to give heed to these very problems had resulted, if one may judge from the congress record, in an impoverishment of understanding and leadership within the party on the rather complex problems and needs of Swedish education. The party, it was agreed, must do better. Because of the seriousness of the educational problems, they would undoubtedly become a postwar matter of public concern, and the Social Democrats, as the dominant political party, would be forced to take the lead in reform activities. Greater unanimity within the party on ends and means in school reform therefore became imperative and the congress referred the matter to a committee for further attention. In the meantime the surprisingly mild party program stood as mute testimony to the confusion attending the Social Democrats' first efforts to achieve somehow "democratic schools for a democratic society."

Although the Social Democrats—with considerable hesitation and some reluctance—took the lead in attempts to reformulate a national program for school reform, all the other political parties as well—to a greater or lesser degree—also began to turn their attention to educational problems. By 1944 optimism was on the rise, with hopes that the war would soon be over, and a common understanding grew in Sweden that the long neglect of deficiencies in education during the 1930's and the war years would make postwar school reform imperative. The findings of the 1940 School Committee left little doubt as to the need; the reemergence of the old controversies about differentiation left little doubt that the problem of a comprehensive school, whether for six or nine years, would be the focus of contention in any postwar school reform.

A Liberal party (*Folkpartiet*) congress convened in Stockholm on June 11, 1944, and, in the creation of a comprehensive program for postwar reforms, paid serious attention to educational matters.[51] The party supported—as had the Social Democrats—the general position of the Folk School Teachers Association and recommended, in a rather

[51] Folkpartiet, *Liberal syn på skolfrågan*, 1948, p. 7. [11]

imprecise way, that "the *folkskola* should be extended and developed into the public comprehensive school (*grundskola*) of a richly diversified school system." [52]

It may be appropriate at this point to review some of the Liberal party's contributions to school reform and their chequered record of support for comprehensive schooling. Early Liberals had been instrumental in securing the legislation for *folkskolan* in 1842 and had frequently—as in the case of S. A. Hedin—worked to see it improved in the decades that followed. During this period *laissez-faire* liberalism was primarily concerned with the removal of restrictive trade regulations and with the tariff issue in general. But in the last quarter of the nineteenth century, Liberals began to think in terms of social reforms, of the democratization of the *riksdag* and the introduction of parliamentary government. [53] It was not, however, until the appearance of the radical Liberal Fridtjuv Berg and his program for "the elementary school as a comprehensive school" (*Folkskolan såsom bottenskolan*) that the Liberal party itself actually became embroiled in attempts to introduce longer common schooling. But it should be recalled that although Berg was able to make the demand for a comprehensive *bottenskola* a Liberal program point, the idea remained highly offensive to many of his fellow party members and with Berg's death, the *bottenskola* plank disappeared from the Liberal program. [54]

The Liberals eventually did, however, in 1927 swing their support to Värner Rydén's compromise "double connection" plan that favored a six-year common school and they continued to support the idea even during the depression when, it might be noted, the Social Democrats had become disenchanted with the desirability of reforms in education. At the 1934 congress, for example, the Liberal program continued to urge—if only in a rather vague way—that the *folkskola* be made a "great comprehensive school . . . to give all Swedish youth an education more in keeping with the demands of modern life." [55]

Although agreeing in principle with the need for longer compulsory schooling and a common elementary school, the Liberals in their 1944 program emphasized the need for adequate planning and experimentation before any changes were made. They were more concerned with the practical problems of expense, of adequate teacher resources, and of the total demand and supply of education, whereas the Social Demo-

---

[52] *Ibid.*, pp. 17–18.

[53] Nils Andrén, *Modern Swedish Government*, 1961, p. 26. [52]

[54] See the article by the conservative professor and 1940 School Committee member Erik Wellander on the absence of popular support for Berg's comprehensive elementary school program in *Svenska Dagbladet*, August 30, 1940, p. 2.

[55] Folkpartiet [11], p. 7.

crats were more concerned with the socio-political utility of school reform.[56]

Sweden's two other major political parties, the Conservatives and the Agrarians, took varying positions in the last years of the war on the question of priorities for school reform. The Conservatives, who had reluctantly come to accept many of the basic tenets of the welfare state, fully agreed that a major modernization of the school was long overdue. They also—as did all the other political parties—gave qualified approval to the proposed extension of compulsory schooling to nine years.[57] The Conservatives had no use, however, for the idea of an inflexible common school that would, they believed, penalize the abler students by forcing them to remain in nongrouped classes well past what they, the Conservatives, generally held to be the point of optimum differentiation into "theoretical" studies in the secondary *realskola* at the age of eleven.[58] Their interests and point of view were well represented by Minister of Education Bagge who as Chairman of the 1940 Expert School Committee had led the majority decision to recommend the continuation of differentiation after the fourth year of elementary schooling. Bagge and his fellow Conservatives, however, were, as noted, willing to compromise to the point of accepting a "multilateral" school that would place separate theoretical and practical curricula under one roof.

The Agrarian party (*Centerpartiet*), on the other hand, had good reasons to support the 1940 Committee's minority view that supported late differentiation and a six-year common school. The farm party had, it may be recalled, regularly aligned itself with the Conservatives before the depression and entered into coalition rule with the Social Democrats only in 1932.[59] Since that time they had in the main, al-

---

[56] See Ola Ullsten, *Folkpartiet och reformerna: liberala riksdagsinitiativ, 1902–1960*, 1960, pp. 9–16 and 92–100. [47] Some idea of the empirical and rational orientation of the Liberals in contrast to the ideological bent of the Social Democrats in defining school reform goals and priorities may be gained from Folkpartiets Delegation i Utbildningsfrågor, *Rätt till utbildning: liberala framtidsperspektiv*, 1959. [12] See especially Chapter 10, "Rationaliserad expansion."

[57] Sveriges Konservativa Studentförbund, *Grundskola: ett alternativ*, 1962, pp. 11–12. [34]

[58] The judgment of Rector Gideon Danell expresses this position: "The *folkskola* gives one type of instruction, the *realskola* another . . . and the solution seems clearly to be that . . . we have already heard more than enough of the comprehensive school." See his article in *Svenska Dagbladet*, November 20, 1940, p. 3. [78]

[59] The majority of the farm-party voters were independent farmers who did not, despite earlier coalition governments, identify as strongly with Social Democratic egalitarian reforms as did the diminishing number of agricultural laborers who in the main voted the Social Democratic ticket. See Gunnar Heckscher and Verner Helti, *De politiska åskadningar och partierna*, 1950, p. 81. [99d]

though frequently with reluctance, supported Socialist programs in return for crop subsidy bills and other favorable legislation. Because of the plight of rural education at the war's end and its many fundamental problems caused by the very nature of a dual system of education, the farmers in general warmly concurred with the sentiment for longer common schooling but, as usual, balked at the thought of increased costs.[60]

As a result of their remarkable gains in the elections of 1944 and 1946 the Swedish Communist party became for a few postwar years a major political group. Because the Communists had been excluded from the coalition government, they were able to exert an influence much greater than their 10 to 11 per cent of the popular vote might indicate. By agitating against unpopular wartime controls which the Social Democrats as the major coalition party were duty-bound to support, the Communists undoubtedly forced the Social Democrats to move farther left when formulating their program for postwar reforms.

In the school reform question the Communists capitalized on their governmental exclusion by urging upon the *riksdag* a highly controversial solution to end the stalemate between the Conservatives and the Socialists on the problem of differentiation. Rejecting the conclusions of the 1940 School Committee as "vague and indecisive" and "totally unacceptable because of their pronounced upper-class flavor," Communist Gunnar Gunnarson presented his party's concise nine-page motion for bold innovation to eliminate all parallelism in compulsory schooling.[61] Following directly after the inconclusive deliberations of the Socialist party congress on the same subject, the motion is perhaps most notable for the scant attention it received, and for its close similarity to later school reform proposals made by the 1946 School Commission.[62] Because the motion clearly marks the break between the early reform proposals that attempted to modify the parallel system and the later proposals that would abolish early differentiation, Gunnarson's plan merits close attention. Its major points are as follows:

1. Every year the schools lag further behind new social norms and achievements. In spite of this the 1940 Committee proposals clearly evidence a lack of sound leadership to rebuild the schools so as to reflect democratic principles in form and content. The trade unions

---

[60] An analysis of the farm party structure and program in and out of Parliament is included in two works by the Swedish historian Elis Håstad: *Partierna i regering och riksdag*, 1949 [97b]; and *Det moderna partiväsendets organisation*, 1949 [97a].

[61] Gunnar Gunnarson, "Förslag till motion i skolfrågan," 1944. [17]

[62] See Riksdagen, *Riksdagens protokoll. Andra Kammaren 1944*, No. 4, p: 221. [391]

must therefore take the lead in this task and follow two guiding principles: (1) education must reflect the state of current social development; and (2) all education must be equally available to all students without social, economic, or geographic limitations. A new school commission should carry out these directives.

2. *Folkskolan* should be extended and made a nine-year comprehensive school for all children. *Realskolor*, municipal middle schools and the like should all be incorporated into the elementary school. Two voluntarily elected courses of theoretical and practical studies beginning after the sixth grade should carry students to three- or four-year *gymnasia* for practical, academic, technical, commercial, agricultural, and general studies. These schools must in turn be linked with various kinds of higher education.

3. The state through grants for board, clothing, and other necessary expenses must guarantee equality of educational opportunity to all Swedish children. The principle should be "free schooling for all, pay for higher studies." Any stigma of charity or "poor relief" must be guarded against.

4. The school's curriculum must be completely changed: adoption of *arbetsskola* methods; maximum class size of twenty pupils; elimination of homework before grade seven; and abolishment of all examinations—even the *real* and *gymnasium* leaving exams.

5. Undemocratic tendencies must be purged by replacing privately printed textbooks with state-made texts; sociology and citizenship courses should be introduced; and the study of religion changed from brazen propaganda to objective history.

The bravado of this revolutionary motion found no echo in its quiet reception and speedy dismissal. The work is so little known that the writer has been unable to find it mentioned, even in passing, in Swedish secondary sources on the history of national school reform. This is not to say that the motion was without significance; on the contrary, it foreshadowed the general direction of all subsequent Swedish school reform formulations, and by outflanking the coalition-hampered Social Democrats, it spurred their planning for educational reconstruction.

Popular Movements (Folkrörelser)

A third major force supporting comprehensive schools at this time—although in a less defined and articulate manner than the vested interest groups and the political parties—were the long-standing and highly developed Swedish popular organizations. The populist movement came to play an ever greater part in the formulation of public life in the nineteenth century, but not until after the electoral reforms that followed World War I did the various popular movements begin to exert any noticeable influence on the Swedish polity. Then the labor movement, the adult education movement, and the cooperative movement came to play an ever greater part in the formulation of public policy.[63] It might even be argued that because of the school's failure to teach youth the values and techniques of a modern democratic society, the *folkrörelse* (folk movement) and its vast network of popular educational and civic activities became the very backbone of the Swedish democratic system.

The folk movement grew out of popular initiative to seek rational and lawful solutions to problems that the government was either unable or unwilling to remedy. It constituted the organized—if before 1918 to a great extent disenfranchised—proletariat seeking mutual support against the established autocratic social order. After 1918, with a large membership drawn mainly from the working and lower middle classes, these groups formed the majority of adherents to the Social Democratic cause. By and large, they looked upon this party as the spokesman of their vital interests and as the champion of their common egalitarian goal to make Sweden *folkhemmet,* the "people's home," where no person would be driven out because of starvation or lack of opportunity.[64]

By the very conditions of their existence these popular movements had largely bypassed the more traditional and conservative institutions in Swedish society to gain their objectives. The labor and cooperative movements successfully circumvented the financial and commercial communities. As already mentioned, the adult education movement attempted and succeeded to an astonishing degree in supplementing the national norm of six years of frequently very elementary compulsory schooling and in providing what was in fact a type of practical and voluntary "people's secondary education" in the folk high schools.[65]

Although the popular movements in general had been slow to take

---

[63] In what has come to be called the estate thesis, a number of observers have commented on the close links between the popular movements and the Socialists on the one hand and the various other national organizations and their political counterparts on the other. According to this interpretation the four estates, abolished to permit a more representational and individualistic system, have gradually reappeared with new names: i.e., conservatives for nobles, liberal for clergy, agrarian for burghers, and socialists for peasants, each party enjoying support from the related occupational or interest organizations. See Rustow [150] p. 157 and James J. Robbins, *The Government of Labor Relations in Sweden,* 1942, pp. 42–43 [145].

[64] For a detailed history of the growth and activity of Swedish popular movements, see the comprehensive three-volume study by Sigfrid Hanson (ed.), *Svenska folkrörelser,* 1936–1937. [95] A more modern and concise study of this phenomenon is given by Gunnar Heckscher in *Staten och organisationerna,* 1951. [99c]

[65] See, for example, a description of this work in Wagnsson [176], pp. 386–398.

an interest in school reform, they were fully aware of the need for fundamental changes in the school system and, following the Social Democratic lead at the 1944 party congress, they began to devote increasing attention to the problem in their many publications and group instructional activities.[66] In addition to stimulating folk movement support for longer and more relevant common schooling, the Workers Educational Association (ABF) also began a program for direct action. In September of 1944, ABF inaugurated a course for study circle leaders at the trade-union-operated folk high school in Brunnsvik. The course, titled "The School of the Future" (*Den framtida skolan*), had a twofold purpose: (1) to prepare teachers as leaders in study circle discussions of the history of educational problems and controversies, which had culminated in the 1940 School Committee; and (2) to encourage an "enlightened opinion to seek a popular solution of public school questions." [67]

The author of the course text, Victor Fredriksson, a *folkskola* inspector and a member of the 1940 Committee, had for decades been an active supporter of the comprehensive school idea.

Fredriksson, in his plan for "the school of the future," reiterated the basic recommendations of the elementary school group on the 1940 Committee, namely, that the *folkskola* should become a common six-year citizenship school followed by a three-year *realskola* or by two compulsory years in vocational schools or in the higher *folkskola*. The "new school" would thus—if it were realized according to the radical formulations of the folk movement leaders—be little different from the "bottom school" advocated idealistically by Berg in 1883. For, aside from the Communist proposal, neither the experts, the political parties nor the popular organizations were able to envision so radical a departure from tradition as to make the *folkskola* and all it represented an extended common school.

However, with its expanded export trade and its commitment to international causes after World War I, Sweden had frequently observed foreign practice in economic and social problems. It was therefore not surprising that groups involved in planning school reforms should cautiously begin to seek possible answers to Swedish educational problems in the theory and practice of certain democratic foreign educational models.

---

[66] Growing popular interest in education is evident in the exhortations to young people to present these various school problems as discussion topics in their group meetings. See, for example, the study circle manuals by Herman Stolpe, *Ungdomen och folkrörelserna*, 1944, pp. 42–44 [161]; and S. Wahlund, "Utbildningens demokratisering," in *Ungdomen bygger framtiden*, 1944, pp. 5–19. [177]

[67] Viktor Fredriksson, *Den framtida skolan: en orientering i organisationsfrågan*, 1944, p. 3. [14]

FOREIGN INFLUENCE IN POSTWAR EDUCATIONAL PLANNING

In the closing years of World War II and in the years immediately following, the influence of the victorious democracies, especially the United States and England, grew notably in Swedish educational and political circles. In the realm of educational reform, many Swedish planners looked with renewed—and sometimes critical—interest at the school systems and current reforms under way in these two countries, hoping thereby to discover guide lines for the further democratization of Swedish education.

Although educational accomplishments in both the United States and Britain had occasionally been held up by Swedish school reformers in the nineteenth century as examples to be emulated, the strong cultural ties with Germany, since the Middle Ages, had continued to dominate foreign influences in Swedish education.[68] This situation was drastically changed, especially for the *folkskola*, after World War I when the elementary school teachers became increasingly alert to developments in the American progressive education movement.[69] The academic secondary school, however, by and large remained loyal to its Germanic tradition right up to the catastrophe of Hitlerian aggression.[70]

During the great debates of the 1920's on the question of a six-year comprehensive *bottenskola*, the Folk School Teachers Association attempted to gain support for their common-school cause by citing, in a variety of publications, the achievements of American common schools in building a democratic society and in realizing individual potential through "scientific" teaching theory and practice through child-centered education activity methods.[71] The reaction of the Con-

[68] Siljeström's unsuccessful attempts to propagandize the American common school in Sweden in the mid-1800's is a notable example in this respect. See *supra*, p. 30.

[69] For one of the first major attempts to interest Swedish educationists in modern American practice in educational psychology and philosophy, see Nils Hänninger, *Den amerikanska uppfostringsvärlden: studier och strövtåg,* 1922. [94a] For many years Hänninger edited the principal *folkskola* journal.

[70] Following the fall of the Weimar Republic and the rise of National Socialism in Germany, Swedish Social Democrats—although nominally tolerant of their bipartite national school system—grew increasingly antagonistic to what they characterized as Germanic aspects of the secondary schools. A motion carried at the Socialists' 1936 party congress, for instance, called for the "democratic conquest of the secondary school" on the grounds that (1) it was dangerously elitist in character; (2) that in secondary school texts Socialists and Marxists were unfavorably represented although the Fascist dictator Mussolini received praise; and (3) that in many cases "Nazi organizations in our land have been recruited from students of the secondary schools." See *Kongressmotioner 1936,* pp. 59–64. [35a]

[71] A summary of references to American education in the school reform controversies from 1918 to 1927 is included in Bogoslovsky [64], pp. 165–168. See also Oskar Olsson, *Demokratiens skolväsen: iakttagelser i amerikanska skolor,* 1926. [140a]

servatives and of the other political parties—indeed, the greater part of the population—was derisive and scornful of what they believed to be the methods and results of American progressive education.[72] The elementary school teachers continued, however, to publish in their own journals the translated work of John Dewey, G. Stanley Hall, William Kilpatrick, Edward Thorndike, and others, as well as the glowing accounts of Swedish *folkskola* teachers who had visited American schools with the aid of travel grants from the government and from their own association. The wartime publication of an influential book on American institutions by Gunnar and Alva Myrdal included a long and highly favorable chapter on the effectiveness of comprehensive schools in inculcating democratic attitudes and behavior in American youth.[73]

But the United States, remote and unhampered by class-linked parallel schools, had little in common with the fundamental problems in Swedish education. England on the other hand, with a dualistic school system, offered an example of a nearby and admired European country that to a large extent shared the same matrix of educational problems. Thus, among many Swedish groups (especially the educational profession and the political parties) there existed a marked interest in and identification with English wartime planning and enthusiasm for reforms to make available in the postwar period "secondary education for all." [74]

Foreign influence undoubtedly played a contributory role in Swedish

[72] The remarks of the leading upper-chamber Conservative K. J. Ekman on American schools during the debate on the 1927 school reform bill are illustrative: "They call it the work-school (*arbetsskola*), because no work (*arbete*) is ever carried on there. The origin is not so much German (*die arbeitschule*) as American. Our honorable friend Oskar Olsson has been over there and observed how the sons of millionaires and also of some simpler folk get their education together. About this education he has wonderful things to tell. I am not going to contradict him. I have heard from America, however, that children, having passed through such modern schools, are called 'cake eaters.' They are not good for anything but to eat cakes in tearooms." Riksdagen, *Motioner i Första Kammaren 1927. Förhandlingar onsdagen den 18 maj angående omorganisation av det högre skolväsendet*, No. 31, 1927, p. 36. [39g]

[73] Gunnar and Alva Myrdal, *Kontakt med Amerika*, 1941, pp. 89–132. [133c] See also the descriptive professional publications of the same period published by the Folk School Teachers Association: Ester Hermansson, *I amerikanska skolor*, 1940 [103a]; and Elsa Skäringer-Larson, *Demokratisk fostran i U.S.A.*, 1941 [156].

[74] For examples of Swedish interest in English school reform plans, see among others: Alva Myrdal, *Efterkrigsplanering*, 1944. [24b] Pages 98–100 contain an analysis of the Fleming Committee in England and its significance for Swedish "plans to democratize the school"; see also Fredriksson [14], p. 39; Sveriges Socialdemokratiska Arbetareparti, *Protokoll 17e. kongress*, 1944, p. 144 [35b]; and Anna B. Bergstrand, *Demokrati och skolväsen i England*, 1940 [60]. Of special interest in this regard is the 1940 School Committee's discussion of the 1944 English school reform as a positive example of how to improve the relationship between the elementary and secondary school branches in Sweden. See Ecklesiastikdepartementet, *Skolpolitikstidens skolformer: I. Allmänn organisationsplan*, 1945, p. 35. [38h]

school reform by intensifying demands for a more unified and rational school system. It is difficult, however, because of a common reluctance to acknowledge indebtedness, to determine with any degree of precision the scope or importance of this influence.

But in light of subsequent reform action, it is fairly safe to assume that foreign influences were in the main negligible.[75] The political leaders who were ultimately responsible for the resolution of the serious problems in the Swedish school structure and content had begun to recognize the pressing need to formulate school reform not around foreign examples or solutions but within the context of the fundamental democratic goals and the accomplishments of the on-going changes in the Swedish social welfare state.

[75] See the corroborative evaluation by Halvdan Koht, *The American Spirit in Europe: A Survey of Transatlantic Influences*, 1949, p. 221. [117]

Chapter 5

POLITICS, REFORMULATION, AND THE *ENHETSSKOLA* PROPOSAL 1946–1950

The time now seems to be ripe for the abolition of dualism and the realization of the comprehensive school idea [enhetsskoletanke] *proposed by the 1918 School Commission.*[1]

[1] From the 1946 School Commission's seminal report, *1946 års skolkommissionens betänkande med förslag till riktlinjer för det svenska skolväsendets utveckling* (Ecklesiastikdepartementet [38a]), p. 8.

The postwar years in Sweden witnessed a period of explosive expansion in the development of Swedish social welfare measures—a so-called harvest time for critical legislation that had perforce been postponed during World War II. With the arrival of peace, educational problems also moved into the forefront of national interest, and the ruling Social Democrats—newly committed to the belief quoted above—for the first time promoted the comprehensive school as an imperative goal of the expanded welfare state structure. This turnabout from previous policy was in part the result of wartime changes that had stimulated an unprecedented growth in demand for education and in part the result of the desire—and a fresh awareness of the necessity—to reduce the only remaining major social institution that retained markedly elitist characteristics in a society long governed by a political majority committed to social democracy and egalitarianism.[2]

This chapter seeks to ascertain the validity of Alfred North Whitehead's dictum that any serious fundamental change in an intellectual outlook on human society must necessarily be followed by an educational revolution. To this end we shall look first at the postwar situation in Sweden and the on-going drive for a variety of social reforms

[2] Torsten Husén has pointed out that "after 1945 a rapidly growing number of pupils completing seven or eight years' elementary schooling went on to lower secondary academic school (*realskola*) and in so doing 'blew it up from the inside'—not only because of the greater pressure of numbers, but also because the *realskola* curricula could cater for the educational needs of only a minority of boys and girls." About 9 per cent of an age group entered the *realskola* in 1929; by 1950 this percentage exceeded 46 per cent (corresponding figures for entrance into the upper secondary *gymnasia* are 4 per cent and 11 per cent). See his article "The Educational Explosion in Sweden," in *The World Yearbook in Education 1965: The Education Explosion,* 1965, p. 297. [111g]

105

and then turn to the related and revolutionary plan of the 1946 School Commission and the reactions that it provoked.

HARVEST TIME: THE POSTWAR SITUATION

In the elections of 1946 and 1948 the Social Democrats remained the largest and most powerful party in the *riksdag*. But because their margin on joint votes of both houses was not great, their rush to make up for five years of enforced inactivity in social reform legislation was tempered by the necessity of compromise. Because the Socialist postwar program goals for major social and educational reforms aroused only minor opposition, they were pursued with vigor.[3] In contrast, the non-Socialist opposition parties severely criticized the government's program demand for "socialization where private enterprise entails abuses or monopolism." The ruling Socialists, however, took no significant steps—to the consternation of the more extreme left—toward realizing this demand for selective and limited nationalization.[4]

The death of Per Albin Hansson in October 1946 at the age of sixty ended his long tenure as prime minister, a post he had held almost continuously since 1932. Tage Erlander, son of a school teacher, in his forties, who had recently accepted the educational portfolio, took Hansson's post as premier and party leader.[5] While Minister of Education, Erlander had officially put in motion the parliamentary machinery that some two years later in 1948 produced a plan for a new nine-year comprehensive school. At the request of the Social Demo-

---

[3] Important postwar reforms included (1) the Old Age and Disability Pension Act of 1946; (2) child allowances (of 260 crowns or about $72 per annum) paid to parents for each child under 16 years (allowances replaced tax exemptions for dependents, which were held to favor upper income groups); (3) the National Health Insurance Act of 1947; (4) longer vacations for workers (and for housewives at government expense); (5) a major revision of the national penal code (the first since 1864); and (6) among others, the 1950 comprehensive school reform, the first major reorganization of Swedish education since 1842. The programs are described in Karl J. Höijer, *Social Welfare in Sweden*, 1949, pp. 126 ff. [107a]; and Social Welfare Board, *Social Sweden, passim* [41a].

[4] Landsorganisationen, *The Postwar Program of Swedish Labor*, 1948, p. 28. [21a] For a survey of similar developments in other Scandinavian countries during the postwar period, see Henning Friis, "Social Welfare," in *Scandinavia between East and West*, 1950, pp. 139–168. [87]

[5] Erlander, along with former Prime Minister Rickard Sandler, represented the traditional prominence of teachers within the inner circle of the Social Democratic party. Another who might be mentioned was Ernst Wigforss, Minister of Finance in the 1930's and 1940's. University professors, on the other hand, such as Gunnar Myrdal and Östen Undén, served the Social Democratic cause but they were never looked to for party leadership. For an interesting study of the occupations of Socialist members of Parliament and their lineal ancestors, see Elfred Kunn, "Vem var Per Albins farfars far?" *Tiden*, 1945, pp. 490–493. [118]

cratic government, Erlander in January 1946 appointed a new school commission which represented all political parties in parliament. The group was clearly dominated by the Social Democrats and by the optimistic spirit of the time for thoroughgoing solutions to old problems. In his selection of politicians from the opposition parties sympathetic to the Socialist school reform position and in his instructions to the commission, Erlander should be credited with charting the course of that commission to a political solution of the problem of educational parallelism. From January until he became premier in October, Erlander was the active chairman of the so-called Political School Commission.[6]

Although the 1940 Expert Committee continued for some months after the appointment of its successor in 1946, the experts' task was nearly done and their limitations had become all too evident. The committee, created during unusual wartime conditions, was ill suited to propose sweeping correctives for the many problems in Swedish education: perhaps one should not look to the representatives of a system for such proposals. Moreover, as an essentially specialist body, the 1940 Committee from its inception had functioned only in an advisory capacity. Only Parliament as representative of the entire nation could in the last analysis make final decisions on school reform proposals.[7] The Social Democrats therefore, when finally free of the wartime coalition government and with a ruling majority in the *riksdag,* were quick to seize their prerogatives of power in a new attempt to reformulate earlier proposals for unifying Swedish schools.

The problems of supply and demand in Swedish education during the postwar years were greatly intensified and complicated for a number of reasons. Economic expansion, an increasingly severe labor shortage, and growing dependence on quality exports all tended to put pressure on the school system to satisfy more adequately the changing demands of the labor market. Severe dislocations arising from an ever increasing internal migration from rural to urban areas also compounded educational problems in both areas. The growing number of working wives, substantial increases in family per capita income, the improvement of transportation and the extension of the mass media as well as the rising birth rate (from 85,000 in 1934 to 135,000 in 1946) all tended to exacerbate existing educational problems and to demand immediate attention and long-range planning.[8] Most

[6] See Ingemar Düring (ed.), *The Swedish School Reform: A Summary of the Government Bill at the Request of the 1946 School Commission,* 1951, p. 31. [8]

[7] *Ibid.*

[8] For a succinct analysis of how these factors influenced the educational activities of the central and local governments, see Erik Westerlind and Rune Beckman, *Sweden's Economy: Structure and Trends,* 1965, *passim.* [179]

important, however, the full impact of economic reforms and social welfare programs was reflected in the marked increase of aspiration for schooling at all levels, especially for vocational and secondary education.[9]

Sweden shared this development with most modern industrial countries, although not all shared similar backgrounds of social reform experience. That Sweden experienced a strong surge in demand for secondary schooling—and particularly by children from working-class families—can only partly be attributed to earlier measures of socio-economic reform and to the influence of the war and the changes it generated or intensified.[10] We can, however, see in the radical solution to Swedish educational problems proposed by the 1946 Commission the direct influence of the extent, scope, and continuity of the on-going democratic revolution in Swedish attitudes and institutions and in the Social Democrats' commitment to carry this revolution into the schools.

THE 1946 POLITICAL SCHOOL COMMISSION

The 1946 School Commission differed from the 1940 School Committee in almost every conceivable way. It worked in open sessions under conditions of widespread postwar enthusiasm for social and educational change rather than *in camera* during a "siege" period of political inactivity occasioned by the demands of a wartime coalition. Its members were drawn from the more progressive sections of all political

[9] Ester Hermansson, "Swedish Education during the 1940's," *Harvard Education Review*, Fall 1951, p. 236. [103b] The long-term expansion in Swedish school attendance is also clearly indicated in the following data on "School Attendance by Age Groups 1940–1960 and Predictions for 1965 and 1970":

Age	1940	1950	1960	1965	1970
7–15	79%	83%	92%	95%	95%
16–18	10	16	34	46	62
19–24	5	8	16	18	22

See Ulf Larsson, "Skolplikt och Skolrätt," in Ingvar Carlsson (ed.), *Ung mening,* 1964, p. 59. [70]

Note: The 1965 estimate for the 16–18 age group is low and 1970 figures have been revised upward. See Husén [111g], pp. 297–300.

[10] For an excellent study of the several factors that stimulated educational demand in postwar Sweden, see the study begun in 1948 by Torgny T. Segerstedt and Agne Lundquist, *Man in Industrial Society,* 1956. [153b] The authors found that (1) migration to urban areas, (2) participation in popular movements, and (3) need for increased job skills all tended to increase demand for post elementary schooling—as did the fact that workers, who in the main regarded themselves as members of the most influential social class, were discontented with their role in the working group. See pp. 15–23.

parties, with a clear majority representing the Social Democratic party. Moreover, the members of the 1946 Commission were by and large politicians or representatives of the large popular organizations, rather than educators or educational experts; and they proceeded with a wealth of factual data on controversial problems (such as differentiation) in large part gathered by their predecessors. They were united in a commitment to the need for sweeping educational reforms, with a social rather than an educational justification for their master plan. They were able, moreover, to reformulate earlier demands for comprehensive schooling so that previous objections (such as making the *folkskola* the only common school at the expense of the *realskola*) were either eliminated, avoided, or obscured. The deadlocked 1940 Committee, with its partisan groups of elementary and secondary school teachers, had utterly failed to accomplish this.

In an unusual move Minister of Education Erlander personally took charge of the commission's work and served as its chairman for ten months until he relinquished his post to become premier. A leading intellectual in the Social Democratic inner circle, Stellan Arvidson, was appointed to the influential position of secretary to the commission. Having revised his earlier views on the overriding importance of vocational education, Arvidson became a leading supporter and propagandist for the nine-year common school.[11] Also notable among the majority of Socialist members on the commission was the educator and social scientist Alva Myrdal, a party intellectual and an admirer of American "progressive" education and prolonged common schooling. It may also be recalled that of the psychologists reporting to the 1940 Committee on the desirability of early or late selection, only Professor John Elmgren concurred with the latter alternative. The commission chose Dr. Elmgren as its psychological consultant and he alone conducted its extensive research program at the University of Gothenburg.[12]

With a mandate from the Minister of Education to produce a blueprint for the complete reorganization of the national school system, the commission worked openly and in an atmosphere of public attention and concern. Under the leadership of the Social Democratic majority,

11 See for instance Stellan Arvidson, *Skolreformen: en sammanfattning av skolkommissionens betänkande,* 1949 [4c]; Stellan Arvidson, Ivan Blomberg and Britta Stenholm, *Enhetsskolan växer fram,* 1953 [55b]; Stellan Arvidson, "Den nya skolan söder om Söder," *Aktuella Information,* No. 4, 1954 [4a]. A criticism of Arvidson's "proletarian idealism" is included in the article by Ragnar Oldberg, "Idealisten och skolreformen," *Perspektiv,* No. 2, 1953, pp. 59–62. [139a]

12 See his report, *School and Psychology,* 1952 [10], for the controversial results derived from a study of some 6,000 Swedish school children.

the thirteen commission members completed their assignment in considerably less than two years.[13] In contrast to earlier parliamentary
committees, the commission's 561-page report, largely the work of
Secretary Arvidson, speaks with authority and with one united voice
for the proposed new nine-year comprehensive school. If important
major differences of opinion arose during the commission's deliberations—as so disruptively happened with its predecessor—such a situation is not noted nor evident in the report. On the contrary, this well
written and well organized report exudes an instructive confidence and
single-mindedness of purpose.[14] The work, for example, confidently
opens with the statement quoted at the outset of this chapter, a
quotation illustrative of the commanding tone of the report.

This is not to imply, however, that the commission completely disre-
garded the position tenaciously held by the still powerful supporters of
early differentiation, who were generally to be found in the upper
classes and in their most representative educational institutions and
political organizations. In this respect it is instructive to note that the
commission's report, submitted to the Minister of Education in June
1948, devotes a considerable amount of space in its initial chapters to
a recapitulation of the divergent proposals and commentary of the
1940 Committee.[15] In a sense this earlier group, because of the numerical dominance of members supporting the academic secondary
school (and the concurring opinions of the psychological experts), had
represented a holding action on the part of conservative interests for
the status quo in the long and sporadic controversy over comprehensive
schooling. Yet, in the selective inclusion of suitable excerpts from the
committee's voluminous writings, the commission (and one suspects
here the hand of Arvidson) implied that its radical plan constituted
merely a logical outgrowth of earlier prolonged investigation and study
by the experts, the majority of whom, it should be recalled, actually
supported early selection (at the age of eleven) into different schools.

For example, the 1940 Committee acknowledged as the basic reform
problem "to find a solution that while allowing for necessary differentiation, permits the greatest possible unity." [16] In reply, the 1946 Commission, ignoring any mention of differentiation, stated its support for
the committee's desire for greater unity in the Swedish school system:
"The Commission however is prepared to go a step farther than the
Committee in the question of unity in the school structure." Where

[13] Ecklesiastikdepartementet [38a], p. 4.
[14] See, for example, *ibid.*, Chapters 2, 3, 15.
[15] *Ibid.*, pp. 18–45.
[16] Ecklesiastikdepartementet, *Sammanfattning av allmänn organisationsplan,*
1945, p. 7. [38c]

the experts had struggled with various plans to bring into closer contact yet at the same time preserve the essential theoretical and practical nature of the two parallel school branches, the commission proposed their total abolishment and gradual fusion into a nine-year *enhetsskola.*[17]

The commission took pains, particularly in the first section of Chapter 3, "The Concept of a Comprehensive School" (*Begreppet enhetsskola*), to demonstrate that its radical proposal was the logical outgrowth and consequence of a central two-part historical development in Swedish education: (1) the implementation of the idea of unity and democracy; and (2) the progressive extension of compulsory schooling. Contributions of Comenius, Pestalozzi, Fichte, Süverns and Diesterweg are selectively touched upon to illustrate early continental concern with the problems of educational and social duality.[18] The efforts of corresponding early exponents of common schooling in Sweden—Anders Fryxell and K. A. Agardh, among others—are also summarized in terms of their contributions to early common school thought. In considerably more detail, the lifelong efforts of Torsten Rudenschöld, P. A. Siljeström, and Fridtjuv Berg to make the *folkskola* an undifferentiated common foundation school are shown to be of increasing relevance to educational problems with the growth and stratification of the parallel system on the one hand and the rise of a folk democracy on the other.[19] The demand for a democratic, undifferentiated *enhetsskola* upon which all other schooling could build had, the commission claimed, grown simultaneously in the past hundred years with the emergence of political democracy and its concomitant requirements for equality of educational opportunity. But because each branch of the parallel system represented different and frequently conflicting educational, teacher and class interests, resolution of educational dualism should favor neither branch at the expense of the other. *All school types* should, therefore, the commission proposed, be abolished and replaced by a new nine-year comprehensive school that might better serve the increasingly complex educational, social, and cultural demands laid upon the school.[20]

Although the commission saw the fundamental justification for this new school in the need to create social and cultural unity,[21] a research program seeking a scientific justification as well had from the very

[17] Ecklesiastikdepartementet [38a], p. 45.
[18] *Ibid.,* p. 39.
[19] *Ibid.,* p. 40.
[20] *Ibid.,* pp. 46 ff.
[21] Note, for instance, the statement that because "the school class is a collective" it is the logical environment "in which to inculcate desired values and solidarity necessary to remold the great collective" (i.e., society). *Ibid.,* p. 3.

beginning (1946) been put into operation under Professor Elmgren. His assignment, "to ascertain the ability structure and factorial maturity in Swedish school children" reflected the commission's interest in the development of "practical" and "theoretical" aptitudes and their interrelation at various age levels.[22] It also demonstrated the commission's desire to justify its proposals, if possible, with the results of research studies in educational psychology, a justification that had been lacking in earlier, vulnerable attempts to achieve structural unity, especially in the pro-comprehensive school arguments in the 1940 Committee.

Elmgren's very extensive studies in this matter were not published until 1952, some two years after the *riksdag* had already accepted the commission's basic plan. The commission nevertheless attempted to bring to bear Elmgren's partial findings (especially in the central question of the possibility of determining various types of ability) and to a considerable extent used the limited knowledge of the outcomes of Elmgren's investigations to develop basic recommendations. These conclusions may be summarized as follows: (1) Because "practical" and "theoretical" aptitudes are positively correlated "an early differentiation can hardly be recommended because, among other reasons, practical aptitude can only be assessed rather late and would result in a theoretical bias in selection." [23] (2) "The earlier sharp distinction between theoretical and practical ability can hardly be valid" and there is no psychological reason why the school organization must have parallel tracks to provide for these so-called parallel abilities. (3) Differentiation must be made more flexible "so that many individual combinations of theoretical and practical ability win consideration" in the school.[24]

The commission further justified the supersession of the selective system by a comprehensive one because the former differentiated on scholastic aptitude and was strongly social-class influenced. It reasoned, therefore, that because of *realskolan*'s elite character and high prestige (vis-à-vis *folkskolan*) it would, with the intensified demand for secondary schooling, tend to "cream off" a goodly number of the students high not only in theoretical ability, but in theoretical and practical ability as well. The growing demand for postelementary education would therefore eventually create a situation in which "the practical vocations would be deprived of people with high general ability, gaps between social classes would widen, and democracy itself would be placed in danger.[25]

---

[22] As used here, "aptitude" refers to potential, and "ability" to manifested potential as defined, using observed achievements. See Elmgren [10], p. 3.

[23] Ecklesiastikdepartementet [38a], p. 68.

[24] *Ibid.*, p. 68.

[25] *Ibid.*, p. 70.

Before examining the sources, content, and effectiveness of the protests that slowly grew to oppose the commission's alleged "undisguised attempts to use the schools for this social engineering" [26] for parity of esteem in intellectual and practical work—and the combination of research and assumptions used to justify their opposition—it will be necessary first to examine precisely what reforms the 1946 Political School Commission put forth in its professed desire to equalize, democratize, and unify Swedish schooling and, at the same time, "develop free human beings for whom cooperation is both a need and a joy." [27]

ENHETSSKOLA: A NEW SCHOOL FOR SOCIAL, EDUCATIONAL, AND NATIONAL UNITY

The School Commission turned in its one-volume report to the Minister of Education and Parliament in the summer of 1948. The main proposals may be summarized as follows.

1. The period of compulsory education should be extended to nine years. This will help to provide a more adequate schooling in light of the requirements of modern society and also put an end to the problems arising from the fact that the period of compulsory schooling varies from seven to eight years depending on the ability and desire of school districts to support longer schooling.
2. All compulsory schooling (i.e., between the ages of 7 and 16) should—granting the obvious exceptions for handicapped children —take place in an "organically integrated" comprehensive school replacing all present parallel schools: the elementary *folkskola,* the lower secondary *realskola,* municipal middle schools, and all girls' schools, vocational and trade schools, etc. By including prevocational training and work experience in the new comprehensive school, the commission believed that more realistic and efficient choices for later work could be achieved through the development of expanded and more efficient vocational guidance services.[28]
3. *Enhetsskolan,* the new school, should be organizationally undifferentiated in the first eight years. Only in grade nine (see Figure 2) should the students be divided into the academic (9G), general (9A), and prevocational (9Y) streams. The absence of streaming and homogeneous grouping in the comprehensive

---

[26] *Svenska Morgonbladet,* March 14, 1949, p. 3.

[27] Ecklesiastikdepartementet [38a], p. 4.

[28] The confused situation in Swedish vocational training at this time (because of inadequacy and duplication of services, and faulty articulation of schools) is described in two publications of the Labor Market Board (Arbetsmarknadsstyrelsen): *Skolor för yrkesutbildning,* 1949 [37c]; and *Att välja yrke,* 1949, *passim* [37a].

Figure 2. Structural Reorganization of the Swedish School System Proposed by the 1946 School Commission and Adopted by Parliament in the 1950 *Enhetsskola* Act. (*Source:* Ecklesiastikdepartementet, *1946 års Skolkommissionens betänkande med förslag till riktlinjer för det svenska skolväsendets utveckling,* 1948, pp. 48–50. [38a])

School Year				Age
	To higher education			
12				19
11	Gymnasium	To continuation schools		18
10		(to be arranged)		17
9	9G Academic stream	9A General course stream	9Y Prevocational stream	16
8	28 hours of required subjects + 9 hours electives			15
7	32 hours of required subjects + 5 hours electives (grades 7-9 taught by subject teachers)			14
6				13
5	Introduction to compulsory English instruction			12
4				11
3				10
2				9
1	(Grades 1-6 taught by elementary school teachers)			8
				7

school's first six years would prevent any "anticipation of future choice of electives" and would thereby guard against "a bias in a more theoretical or practical direction."

4. *Enhetsskolan* would be examination-free and replace selection with election. Beginning in grade seven all students would be free to choose elective subjects with guidance from teachers and parents. The school was to be divided into three sections, each of three years' duration, but no selection by examination would take place at any time. All children would have teachers meeting the same professional requirements. Teacher training would be completely reorganized and unified with greater stress on pedagogical techniques than had previously been the case. Teachers for the first six grades would be trained in new training colleges which would replace the existing normal schools. Higher-form

teachers in grades seven through nine would continue to be university educated and would then receive professional training in the new teacher colleges.

5. The curriculum of the school would be totally changed in both content and purpose. A "child centered approach" and activity methods would replace instruction of the class as a whole. Pedagogical differentiation should be attempted only through grouping by student-chosen electives and through the use of standardized basic and enrichment syllabi.

Additional proposals dealt with provisions for guidance, social services, and the increased need for psychological testing. New and better programs must be developed in these areas if the comprehensive school is to meet adequately the requirements of a modern, technical society. The point is strongly made that a firm basis of general education for all children is the only logical educational solution in light of an uncertain future fraught with a shortage of labor, a heavy dependence on the export market, and rapidly changing demands for various types of vocational and technological competence.[29]

The commission also devoted a large section of its report to the problems of the *gymnasium;* its aims, its streams and inner work; and how it might most efficiently be linked to the new school and the universities.[30] As might be expected from the proposed extension of compulsory schooling to provide all children with three years of lower secondary schooling (grades 7–9), the commission envisioned drastic changes in the elite character of the *gymnasium* as the comprehensive school and extended lower secondary schooling would gradually come into being.[31] Latin, for instance, would be deemphasized, new modern and general studies should be offered, and even the prestigious *student examen* was called into question. As in the demand for reform of teacher training a future committee might well, the commission believed, soon begin work ·on the task of "democratizing the *gymnasium.*"[32]

[29] Ecklesiastikdepartementet [38a], pp. 11, 48 f., 223, 287.

[30] A study of the problems in relating the *gymnasium* to labor market needs is included in Arbetsmarknadsstyrelsen, *Gymnasisternas ämnesval,* 1948. [37b]

[31] Ecklesiastikdepartementet [38a], pp. 270–280.

[32] *Ibid.,* p. 281. Fears that an undifferentiated *enhetsskola* would eventually lead to demands for an undifferentiated *gymnasium* were widely expressed in the following years. See, for instance, the representative article in the secondary school teachers' journal by Ragnar Oldberg and Adolf Söderlund, "Skolkris och—krisskola?" *Pedagogisk Tidskrift,* Vol. 9, 1952, pp. 169–178 [139b], and the debate, as published by the faculty of the University of Gothenburg (Göteborgs Högskola), *Skolreformen, Göteborgs Högskolas lärarråds yttrande över skolkommissionens betänkande,* 1948. [16]

The reform of teacher training and the need to decentralize school control so that local districts might assume more responsibility for school management and financial support were subjects that, in the opinion of the commission, warranted separate study because of their crucial importance to the success of the *enhetsskola* proposals. Both topics were dealt with in detail by later committees.[33]

As instructed, the School Commission in its proposals for a new comprehensive school formulated a general and far-reaching plan for the future development of Swedish education. For the first time since the founding of the *folkskola* in 1842 the problem of parallelism in compulsory education would be eliminated and the entire national school system would face a revolutionary reorientation of purpose and reorganization of structure. Few Swedes in light of the changing times and the demonstrated need for educational reform questioned the basic goals sought by the reformers: (1) the expansion of compulsory education to provide a measure of secondary education for all; (2) the equalization of educational opportunities for all students irrespective of social class, sex, or domicile; (3) the modernization of the work of the school, its methods, its curriculum and its social-psychological services, or even the commission's somewhat doctrinaire goal of making the school "more democratic." Indeed, the very unanimity of the commission underscored the general public recognition of the need for thoroughgoing reforms to meet more efficiently present and future demands on the schools.[34]

FOR AND AGAINST *ENHETSSKOLA*

In accordance with Swedish practice, the government sent copies of the commission's report to a wide variety of professional educational organizations, institutions, and diverse national bodies for their written comments and suggestions (*remisser*). In 1948 the report was published and found a wide audience. The commission's work aroused considerable public interest for several reasons: because of its radical proposals, and because, in contrast to traditional practice, the group

[33] See Stellan Arvidson, *Enhetsskolan: skolan vi skall få*, 1950, pp. 12 ff. [4b]

[34] Members of the School Commission, it should be noted, divided only on the question of religious instruction. Sweden has a Protestant state church and all elementary school teachers were required to be members. School began with prayers, and ethically and historically oriented instruction in Christianity was given. With the deciding vote of the chairman, the commission recommended a continuation of morning devotions and religious instruction rather than, as the minority wanted, the total abolition of state church influence. See Ecklesiastikdepartementet [38a], pp. 176–177.

had made no effort to keep the proceedings secret. On the contrary, the Secretary, Stellan Arvidson, had as early as 1947 revealed in a speech the basic outline of the commission's plans. His speech in Gothenburg on September 16, 1947, should be noted in some detail. By explaining the procedures of the commission's deliberations, Arvidson attempted to correct several earlier confusing and somewhat critical statements concerning the group's progress. At the same time he gave an authoritative overview of the reformulated plans for a nine-year comprehensive school and the rationale behind them.[35]

In March, Bertil von Friesen, a Liberal member of Parliament and member of the commission, had given strong intimation in a newspaper article that the commission's work would be both thoroughgoing and united. But his announcement of the direction of reform development was somewhat premature and confusing.[36] He noted, and it was true enough, that because discussion differed only on details and did not follow party lines, the eventual plan would represent a unanimous decision of the members. Erroneously, however, he said that the new comprehensive school would contain three stages of three years each, corresponding to the existing primary (*småskolor*), elementary (*folkskolor*), and lower secondary schools (*realskolor*), and that it would terminate "with something corresponding to the present *realskola* exam," which qualified students for the *gymnasium* (and the right to wear a special grey cap).[37] Arvidson took pains to point out that the new school would be free from any terminal exam and that because

[35] *Göteborgs Handelstidning*, September 16, 1947, p. 3. This newspaper supports the Liberal Party.

[36] *Göteborgs Handelstidning*, March 1, 1947, p. 3.

[37] On the contrary, one of the basic purposes of the new nine-year school would be to provide a practical citizenship school for all students including those who previously would have been unable to pass the entrance examinations for the *realskola* and other forms of academic lower secondary schooling. A study by Torsten Husén, then a young educational psychologist, who some years later played a vital role in implementing the reform, showed that only about 33 per cent of Swedish boys had the intellectual ability to qualify for *realskolan*, a school that, according to the 1940 Committee, "addresses itself to a clientele with marked gifts for study and consequently with the power to absorb the comprehensive theoretical knowledge that it imparts at such a high tempo. Pupils who enter *realskolan* without possessing the requisite powers of study find that they are unable to continue to the end." The study points out that in 1948, 31.7 per cent of an age-cohort transferred to various types of secondary schools and concludes, "It is clear that a quantitative expansion of the present middle-school organization together with the retention of the standards . . . hitherto demanded for all pupils cannot provide a solution to the much wider program of popular education, which has arisen as a result of the striving of *all* strata of the population . . . for more knowledge as a start in life." See Torsten Husén, *Begåvning och miljö: studier i begåvnings-utvecklingens och begåvningsurvalets psykologisk-pedagogiska och sociala problem*, 1948, p. 104 [111a]; and Ecklesiastikdepartementet [38a], pp. 93–94.

of its planned practical character, its upper stage would not correspond to the *realskola* in any substantive way.

The contention of the director of the Royal Board of Education Otto Holmdahl that "the School Commission has not provided any convincing proof that the solution [to the problem of when to differentiate] lies in the new *'elementarskola,'*" also required rebuttal and clarification by Arvidson, who by this time had clearly emerged as the government's foremost ideological and pedagogical spokesman for *enhetsskolan*. The *"elementarskola,"* according to Holmdahl's erroneous belief, would be the commission's plan for a lower undifferentiated *folkskola* with a higher differentiated *realskola* as adjunct: ". . . it will certainly be called a comprehensive school," he complained darkly, "but it will not be comprehensive." [37]

In retrospect, Arvidson's speech may be seen as an attempt to correct the misunderstanding caused by faulty interpretation; to chart the course and goals of the reform; and to solicit support from those who either doubted or looked passively on these goals. The "basic theme in the Commission's work," said Arvidson, "is obviously the democratization of the school." [38] With this objective firmly established, concrete requirements, he continued, become clear: (1) state scholarships, student social services, and school psychological services must be expanded and improved; (2) seven years is too short a period in which to provide knowledge adequate for our modern, complex life; therefore schooling must be lengthened—and only a minimum of nine years will suffice to provide the new courses needed in Swedish, social studies, practical studies, and foreign languages; (3) "another point in the democratization program is the decentralization of the national school system"; and (4) differentiation must be postponed until after the eighth grade because, with the growing demand for secondary education and the resultant pressure to enter the *realskola*, continued early selection will eventually starve practical and manual occupations of intelligent new members. This would, Arvidson cautioned, gradually deprive Sweden's large popular movements of intelligent leadership to such an extent that they would no longer be able to serve as the foundation for a democratic society. He did not say so, but it was quite clear (and most significant) that Arvidson and the Social Democratic party he supported had come to see early selection as detrimental to the continued political dominance of the Socialists and the folk movement.

Awareness of this danger is also evident in the position taken by

[37] *Sydsvenska Dagbladet*, May 22, 1947, p. 4.
[38] *Göteborgs Handelstidning*, September 16, 1947, p. 3.

the Central Federation of Trade Unions (Landsorganisationen or LO).[39] In its *remiss* to Parliament this powerful group of 1,251,000 workers expressed its opposition to differentiation even in the ninth year of the proposed new school.[40] This objection had the warm support of the trade unions whose members were increasingly looking to the state rather than to their own workers' high schools and study circles to provide their children with some measure of secondary education.[41] As might be expected, the trade unions' demand was strongly opposed by all the teacher organizations and by all political parties with the exception of the Communists.[42]

Overriding the objections of the trade unions, the eighteenth congress of the Social Democratic Party (which represented not only labor but all the diverse groups comprising the popular folk movement) placed itself fully in accord with the proposals of the commission. The party program was accordingly revised to reflect this support and numerous motions from the floor dealing with problems in education were tabled with the explanation that they would eventually be resolved by the commission's proposed reforms.[43]

Support by the large and influential Folk School Teachers Association (Sveriges Folkskollärarförbund) for the idea of comprehensive citizenship schooling had been traditional since the founding of the organization in the 1880's. It is not surprising therefore that this group in the main responded with great enthusiasm to the commission's proposals.[44] If the prestigious *realskola* were abolished, there would then be some chance for a partial reduction of dualism in the two teacher levels, for more favorable professional conditions of work and advancement, and for the long-cherished goal of the normal-school-trained elementary teachers to achieve parity of prestige and training with the

[39] The Social Democrats and the trade union movement have since their beginnings in the 1880's cooperated closely and disagreements, when they have arisen, have usually concerned details and not basic goals. For example, the postwar program of the Federation of Trade Unions was issued jointly with the Social Democrats—and also accepted *in toto* by the Swedish Communist Party. The program gave strong support to the idea of a nine-year comprehensive school. See Landsorganisationen [21a], p. 45.

[40] Landsorganisationen, "Remiss rörande 1946 skolkommissionens betänkande," 1948. [21c]

[41] Personal interview with Nils Ramsten. Stockholm, August 14, 1965.

[42] The editor, and Communist, Knut Olsson, a member of the 1946 School Commission, did, however, support the commission's proposals.

[43] *Protokoll från artonde kongress i Stockholm den 12–20 februari 1948*, pp. 130–135. [35b]

[44] For an example of the uncritical and enthusiastic support of the association for the commission's proposals, see Sveriges Folkskollärarförbund, *Skolkommissionens principbetänkande*, 1948 [33a] and *Sveriges folkskollärarförbund om skolreformen*, 1948 [33b].

elite corps of university-trained secondary school teachers. The association saw, moreover, in the practical, progressive nature of the proposed new unified school, not so much the fusion of all parallel branches but, rather, the old *folkskola* extended and modernized, and the *realskola* vanquished.[45] This combative spirit, which was also obvious among the secondary school teachers, is evident in numerous articles in the elementary school teachers' press supporting the reform proposals; an example of this can be seen in the banner heading announcing the successful passage of the *enhetsskola* bill in 1950: "Parliament Unanimous: The *Folkskola* Has Won" (*Riksdagen enig: folkskolan segrade*).[46]

The popular folk movements that represented well over half the families in Sweden were another influential source of support for the proposed *enhetsskola*. Since their introduction of nationwide courses in Swedish educational problems after 1944, these organizations and their members had become increasingly vocal in demands for expanded and more democratic schooling.[47] The Cooperative Society, for example, published a number of books on this subject. One series of three volumes developed the theme that comradeship should be encouraged in both the proposed egalitarian society and the *enhetsskola*, and that this solidarity would "ripen into democratic understanding."[48] A similar work in a more militant vein presented the struggle to democratize the school as "The New Front" (*den nya fronten*) in the folk movement's battle against institutionalized privilege.[49] The author points out that the present crisis in postelementary education for lower-class children —a crisis, in fact, for the entire folk movement—had ironically been fostered by the supplementary educational activities provided by many of the organizations in the movement itself.[50]

The Social Democrats functioned as the main political arm of the folk movement. Although the relationship was only a loose arrangement, the solidarity of interests between the movement and the party was perfectly understood by all organizations involved.[51] Clearly, as pointed out by Arvidson in his 1947 speech and in the 1946 School

[45] *Svensk Skoltidning*, No. 5–6, 1948, p. 5.

[46] *Svensk Skoltidning*, No. 9, 1950, p. 3.

[47] Interview with Rektor Stellan Arvidson. August 31, 1965.

[48] See Carl Cederblad, *Kamratskap*, 1951. [72] Cederblad had earlier participated in spelling reform activities.

[49] See Tage Lindbom, *Den nya fronten*, 1949. [123] Lindbom believed that the protracted resistance of the secondary school to fundamental change could only be constructively overcome through a united effort of the total movement. See Chapter 3, "Folket och folkrörelserna."

[50] *Ibid.*, p. 50.

[51] Dankwart A. Rustow, *The Politics of Compromise: A Study of Parties and Cabinet Government in Sweden*, 1955, p. 76. [150]

Commission's *enhetsskola* report itself, the proposed extension and unification of Swedish compulsory schooling lay in the best interests of the common folk and their continued political dominance. For too long, he cautioned, the folk movement had ignored the benefits of academic secondary education because of its inaccessibility and the impression it gave of an almost foreign culture to the majority of working-class parents and their children. As a result, the popular branch of the bifurcated school system with its *folkskola* and compensatory folk high schools had become increasingly anachronistic with the rise to political dominance of this folk movement in 1932 and the successful implementation of its welfare state program in the following decades.[52]

The principal themes of opposition to the School Commission's proposals are revealingly documented in the collective *remisser,* in various publications of the postelementary teacher organizations, and in the conservative press.[53] Some of the most significant arguments can be categorized and analyzed according to their emphasis on the psychological, educational, or social problems that would follow, according to the critics, the adoption of the commission's blueprint for school reform. It should be stressed, however, that those who viewed the proposals as trifling or worse held a minority position. Although they frequently spoke with the weight and influence of high academic position or expert knowledge, the critics were opposing a popular cause. Moreover, their attack was fragmentary and unfocused, without overt support from any political party or large national institution or organization. Although criticism of the proposed reform in many instances was perceptive and, understandably, expressed well-founded doubts, the arguments of the opponents of the comprehensive school plan and their lack of effect tended to confirm the commission's claim that the time to replace educational dualism with unity had indeed arrived.

Because Elmgren's detailed research report was not published until 1952, psychological questions were raised not only concerning the validity of the findings cited in the commission's report, but about their interpretation as well. Torsten Husén, an unflagging adherent of the school reform, believed that "it is not quite clear what conclusions Elmgren himself is inclined to draw from the findings presented in his research report" and, more serious, that "the conclusions drawn by the

52 *Göteborgs Handelstidning,* September 16, 1947, p. 3.
53 Replies from 160 local school boards, 44 out of 51 school inspectors, nearly 300 secondary school faculties, and others, concerning the suitability of the proposals may be found in Ecklesiastikdepartementet, *Skolöverstyrelsens utlåtande över vissa av 1940 års skolutrednings betänkanden och 1946 års skolkommissionens principbetänkande jämte sammanfattning av avgivna yttranden,* 1949, *passim.* [38g]

School Commission [in the matter of differentiation] do not gain support throughout in the findings of the research projects sponsored by the Commission." [54] This evaluation by a supporter may help to explain the plethora of critical interpretations concerning the problem of determining theoretical and practical aptitudes and the proper conclusions to be drawn therefrom.

Most of the evaluating specialist bodies that collated and summarized the *remisser,* including the Royal Board of Education, were in one way or another critical of the commission's conclusions in the matter of differentiation. They might sympathize with the goal of the reform but judged it dangerous to rush ahead with a total reorganization of the school system based on debatable conclusions and "billowy speculations" instead of hard empirical data. [55]

Criticism of a pedagogical nature concerning educational efficiency emphasized the many possible difficulties for teachers and students alike in the commission's proposals for ungrouped classes, free selection of electives, and a "child-centered approach" to instruction. Research in curriculum development and teaching methods was relatively new in Sweden and the debate between the champions of the new "activity school" and the old or traditional "cramming schools" (as the report described them) was carried on without much benefit of "expert" evaluation. [56] Rather, it was a debate of opinions drawing heavily on the relationship between two types of learning and knowledge that represented diametrically opposed philosophical positions. The first, which might be called the "progressive" or "child-centered" opinion, believed that all learning must be closely associated with the child's own personality growth and that it was infinitely better to learn techniques of information retrieval than merely to memorize facts. [57] The academic opinion, on the other hand, was basically essentialist; it held that there must be a skeleton of firm knowledge upon which one could hang acquired facts and a personally adapted cultural tradition transferred from adults to the new generation and especially to the most able of each new generation. [58]

Not surprisingly, the *remisser* from the elementary school teacher

[54] Torsten Husén, *Problems of Differentiation in Swedish Compulsory Schooling,* 1962, pp. 25–26. [111e]

[55] Ecklesiastikdepartementet [38g], pp. 32–33.

[56] Gunnar Helén, "Present Trends and Political Issues," in *Differentiation and Guidance in the Comprehensive School,* 1959, pp. 33, 34–35. [101]

[57] Indeed, with reference to new teaching methods, the commission observed that "a touch of radicalism does no harm: respect for tradition should never go so far that the pupil is overwhelmed by masses of knowledge, or that orientation becomes out of date, and neglects the community that is coming into being for the one that has passed away." See Ecklesiastikdepartementet [38a], pp. 115–116.

[58] Helén [101].

organizations and faculties, who had looked most favorably on progressivism in American schools and had pressed for similar innovations in Swedish schools, warmly approved of the commission's proposals. In contrast, the secondary and university *remisser* almost unanimously rejected the proposals as educationally unsound and undesirable. The higher the type of school, the more numerous and disapproving were the criticisms.[59] The *läroverket* faculties were, with only one exception, united in their disapproval of the commission's proposals and highly skeptical about, for example, the possibilities of postponing organizational differentiation until the ninth grade. The representatives of the university worried lest the prestigious *student-examen,* which qualified graduating *gymnasium* students for university admission, might be weakened by a poorer foundation for scientific studies and research.[60]

The pervading concern of these evaluating bodies revolved around the commission's proposal for heterogeneous classes and the supposedly detrimental effects they would have on teaching because of "heaviness." Many evaluators contended that the gifted would be unnecessarily restrained, would become bored, and would run the risk "of not obtaining the firm basis of hard knowledge they will need when moving up to the *gymnasium*." [61] A related negative influence would, it was also frequently stressed, affect less able students who might develop feelings of inferiority and "school weariness." Nor were the commission's proposed remedies for these problems (i.e., activity methods and the individualization of instruction) seen as adequate to alleviate properly these anticipated problems. They might, according to Rektor Sefve, produce a satisfactory kind of *arbetsskola* for the less able, but they could never neutralize the time factor inherent in heterogeneous classes. In short, "the *enhetsskola* would be a waste of time for the gifted children." Sefve asked rhetorically why, if able students benefited from selection in the fourth school year, this should not be continued? There is more than a hint of suggested class self-interest in his answer: "Several reasons can be drawn upon to show the advantages of the School Commission's suggestions, and each in its own way will especially impress persons of a certain social class and political opinion." [62]

Professor Erik Wellander, an old foe of the comprehensive school proposals in the 1920's and a member of the 1940 School Committee, in a manner somewhat more mellow than in his earlier attacks, pointed out that Sweden, dependent on quality exports, could ill afford the

---

[59] Ecklesiastikdepartementet [38g], pp. 43 ff.
[60] *Ibid.* See also Göteborgs Högskola [16], *passim.*
[61] Ecklesiastikdepartementet [38g], p. 231.
[62] *Svenska Dagbladet,* March 31, 1948, p. 2.

debilitating influence on language instruction and on efficiency in general that would surely follow in the wake of the new school.[63] In a similar vein Rektor Ragni Kjellberg pointed out in her article "Culture and the Comprehensive School" ("Kultur och enhetsskolan") that "exact knowledge and character training" are the school's dual goals and that they will be put "into the shadows" by the enhetsskola and its "ethical-social program designed to attract public (folk) sympathy." [64]

The lively battle over the "new" school in the press during the years 1948 and 1949 suggested that a number of critics identified the enhetsskola with what they believed to be certain less than desirable foreign influences. Harald Alm, for example, attacked the proposal as an attempt to decentralize school administration and thus "Germanize" the system.[65] Gösta Adeler, on the other hand, saw in the commission's work a deliberate attempt to "progressivize and Americanize" Swedish schools.[66] A secondary school teacher, Dr. Melker Johnson, who had just returned from a study of American comprehensive schools, concurred in this opinion. The charge made by Johnson and many other critics that the School Commission had been unduly influenced by American progressivism cannot altogether be dismissed. It is, however, difficult to identify the precise nature and extent of American influence and almost impossible to prove that it swayed the commission—as the reform opponents claimed—in its emphasis on "freedom and inner growth" at the expense of "strength of character, firmness of standards, and acceptable quality of attainment." [67]

According to Dr. Otto Holmdahl, the Americans, without a culture of their own, could well afford to experiment with mass secondary education whereas Sweden must continue to enrich and perpetuate her cultural traditions in the secondary schools and universities.[68] An example of a true enhetsskola, he observed, would be the medieval grammar schools that synthesized the classical tradition and the Christian Weltanschauung to produce a common western European spiritual culture. Only in a "multilateral" system with separate parallel streams, asserted Holmdahl, will the school be able to continue as an efficient agent for cultural service: We should not, therefore, "destroy what we have before we know that the replacement is better." [69]

[63] Ibid., July 8, 1948.
[64] Svenska Dagbladet, November 16, 1948, p. 2.
[65] Göteborgs Handelstidning, January 26, 1949, p. 5.
[66] Svenska Morgonbladet, March 14, 1949, p. 3.
[67] Ibid. American progressive educational philosophy influenced Swedish school reformers to a much greater degree than did American educational practice. Interview with Stellan Arvidson, August 31, 1965.
[68] Sydsvenska Dagbladet, May 22, 1947, p. 3.
[69] Ibid., May 22, 1947, p. 3.

The activities of the commission and the rapid pace of its work were also subjected to criticism. Minister Erlander had no more than called the commission into being in 1946 when he was berated by the Secondary School Teachers Association at their congress of that year for his supposed hurry to accomplish a common school reform. Stellan Arvidson attempted to answer this charge several years later when the rapid tempo of reform had become apparent to all and was a matter of growing concern and criticism not only in opposition quarters.[70] The reasons for speed, Arvidson explained, were the result of the increased wartime and postwar birth rate and the logical need to key new investments in staff and plant to a rational long-term plan, a plan that was obviously missing. Yet the great rush had only been concerned with details—not principles. "It is to Erlander's honor," he contended, "to have seen the need to act and the need to rush." [71]

As early as 1948 the School Commission in accordance with its mandate for speed had already sent out invitations to over two hundred communities inviting them to join in experimental activities for a limited implementation of the proposed comprehensive school.[72] This move can only be seen as unusual and irregular in light of the fact that evaluations (*remisser*) were not available to members of Parliament until 1949 and that there was a paucity of research findings even faintly indicating the pedagogical desirability of such a cataclysmal reform program. Rektor B. Ernestam bitterly complained in the conservative press that despite the lack of *remisser* "the School Commission is eager to show with this move that much of the country supports its proposal. Shame! This is a bid for popular support even before the plan has been proposed or accepted by Parliament! What's the terrible hurry? Should even the *riksdag*, the deciding authorities, be simply presented with a *fait accompli?*" [73]

[70] *Morgontidningen*, November 1, 1948, p. 1.

[71] Arvidson mentions "democratization" as the principal reform objective. The details were (1) length of school; (2) age of differentiation; (3) organization; (4) teacher areas; (5) goals of instruction; and (6) local responsibilities. *Morgontidningen*, November 5, 1948, p. 1.

[72] Within the districts finally accepted for tryouts, there were 172 experimental classes with 2,483 pupils in the school year 1949–1950. See Skolöverstyrelsen, *Försöksverksamhet med nioårig enhetsskola: sammanfattande redogörelse 1949/50–1958/59*, 1959. [40b]

[73] *Svenska Morgonbladet*, November 10, 1948, p. 35.

Chapter 6

THE *ENHETSSKOLA* ACT: STEPS TO
PARLIAMENTARY ADOPTION
1950

*Members of Parliament, don't ride so fast; your
chance to decide has already passed.*[1]

[1] Old Swedish saying.

When the School Commission's proposals reached Parliament in 1950, pressure for school reform in Sweden had grown to an unprecedented high. With the passing of each postwar year, the problem of coordinating a vertical extension of the elementary school with a corresponding horizontal expansion of the lower secondary school—not to mention the ever greater need to expand facilities for vocational training, the *gymnasium,* and higher education—grew more tangled and demanding of a solution.[2]

The need for educational reform was also seen by the Social Democratic government as constituting an integral part of the postwar program of long-term economic planning. An early assumption of the 1944 Economic Planning Commission was that school reform could play an important role in alleviating an expected postwar depression. The Planning Commission therefore recommended (1) extended compulsory schooling to keep students in school longer and out of the labor market and thereby lessen problems of youth unemployment; (2) replacing early vocational specialization with longer general education for all pupils so as to prepare more efficiently for an uncertain future.[3]

---

[2] Torsten Husén, "The Educational Explosion in Sweden," in *The World Yearbook in Education 1965: The Education Explosion,* pp. 297–298. [111g]

[3] Cf. SOU 1944:7 and 12, *Utredningar angående ekonomisk efterkrigsplanering,* I and II, p. 39 [36g]; SOU 1948:45, *Svensk långtidsprogram 1947–1952/53,* pp. 78–81. [36f] This erroneous position may be seen as a projection of the "depression mentality" still dominant in the Socialist and trade union leadership at that time. For instance, Socialist Minister of Commerce Gunnar Myrdal (1945–1947) attempted to prepare Sweden for a worldwide depression (to be triggered, he believed, by the United States) with (1) a billion-crown ($280,000,000) credit to the USSR and (2) an expansionary policy of cheap money and easy credit at home. The year 1947 saw posters on Stockholm walls warning "Save for worse times ahead"; the exhaustion of wartime foreign exchange reserves; and an unprecedented foreign demand for Swedish exports. By 1948, indirect Marshall Plan aid of $106,000,000, full employment, and a favorable trade balance helped to restore confidence in the future. See Elis Håstad, *Sveriges historia under 1900-talet,* 1958, p. 59. [97c]

Another factor supporting adoption of fundamental school reform at this time was the commanding position held by the outspoken Socialist partisans for a change-over to comprehensive schooling. Their plan to attempt a solution of national educational problems through the adoption of longer and unified compulsory schooling, had strong governmental and popular support. Moreover, the move to eliminate educational dualism constituted a logical counterpart of the Social Democrats' postwar campaign to eradicate and replace dualism in national cultural affairs with a new egalitarian theory and program for enlarged popular participation in all areas of national life.[4]

Opponents of the proposed school reform—in the main Conservatives with a sprinkling of Liberals and Agrarians—fully accepted the need for a renovation of the school system, yet balked at the ideological and doctrinaire aspects of the proposals. They alleged (1) that the plans were pedagogically weak and (2) that instead of concentrating on pedagogical problems and solutions, the Social Democrats sought to capitalize on the educational crisis to foist an ideological revolution on the schools.[5] But because none of the political parties took an arbitrary position against the proposal, the burden of opposition fell largely to individuals who, at the most, could only hope to fight a limited holding action and prevent the unqualified acceptance of the government's school reform bill.[6] They did, nevertheless, succeed in forcing a compromise of sorts to provide a measure of consideration for their two principal demands: (1) that any change must be proven superior to existing practice—the need for "scientific" evaluation; and (2) that because a truly "democratic" school does not willy-nilly force all children irrespective of their ability and desires into a common track, adequate arrangements must be made for differentiation.[7]

This chapter traces the route of the school reform bill through the various legislative steps of the *riksdag* to the passage of the final *enhetsskola* act in 1950.

[4] For the position of Socialists, the popular movements and others on the need to replace a "capitalistic" culture with a socialistic "folk" culture, see, for example, the monthly journal *Folklig Kultur*, published jointly by the study-circle organizations in Sweden; and Nils Elvander, *Role of the State in Sweden's Cultural Life*, 1965, pp. 3 ff. [83]

[5] The Conservative position is presented in detail in Höger Partiet; *Fakta om enhetsskola*, 1955, pp. 1–10. [18a]

[6] After 1946 the Conservative party left *enhetsskola* opposition largely to individuals and related action groups. One such group was the Konservativa Skolungdomsförening (comprising nearly 3,000 secondary school students in 1950), founded in 1945 in protest to the party's "apolitical" attitude toward school reform. See their publication, *Skola och politik*, 1952, pp. 1–13. [18b]

[7] Ecklesiastiksdepartementet, *Skolöverstyrelsens över vissa av 1940 års skolutrednings betänkande och 1946 års skolkommissionens principbetänkande jämte sammanfattning av avgivna yttrande*, 1949, p. 231. [38g]

THE ROLE OF INTEREST GROUPS

Because Swedish society is more completely organized than most Western societies, and because these organizations or interest groups have every opportunity to influence political parties—and thus, indirectly, the legislative process—it may be fruitful at this point to make some general observations on Swedish interest groups and, more specifically, on the extent to which they influenced the 1950 comprehensive school reform legislation.[8]

The development of popular organizations in Sweden had paralleled the growth of democracy in both the political and social sense of the word; the popular organizations can only be properly understood as part of the Swedish folk movement. The trade unions, the agricultural producers' and consumers' cooperatives, the free-church groups, the temperance groups, and others represented formally organized interest groups enrolling well over half of the nation's voters.[9] Perhaps the single most common characteristic of these diverse groups—aside from their earlier common opposition to the bureaucratic and autocratic character of the established social order—has been their continuous interest in developing specialized educational opportunities for their members.[10] These programs also provided several other valuable services for their groups by aiding in the development of ideologies and the formulation of long-range objectives, and by preparing future leaders.[11] After World War II, however, the popular movements became less willing and able to provide compensatory education.[12] They

[8] For contrasting interpretations of the role and importance of interest groups, see Gunnar Heckscher, "Interest Groups in Sweden," in *Interest Groups in Four Continents*, 1958, pp. 154–172. [99a] (Heckscher is professor of political science at the University of Stockholm and past chairman of the Conservative party.) See also Albin Lind, *Popular Movements in Sweden*, 1940 [121], which presents the trade union point of view.

[9] The numerical strength of the popular organizations is in large part an illustration of their political strength. For example, membership in the Consumers Cooperative rose from 567,000 in 1934 to nearly a million in 1949; membership in the trade unions rose from around 650,000 in 1934 to an estimated 1,400,000 in 1942 (equivalent to about 45 per cent of the labor force of about 3,000,000 at that time). When one also includes the 350,000 members of the Agricultural Producers Cooperative it becomes evident (even allowing for some multiple memberships) that considerably over one-half the Swedish working and voting population belongs to one or more of these popular organizations. See Heckscher [99a], p. 165.

[10] *Ibid.*, p. 167.

[11] It should also be noted that popular movements play an important social role —especially against the background of heavy migration to urban areas in the decades after World War II—for their members and create feelings of personal belongingness and emotional satisfaction. See Ann Lisa Kälvésten, *The Social Structure of Sweden*, 1961, pp. 19–20. [113]

[12] SOU 1946:68, *Betänkande om det fria och frivilliga folkbildnings arbetet*, pp. 19–20. [36c] After a postwar study of the Swedish folk high school, David

were also well aware that the burgeoning demand for secondary education could—under the existing parallel system of practical and theoretical tracks—only lead to greater disparities of prestige between these two educational branches and the social classes they represented.[13]

The popular organizations exerted pressure on legislation in two basic ways. One was through group identification with a political party. The best example is the close relationship between the Social Democrats and the trade union movement. Another example, although less distinct, is the link between the Agrarian party and the producers' cooperatives. Other relationships are more diffused, with members of the temperance movement dividing their political support between the Liberal party and the Socialists, and the much smaller free-church group fairly equally represented among the Conservatives, Liberals, and Agrarians.[14] Thus it may be assumed that popular support for the new school was not restricted to, but only concentrated in, the left political groups. This factor may have tended to unite all parties to a certain degree on the need to accept the basic desirability of school reform and perhaps militated against the proposals' becoming a clear-cut party issue.

The second major influence of interest groups on the school reform plan occurred (1) in the Political School Commission of 1946, in which representatives of all political parties and major folk groups participated; and (2) in the *remisser* submitted by, for example, the labor (LO) and cooperative (KF) movements, which with certain minor reservations warmly supported the School Commission's proposals. Thus, when the *riksdag* made a final decision in 1950, the members had before them not only the government's bill, but also relevant committee amendments and a considerable body of evaluations from official agencies and popular organizations that either had participated or had been consulted at preliminary stages of the formulation of educational reform policy.

The influence of popular group support on school reform legislation is, of course, difficult to evaluate. It must, however, have been considerable because Sweden, in terms of population, is a small country

---

Östergren concluded in 1949 that these institutions "as arsenals of democracy are failing to function effectively because of growing tendencies toward lectures, a subject-centered curriculum, and paternal attitude." In addition, because emphasis of study was shifting from a general culture training to preparatory training, the folk high schools "are not functioning adequately in their program of personality development and citizenship training." See David L. Östergren, "The Folk High Schools of Sweden," 1949, pp. 163–164. [141]

[13] *Östergren* [141], p. 46.

[14] B. Bolén, "Organisation och riksdagen," *Tiden*, 1954, pp. 9 ff. [65]

and the scale of political interaction is small indeed. It is definitely in the interests of the political parties not arbitrarily to oppose or take lightly any legislation given high priority—as in the case of the school reform—by the large mass organizations.[15] Conflicts are therefore rare and are in most cases resolved by a legislative system that is designed to facilitate compromise of one kind or another.

THE LEGISLATIVE PROCESS

Compromise has long been the key to orderly change in the Swedish political structure. The peaceful abolition of the Estates in 1866, the final granting of universal suffrage after World War I, and even the transformation of the Socialists from revolutionary Marxists to welfare state bureaucrats, all point to a basic unity of Swedish society that makes compromise possible, as well as to its ingrained diversity of class structure that makes compromise necessary.[16] Inevitably, this political process has in turn reshaped not only the political parties but also the social setting from which it arises.

Legislative debate on the proposed nine-year comprehensive school began when the School Commission Chairman, Josef Weijne, as Minister of Education, laid the government's bill for a new school law

[15] On the other hand, individual interests occasionally suffer from close administration-organization links since both tend to measure the effects of legislation on a majority of those concerned rather than on the individual. Gunnar Heckscher, "Pluralist Democracy," *Social Research*, 1948, p. 417. [99b]

[16] The early Socialist leader Hjalmar Branting, who constantly faced situations where positive results could only be obtained through compromise, once in a peevish mood described Sweden as *ett kompromissarieridet land*—a compromise-ridden country. Hjalmar Branting, *Tal och skrifter*, Vol. 3, 1927, p. 214. [7]

The extent to which the technique of compromise has been an essential ingredient in Swedish politics in reconciling initial differences and setting the terms on which men can live together is indicated by three types of compromise (determined by the initial differences) recognized in Swedish committee parlance: (1) "invitation"; (2) "amputation"; and (3) "compromise." When conflicting programs offer no area of overlap an *inclusive* (No. 1) compromise has been the logical answer. The political triangle of the 1920's favored *exclusive* compromise (No. 2) to exclude one party, or *split the difference* (No. 3) compromises alternately between the right and the left. With the symbols before the arrow representing the initial positions and those following the resulting settlement, the three types of compromise may be symbolized as follows:

$$A, B \longrightarrow A + B \text{ (inclusive)}$$
$$A + B, B, B + C \longrightarrow B \text{ (exclusive)}$$
$$A, B \longrightarrow \frac{A + B}{2} \text{ (split the difference)}$$

Compromise on school reform legislation, because of its controversial character, has largely been of the first type. See Dankwart A. Rustow, *The Politics of Compromise: A Study of Parties and Cabinet Government in Sweden*, 1955, p. 231. [150]

before an expectant Parliament on February 14, 1950.[17] A massive
document of nearly six hundred pages, the bill comprised not only
the commission's original proposals but a long summary of *remisser*
evaluating the work and a lengthy recapitulation of the contrasting
conclusions of the 1940 and 1946 investigatory groups. In a lengthy
and didactic introduction of the bill, Minister Weijne presented a
summary of his views on Sweden's educational needs and his reasons
for believing that any reform should be guided by the principles of
unity and comprehensiveness, the two conditions required to "create
an organically integrated school system where every growing individual, independent of place of residence or of the social or economic
position of the parents will get (if need be, with public support) the
education which best suits his potentialities." [18]

The minister did not deny that the School Commission's plans for
"an eight-year comprehensive school, without a division into streams
before the ninth grade" had been almost unanimously opposed in the
remisser from faculties of secondary and higher institutions.[19] He even
cited, as a typical comment from the *läroverk* and university faculties,
the accusation that "the School Commission has a Rousseauesque pro-
pensity for populating the future schools with ideal teachers and model
pupils." [20] This said, Minister Weijne proceeded to clarify why he felt
reason favored the commission's proposals as legitimate and necessary
goals for the future course of Swedish education. Most serious, he
explained, was the pernicious and enduring educational parallelism
which, beginning with the School Act of 1842, was an intolerable
situation and completely incompatible with the goal of a truly democratic and egalitarian society to which the Socialists aspired.[21] And
because the old roots of educational dualism were tenaciously entwined
with the interests and prestige of still powerful conservative groups
and institutions, any reform must, he claimed, be revolutionary in
scope:

Between the different types of schools there are barriers that cannot be
destroyed merely by giving an existing type of school a new label and
a new place in the school system. When the staff of one of our largest
girls' schools expresses its satisfaction with a reform that they feel is

---

[17] Riksdagen, *Kungl. Maj:ts proposition 1950:70: angående riktlinjer för det
svenska skolväsendets utveckling,* 1950. [39c]
[18] *Ibid.,* p. 190.
[19] *Ibid.*
[20] Ingemar Düring (ed.), *The Swedish School Reform: A Summary of the
Government Bill at the Request of the 1946 School Commission,* 1951, p. 91. [8]
[21] *Ibid.,* p. 93.

designed to tear out by the roots the worst fault in our school system—its division into various streams that are completely divorced one from another—we can see behind these words a feeling that in the present school system each school type forms a little closed world of its own, and that despite all the statistics on growing attendance in secondary schools, the educational system is not considered by the general public to be the egalitarian democratic system that it ought to be.[22]

Although Minister Weijne carefully avoided any expression of personal preference for one plan of internal differentiation over another, he strongly reiterated his convictions as to the role the future school should play in fostering unity in social and political values. For only within a nonselective *enhetsskola* organization, he stressed, where all instruction and teachers and curriculum and goals are unified and equally available to all children would both the educational structure and the environment support, reinforce and, hopefully, perpetuate the goal of national unity within the concept of social democracy.[23]

A reform that is to bridge the old gulfs in society must see to it that the educational system appears to all social classes as a homogeneous structure with broad highways open for all Swedish youth and where every growing individual, irrespective of his social starting point in life, can learn how best to utilize his personal qualification for his future tasks. Such an aim is not reconcilable with a system of parallel schools, whether open or concealed. It seems certain that a differentiation into different types of schools should not, therefore, be made until it is finally necessary for vocational choice.[24]

After giving a somewhat vague assurance that the new comprehensive school would not be permitted to "neglect its cultural tasks in its pursuit of social ends" (i.e., to "cherish budding talent" and provide for the gifted), Weijne moved to attack opponents of late selection and heterogeneous grouping. He warned that because "comments from secondary school staffs and teacher organizations do not support this opinion [i.e., late selection], it might be thought easy to reject the commission's ideas as impracticable. That, however, would be too hasty a conclusion." [25] For, Weijne postulated, to teach successfully in the proposed schools would require new, but as yet nonexistent, curricula, textbooks, and teaching aids, as well as profound changes in teacher training. He therefore reasoned that

[22] Riksdagen [39c], p. 191.
[23] *Ibid.,* p. 192.
[24] *Ibid.,* p. 190.
[25] *Ibid.*

as long as these prerequisites are lacking, any sounding of teacher opinion can hardly be expected to be otherwise than as expressed. There is nothing surprising in a teacher rejecting a new method of teaching, if he believes he will be required to work it out by himself from scratch, barehanded. It is of course possible that the School Commission underestimated the practical difficulties, but on the other hand it is by no means impossible that the teachers will alter their opinions when once the methodological requirements have been worked out in detail and the new teaching aids more generally tried out in the classroom.[26]

Then, after having viewed the problem of school reform synoptically and having expounded the government's position, the minister conceded the possibility of compromise:

The discussion on the question of differentiation has been carried to a point where it does not seem possible to get appreciably nearer to a solution. The decision must now be made by means of practical experiments. The ten years ahead of us, before the school reform can be implemented on a large scale, should probably be used to confirm the resources of the method, to test the strength of the various types of organization, and to draw definite conclusions about the organization of the comprehensive school on the contested points. *Only by research of this type will we be able to ascertain how far it is going to be possible to carry out the School Commission's intentions;* . . . the experience obtained should be used as the basis for the further development and direction of the work. These investigations could conveniently be directed by the Royal Board of Education . . . *and by the late 1950's it might be time for a comprehensive solution to the problem of differentiation, whereupon it should be possible to combine the practical and scientific findings to provide a firm foundation for the organization that would then be gradually built.*[27]

The comments of individual *riksdag* members following Minister Weijne's presentation indicated that though opposition to the proposition had not yet crystallized along party lines, this might conceivably occur if the government forced an unqualified acceptance of the bill as it stood.[28] A number of Conservative members in the First Chamber rebelled at the idea that Parliament should accept a plan that would abolish the present system and "legalize how our grandchildren and their grandchildren should be educated without any definite knowledge of the new school's curriculum, planning, or cost."[29] Several Liberal

---

[26] *Ibid.*, p. 191.
[27] *Ibid.*, pp. 191–192. Italics added by author.
[28] Stellan Arvidson, *Enhetsskolan: skolan vi skall få*, 1950, pp. 7–8. [4b]
[29] *Svenska Dagbladet*, November 16, 1948, p. 4.

members pointed out that although "the basic problem is differentiation, no real solution has been forthcoming to the problem of classifying children for various types of occupational preparation." [30] Members of the Agragian party, caught in their perpetual dilemma of balancing costs against needs, were worried because too little had been said about the expense of the reform, and asked, "Who will bear these immense costs if national production and income do not in the main continue to rise?" [31] At the same time, the farmers warily supported the measure with the hope that the *enhetsskola* would finally close the still-wide gap between urban and rural standards of schooling.

The government, with only a slim majority in the *riksdag,* did not deem it prudent to force the issue by bringing the proposition to a vote. Not only would this move have tended to crystallize latent opposition in the political parties but it would have put a Socialist stamp on the new school that would undoubtedly have complicated eventual implementation of the reform. Perhaps with the bitter party struggles of the 1920's over the *enhetsskola* in mind, the Social Democrats made every effort to portray the school reform proposal as the logical consequence of evolutionary change in the national school system, and as a measure that served no vested interest and deserved the support of all.[32]

The government therefore quickly concurred with the parliamentary motion that a Special Committee representing all major parties should meet and attempt to reconcile divergent views on the bill before it was put to a vote.

Before describing the compromise on the *enhetsskola* bill achieved by the Special Committee, it may be instructive to examine in some detail the specific functions of these special parliamentary groups in the over-all Swedish legislative system, which by its design is admirably suited to achieve consensus and compromise.

The Swedish constitution, dating from 1809, originally balanced governmental powers between king and Parliament. With the decline of royal power, however, and the rise of the second chamber to equality with the first chamber, the *riksdag* gradually came to be the sole

[30] *Ibid.*
[31] Arvidson [4b], p. 181.
[32] See, for example, the somewhat patronizing and misleading remarks of Prime Minister Erlander that implied the Socialists were merely following the Conservatives' earlier lead in school reform: "The problems that caused the Conservative Party leader Gösta Bagge, as Minister of Education, to call the 1940 School Committee, are the very same that we are trying to cope with today. It is therefore the Conservative Party who took the initiative for school reform while the Social Democrats, in power during practically the entire 1930's, neglected this need. The idea of an *enhetsskola* first originated in the Conservative Party." Riksdagen, *Riksdagens protokoll. Första kammaren 1950,* No. 41, Bilaga 1, p. 93. [39q]

cornerstone of the governmental system. Today the cabinet is wholly dependent on Parliament's confidence or toleration; no popularly elected executive competes with the *riksdag*; nor do regional distribution of powers or popular legislation encroach on its lawmaking power. Even the judiciary, although independent in its own sphere of responsibility, cannot invalidate statutes as contrary to the national constitution. In short, the only effective limitations on Parliament's legislative power are found in its own internal divisions and in its own conception of the public good.[33] Under these conditions consensus becomes highly desirable and is regularly sought through procedural devices such as special committees. The committees representing diverse groups and interests usually deliberate in a secluded atmosphere and generally are content to supplement the data gathered by the cabinet or special commissions (themselves the product of previous compromises) at a few crucial points.[34] A final special committee report will therefore usually reflect a bill more or less acceptable to all parties, and parliamentary debate on committee reports seldom lasts longer than a few hours, or at the most a few days. The debate merely sums up earlier arguments for there is then little time for major textual changes.[35] Thus, on the final vote, the chambers in fact test the acceptability of earlier compromises and usually either adopt or reject the entire bill, or approve it with such amendments as have been recommended in the report of the special committee.[36]

The Socialist government's desire to keep alteration or compromise of their school reform bill to the minimum necessary for acceptance is indicated by the political stature and background of the government's appointee, Rikard Sandler, to chair the Special Committee. Sandler, the "grand old man" in the Social Democratic party, had been a protégé of Branting, a Socialist Prime Minister from January 1925 to June 1926, a minister of foreign affairs and a provincial governor. Moreover, Sandler, a native of the northern part of the country, came from a family which had pioneered the folk high school movement in Sweden. He too continued this work throughout his political career and was instrumental in adapting the *folkhögskola* to the educational

[33] Nils Andrén, *Modern Swedish Government*, 1961, pp. 137 ff. [52]

[34] Heckscher [99a], p. 167.

[35] *Ibid.*, p. 172.

[36] Not long after the passage of the 1950 school reform act, the cry was raised that large special interest groups (such as labor and consumer organizations, and temperance leagues) wielded undue influence because of their inclusion in the committees as pressure groups and because of the government's tendency to negotiate with them separately. Consequently, it was claimed, the government on several occasions presented the *riksdag* with a *fait accompli* rather than a legislative proposal. See "Sweden Clears Bills in Secret: Closed-Door Investigations Pave Path to Compromise," *The New York Times*, May 10, 1964, p. 26. [169]

requirements of the trade union movement and in the creation of new approaches to education (e.g., study circles) for workers and others in the popular movements.[37]

Assisted by the Liberal Bertil von Friesen, Sandler guided the committee's deliberations to a rapid conclusion, and within a few months submitted a tactfully written evaluation of 187 pages amending the original bill. On presenting the amendments Sandler observed that because the Special Committee had carried on its deliberations "in the spirit of teamwork so characteristic of the new unity school," an agreement had been reached that represented according to Sandler, "a compromise between faith and hesitation." [38]

The main reason, apparently, for the committee's agreement and, indeed, the later agreement of Parliament as well, was a brief phrase inserted in the opening section of the bill which in effect made the primary purpose of the legislation highly ambiguous. The original bill read: "measures shall be taken to introduce, within a period to be determined later, a nine-year compulsory comprehensive school designed to replace the elementary, continuation, lower secondary, vocational, municipal middle, and girls' schools." [39] The committee's revision changed this key sentence to read: ". . . a nine-year comprehensive school designed—*in so far as the proposed experiments demonstrate its suitability*—to replace . . ." [40] With this qualifying insertion, many opponents of the proposals felt they could accept the bill. It would provide, according to their interpretation, for no more than experimental activity and would force the new school to demonstrate its alleged superiority over the existing parallel system before any changes could be made. It also eased the apprehensions of some members who earlier had pointed out that because the School Commission's revolutionary plans were "just sketches," they were dangerously inadequate as a blueprint for thoroughgoing educational reformation.[41]

The influential Liberal party leader Bertil von Friesen, who served as vice-president of the Special Committee, wholeheartedly endorsed the committee's solution and in so doing signaled the acceptability of the compromise by his party.[42] He noted that "on the whole the Special School Committee agrees with the Minister of Education," but he

[37] See the chapter by Sandler in Karl V. Hedlund (ed.), *Svensk folkhögskola under 75 år,* 1943. [100]

[38] Riksdagen, *Särskilda utskottets utlåtande,* No. 1, 1950, p. 116. [39u]

[39] Riksdagen [39c], p. 48.

[40] Riksdagen [39u], pp. 115, 179. Italics added.

[41] *Ibid.,* p. 115.

[42] *Morgontidningen,* February 16, 1950. It is interesting to note that Rydén's rejected proposals for comprehensive schooling in the *riksdag* of 1918 also shared a measure of support from the Liberal section of the Liberal-Socialist coalition government.

placed far greater emphasis on "the importance of the experimental activity for the creation of the new school." [43] To this end, the committee also proposed an amendment calling for more detailed and comparative experimentation with various types of comprehensive schools in matters of streaming, grouping, curriculum, and instructional methods. Another major recommendation called for experiments in all "existing types of schools pertaining not only to their continuous development during the period of transition" but also "to problems of general interest related to the purpose of the school type in question." [44] In this way the *realskola* could conceivably maintain an on-going reform and at the same time serve as a comparative institution with the experimental new comprehensive school. And finally, von Friesen congratulated Sandler on their joint efforts and in a highly conciliatory statement concluded: ". . . because this reform is intended to give the largest possible measure of freedom to both teachers and youth . . . I hope I am not insulting the Minister [of Education] as a Socialist if I suggest that this leigslation be characterized as a liberal reform." [45]

THE *ENHETSSKOLA* ACT OF 1950

On this bipartisan note, Parliament approved the amended comprehensive school reform bill in an unusual joint session of both chambers on May 26, 1950.[46] Presiding over the meeting, Prime Minister Tage Erlander congratulated the *riksdag* on its show of unity and observed that this support augured well for the successful solution of the myriad problems that would undoubtedly arise in the new era of Swedish education begun that very day.[47] Erlander left no doubt that the Social Democrats and his government viewed the legislation, despite the amendments added to secure passage, as a mandate for the rapid implementation of the 1946 Commission's proposals—albeit within an experimental framework. Clearly he had little doubt that the comprehensive school finally decided upon after the required decade of experimentation would be the nine-year *enhetsskola*.

The major provisions of the school reform act and subsequent amend-

[43] Riksdagen [39u], p. 118. After 1946, Liberal cooperation in the school reform activities helped to give an appearance of multiparty political effort. Much less interested in an ideological justification for the proposed comprehensive school, the Liberals primarily sought school reform to meet educational needs and to shift initiative for all compulsory education to the local, communal level. For an exposition of the party's position in these matters, see Folkpartiets kommunalpolitiska delegation, *Kommunen och skolfrågorna*, 1956, pp. 5 ff. [13]

[44] Riksdagen [39u], p. 120.

[45] Riksdagen, *Riksdagens protokoll. Andra Kammaren*, No. 2, 1950, p. 184. [39m]

[46] Düring [8], pp. 32–33.

[47] Riksdagen [39m], p. 184.

ment have been described and need not be repeated at this point.[48]
It should be noted, however, that the Act as interpreted by the Prime
Minister did indeed provide a commitment and a general blueprint for
the enormous task of replacing the traditional selective dual educational
system with a new untried common school that would in large measure
substitute electives for examinations, and social-political goals for
academic goals.

Because of the institutionalized nature of education and the frequently conservative bent of secondary school teachers, the radical
reorientation of a nation's educational structure, content and goals
through democratic processes is rare indeed in the history of education.
What is somewhat surprising in the Swedish accomplishment of the
feat, if at this point only in theory, was the ease with which such a
reform proposal—despite its strong ideological implications—once
amended, found unanimous acceptance. The Prime Minister's con-
gratulations had no more than ended, however, when dissenting arguments were put forth in Parliament concerning the proper interpretation
of the recently accepted school reform legislation. It then became
evident that school reform had been secured at the expense of clarity
and mutual understanding.

A Conservative member, for instance, belatedly sounded the war
cry: "The decision we made today did not really endorse the extension
of school duty or the creation of a new school type, but simply experimental work that will indicate whether such speculations should be
carried through." [49] After a number of Agrarian and even Liberal
members of Parliament had expressed similar beliefs, Parliament eventually called upon the Special Committee to clarify precisely what its
amendments linking change and experimentation actually did mean.[50]
Did the qualifying phrase inserted by the committee to achieve consensus actually mean, as some claimed, that the introduction of the
new nine-year school must be entirely dependent on the outcome of the
experimental activities?

According to Professor Georg Andrén, a prominent Conservative
and member of the Special Committee, the ambiguous wording of the
phrase "in so far as the proposed experiments demonstrate its suitability" meant, as he had understood the committee intended, that
the proposed new school was only accepted conditionally; that it
must first prove its superiority over existing schools, especially the
realskola, before it could finally be accepted by Parliament.[51]

The majority of the other committee members, however, expressed

---

[48] For a summary of the main points of the 1950 Act, see pp. 113–115.
[49] Arvidson [4b], pp. 7–8.
[50] *Ibid.*, p. 9.
[51] *Dagens Nyheter,* August 12, 1950.

some very different interpretations. Dr. Bertil von Friesen, for one, could see no logical reason for confusion; ". . . the decision," he said, "is easily understood when one considers both its form and its practical content." If Parliament did not intend to create a nine-year *enhetsskola*, he questioned, why are we working on legislation to reorganize teacher training to provide the requisite conditions for a changeover from parallel to unified schooling? Nor, he continued, is it conceivable that the *riksdag* would in such a momentous project limit itself only to experimental work and leave all the rest open to speculation. "Certainly we have decided on the comprehensive school," von Friesen said sharply.[52]

Governor Rickard Sandler concurred with his committee vice-president that a proper interpretation of intent was simply a matter of reading the amendments with common sense: "There is absolutely no doubt about the sincerity of the intention made clear in the first point of the Act [i.e.]—the decision to carry through a comprehensive school reform. Nor is there any doubt that in the changeover, one ought to be guided by the on-going experimental work."[53]

Professor Sten Wahlund, the Agrarian representative on the Special Committee, had originally proposed the qualifying clause responsible for the confusion. Wahlund tersely protested that the argument was not only senseless, but useless as well:

The decision is clear, it allows no ground for questions of interpretation. If the experimental work is positive, the school reform is accepted as voted. If the experimental work is not positive, the reform will be carried through with those changes called for by experience.[54]

With Parliament's approval secured, the Royal Board of Education moved confidently ahead with the experimental implementation of the new school on a nationwide basis. A new political school commission, appointed in 1957, evaluated the decade of experimental activity, and the nine-year comprehensive school with its new name—*grundskola*—was adopted in final form by the *riksdag* in 1962.[55]

Although sporadic opposition continued to come from the conservative press and from the secondary school teachers who foresaw undesirable changes in both their work and job status, the great majority of Swedes accepted the basic principles of the reform with the "hope

---

[52] *Ibid.*, p. 1.
[53] *Ibid.*, p. 11.
[54] *Ibid.*
[55] See Appendix A. The name *enhetsskola* with its marked ideological connotation (i.e., "unity school," for educational, social, and national unity) was replaced. by *grundskola* ("basic school") with its more pronounced pedagogical flavor.

and uncertainty" expressed by the Special Committee.[56] Moreover, with the general intensification of demand for education in conjunction with the changing nature of the needs of a modern technological society, it became increasingly evident in the decade of experimentation after 1950 that the new comprehensive school was, because of its greater structural flexibility and less specialized instruction, in many ways better able to meet the new functional demands on the schools with the accelerated emergence of the Swedish "educational society." [57]

[56] Conservative opposition to the comprehensive school idea is typified by Professor Erik Wellander's newspaper article entitled "Intellectual Disarmament." Wellander claims that "the new Swedish pedagogical doctrine announced and disseminated by Tage Erlander, Alva Myrdal, and Stellan Arvidson . . . is pure anti-intellectualism," and "poorly suited to the modern-day educational demands of science, commerce, and technology." *Svenska Dagbladet,* February 14, 1956, p. 2. See also the article by the secondary school teachers Ragnar Oldberg and Adolf Söderlund: "That we find ourselves in a severe school crisis is certain, but whether the outcome will be a crisis school it is too early to determine. Everything or almost everything in the school world is to be changed. I ask if we need to change so much, and will the new be better than the old? The old school is said to have been the product of a patriarchal and authoritative society, but now with democratic control, the schools must also be democratized. A democratic society, it is said, must have democratic schools. This is logical in theory, but the question is, is it wise in practice!" "Skolkris och—krisskola?" *Pedogogisk Tidskrift,* 1952, pp. 169–178. [139b]

[57] For studies revealing the high wastage rates in the *realskola,* see Torsten Husén, "Loss of Talent in Selective School Systems: The Case of Sweden," *Comparative Education Review,* October 1960, pp. 70–74 [111d], and Sten Carlsson, "From the Estates to the Educational Society," in *The Intellectual Face of Sweden,* 1964, pp. 12–13 [71b].

Chapter 7

SUMMARY AND CONCLUSIONS

The preceding pages have presented a historical study of the origins and formulations of the concept of compulsory comprehensive schooling in Sweden and its adoption within an organically unified educational system. The direction of change in Swedish education before 1918 was toward greater duality; after 1918 the movement turned increasingly toward greater unity in the organization of the national school system. This latter movement reached a climax in 1950 when the dominant political party secured a rapid and total reorientation of national educational policy and goals from elitism to egalitarianism.

The study suggests a variety of forces giving rise to this change and a number of influential contributing factors. In general, the most significant innovating individuals and groups attempting to move the bifurcated Swedish school system to greater unity have worked outside the system which they sought to change. They comprise a quantitative progression from the dedicated, idealistic, and frequently cosmopolitan individual reformers of the pre-1918 era to the political parties and massive popular interest groups whose activity became especially significant after 1944.

Throughout the nineteenth century and into the twentieth, many individual clergymen, educators, and others significantly not of the "folk" class advocated an organically structured educational system built on a common elementary school that would satisfy what they believed to be the needs of social justice and social mobility. Their idea of common elementary schooling was not altogether new but expressed egalitarian ideals from the Enlightenment, ideals that looked to the school as the agency for social change and correction. By the nineteenth century, proposals for comprehensive schooling had become even more utopian and unrealistic in Sweden, where the firmly entrenched ruling groups of nobles, clergy, bureaucrats, and bourgeois looked to the dualistic, segregated, and class-linked school system to perpetuate their privileged positions.

With the transformation of Sweden from an impoverished rural bureaucracy to a highly centralized industrial state, the ruling classes were forced gradually to extend the franchise until in 1918 all adult Swedes received the right to vote. At that time the Social Democrats joined in the Liberal program to make the *folkskola* a six-year comprehensive school. From 1918 to 1927 the question of incorporating the lower grades of the elite lower secondary school into the low-prestige *folkskola* became a strongly contested political issue that neither the Socialists nor Conservatives could resolve in their own favor.

With the compromise of 1927, political pressure for common compulsory schooling waned as the ruling Socialists devoted their full energies to fundamental social and economic reforms in the creation of a democratic social welfare state.

After 1927 the Social Democrats attempted to equalize, so far as possible, rather than to remold, the traditional parallel school systems. As a result, the large and powerful popular movements were spurred to expand and extend their voluntary systems of worker institutes, study circles, and folk high schools, all of which were indirectly linked with the six-year folk elementary school. The ending of Socialist acceptance of the educational status quo was signaled by, among other factors, the Communist reform proposal of 1944 for a nine-year compulsory *folkskola* that would—in freely chosen streams—incorporate all existing parallel schools in a multilateral-type elementary school stressing social learning.

The subsequent actions of the Social Democratic government in pushing through a similar program would seem to indicate that the Communist initiative served as a catalyst to stimulate and influence the Socialist school reform program, which was eventually accepted unanimously by the *riksdag* in 1950.

Interest groups influencing the movement toward educational unification were widely disparate in size and character. They included the folk elementary school teacher organization (most influential before 1932) and, after World War II, the popular movements (such as the trade unions, the cooperatives, and the temperance groups).

After their organization into a professional corps in the 1880's, the *folkskola* teachers waged a constant battle in their own publications and in those of the folk movement to make the *folkskola*—despite its serious deficiencies—a common citizenship school. Although their strong vested interest in this goal declined with the improvement of the elementary school branch after 1932, their early propaganda for common

schooling no doubt served an important educational function in drawing popular attention to what these teachers believed were the flagrant
injustices of early selection into (or out of) totally different schools
with different purposes and social class associations.

The Swedish popular movement represented the organized interests
of the working and lower middle classes in their fiercely contested rise
to power. Friction and dissatisfaction arising from popular agitation
for improved living and working conditions and economic and social
opportunities led the popular movements to create their own voluntary
folk education system within their own isolated communities. With
the rise to dominance of the folk group under the Social Democratic
banner after 1932 and the widespread implementation of its program
for improved social welfare and economic redistribution after 1946,
the interrelationships of the movement—such as compensatory popular
education—began to disintegrate, and folk values came increasingly to
dominate Swedish institutions. In the "harvest time" of the post-World
War II decade, the popular movements saw the fruition of their goal:
to make Sweden the "people's home," or *folkhemmet,* where all would
be welcome and economically secure—in contrast to earlier decades
when for many emigration offered the only hope for a better life.[1]

The revolutionary changes in the Swedish political system from oligarchy to democracy and from elitism to egalitarianism that followed
the electoral ascendancy of the folk movement may be seen as fundamental factors leading to a parallel revolution in education: the creation
of a new school system, based not upon selection and academic values
but rather on the rationale of *folkhemmet,* "the need for all children to
have equal opportunities, the need for all to feel safe and wanted in
school."

If the primary forces that propelled the movement toward unity
in compulsory schooling are essentially the same as those which sus-
tain the welfare state, then the leadership of the Social Democrats
should be emphasized. Their long tenure and successful rule helped to
bring about conditions that were favorable for popular demand and
political acceptance of congruent social values and for the reformation of the structure, content, and goals of the national school system.

The success of the Social Democratic party in Sweden (it has comprised the largest party since 1918 and has been continuously in power
since 1932) may be attributed to several factors. First, the party represents mainly the interests of the low and modest income groups which
outnumber the other classes. Second, it retains the support of most
Swedish popular movements and especially the powerful and active

[1] See Appendix E for Swedish emigration from 1851 to 1926.

trade union organization with more than one million members in a nation of about eight million inhabitants. Third, the party's policy of social welfare and higher living standards at home and neutrality abroad reflects the attitude of most Swedes.

Although the conscious effort of the Socialists to bring the schools into harmony with the ideological imperatives of the welfare state has been an important factor in educational change, a number of significant objective forces or factors have either facilitated or intensified this development at various stages. One, clearly, is the absence of ethnic, religious, and linguistic diversity, which insures a basic homogeneity of the Swedish nation. Another has been the success of Socialistic rule, per se, with a social policy that all political groups have accepted. Another factor is Sweden's national wealth and ready commitment to invest a sizable portion of it in educational reform which, with its demands for new facilities, materials, and retraining, is of necessity an expensive undertaking.

A fourth contributing factor may be seen in the *Zeitgeist* of post-World War II Sweden when popular enthusiasm for social reform ran high. This period of pressure to harmonize social institutions with the values of the ruling majority is in sharp contrast to the nineteenth century, when individual proposals for similar changes had their origin in conflict and in the impending changes in the social system.

Finally, the expanding demand for education coincided with the postwar popular commitment to egalitarian reforms and the Socialists' ability and readiness to translate reform plans into practice. The willingness of the government to devote its energies to school reform came about for several reasons. One was purely educational. The dual educational structure, originally designed to select only a small elite for secondary schooling, was unable to cope with the intensified postwar demand. Moreover, the work of the 1940 Committee had documented many grave inequalities and malfunctions in the national school system.

Political and ideological considerations were, however, far more important than educational concerns. Social Democratic leaders, for example, warned that the growing demand by working-class youth for selective lower secondary education endangered the Socialist goals of parity of prestige and equality of opportunity. For if the universally recognized need to extend compulsory education to nine years were to be implemented in the traditional system, the Socialists would have a more serious problem, because (1) dualism would be aggravated; (2) demand for and selectivity of secondary education would increase; and (3) the continued dominance of folk democracy would be threatened.

Because vested interests opposed the extension of the elementary school through incorporation of the lower secondary school, the Socialists radically altered the earlier comprehensive school proposals to make the low-status *folkskola* the common school. Taking full advantage of their control of educational policymaking in the centralized Swedish parliamentary system, the Socialists speedily effected a compromise for a new educational structure which, in organization and goals, satisfied the trade unions and the forces on the left and, in its ambiguity and supposedly conditional nature, gained the approval of the bourgeois parties.

The Swedes, however, have shown little inclination for dialectics; no grand design lies behind their social and economic reconstruction any more than behind the movement to unify education through comprehensive school reform. Rather, as a highly practical people, the Swedes in a notably pragmatic manner have adopted specific measures to meet specific needs and situations. Thus, the Social Democratic government, in the matter of school reform after 1918, was guided by no preordained pattern but, rather, by the natural consequences arising from a depression, a world war, and the continued rule of a firmly entrenched and successful political party pledged to the progressive democratization and equalization of opportunity in education as in all spheres of national life.

By 1950 it had become apparent not only to the Socialists but to the great majority of Swedes that these goals could not be realized in a bipartite class-linked school system. As voters, they continued to support the government and its plan to extend, unify, and reorient Swedish schooling, in turning from an emphasis on academic achievement to an emphasis on social-political values so as better to inculcate and foster the underlying attitudes, goals, and dreams implicit in building *folkhemmet*.

BIBLIOGRAPHY

PRIMARY SOURCES

1 a. Agardh, K. A. *Försök till rattfärdigande av det nya skolsystemet.* Stockholm: P. A. Norstedt & Söner, 1844.

1 b. ————. *Om de lägre folkklassernas upplysning.* Stockholm: P. A. Norstedt & Söner, 1837.

1 c. ————. *Slutanförande: betänkande af comiten till öfverseendet af rikets allmänna undervisningsverk.* Stockholm, 1829.

2. Andrén, Ivar. *Det fria och frivilliga bildningsarbetet i Sverige, 1944.* Stockholm: Folkuniversitets Förlag, 1944.

3. Andrews, C. C. "Report on the Educational System of Sweden," U. S. Bureau of Education, Circular of Information. Washington, D. C.: Government Printing Office, 1871.

4 a. Arvidson, Stellan. "Den nya skolan söder om Söder," Stockholms Artetarekommuns serie: *Aktuella Information,* No. 4 (1954).

4 b. ————. *Enhetsskolan: skolan vi skall få.* Riksdagsbeslutet: kommunal planering. Forsöksverksamheten. Lund: C. W. K. Gleerups Förlag, 1950.

4 c. ————. *Skolreformen: en sammanfattning av skolkommissionens betänkande.* Lund: C. W. K. Gleerups Förlag, 1949.

5 a. Berg, Fridtjuv. *Arbetet.* May 5, July 5, 1904.

5 b. ————. *Folkskolan såsom bottenskola: ett inlägg i en viktig samhällsfråga.* Stockholm: Sveriges Allmänna Folkskollärarförening,[1] 1883.

5 c. ————. *Folkskolan såsom bottenskola: nutidsfrågor på uppfostrans område.* Lund: SAF Pedagogiska Skrifter, 1911.

5 d. ————. "Hur tankar mogna," *Svensk Lärartidning,* Vol. 2 (1894).

6. Bergqvist, B. J. *De nya praktiska ungdomsskolorna.* Stockholm: Haggströms, 1918.

[1] Hereinafter referred to as SAF.

147

7. Branting, Hjalmar. *Tal och skrifter.* Vol. 3. Stockholm: Tidens Förlag, 1927.

8. Düring, Ingemar (ed.). *The Swedish School Reform: A Summary of the Government Bill at the Request of the 1946 School Commission.* Uppsala: Äppelbergs, 1951.

9. Edén, Nils. *Den svenska riksdagen under femhundra år.* Stockholm: P. A. Norstedt & Söner, 1935.

10. Elmgren, John. *School and Psychology: A Report of the Research Work of the 1946 School Commission.* Stockholm: Ministry of Education, 1952.

11. Folkpartiet. *Liberal syn på skolfrågan.* Folkpartiets Småskriftsserie. Stockholm: Folkpartiet, 1948.

12. Folkpartiets delegation i utbildningsfrågor. *Rätt till utbildning: liberala framtidsperspektiv.* Stockholm: Folkpartiet, 1959.

13. Folkpartiets kommunalpolitiska delegation. *Kommunen och skolfrågorna.* Stockholm: Westerbergs, 1956.

14. Fredriksson, Viktor. *Den framtida skolan: en orientering i organisationsfrågan.* Skriftserie. Stockholm: Arbetarnas Bildningsförbund, 1944.

15. Fryxell, Anders. *Förslag till enhet och medborgerlighet i de allmänna undervisningsverken.* Stockholm: F. B. Nestius, 1823.

16. Göteborgs Högskola. *Skolreformen. Göteborgs högskolås lärarråds yttrande över skolkommissionens betänkande* (avfattats av H. Hagendahl och K. Michaelson). Göteborg: Wettergren & Kerbers Förlag, 1948.

17. Gunnarson, Gunnar. "Förslag till motion i skolfrågan." Stockholm, 1944. (Unpublished ms.)

18 a. Höger Partiet. *Fakta om enhetsskola.* Stockholm: Högerns Informationstjänst, 1955.

18 b. ———. *Skola och politik.* Stockholm: Konservativa Skolungdomsföreningen, 1952.

19. Laing, Samuel. *A Tour in Sweden in 1838: Comprising Observations on the Moral, Political, and Economic State of the Swedish Nation.* London: Longman, Orme, Brown, Green, and Longmans, 1839.

20. *Landshöfdinge berättelser: Kronobergs län och Jönköpings län.* 1822.

21 a. Landsorganisationen. *The Postwar Program of Swedish Labor.* Stockholm: Landsorganisationen, 1948.

21 b. ———. *Protokoll, elfte ordinarie kongress 9-27 oktober, 1936.* Stockholm: A. B. Arbetarnas, 1936.

21 c. ———. "Remiss rörande 1946 skolkommissionens betänkande." Stockholm, 1948. (Mimeographed)

22. Lindgren, John. *Varför Sverige icke är republik.* Stockholm: Tidens Förlag, 1955.

23. Lunds Stift. *32:a folkskolläraremötet i Malmö, 1906: berättelse.* Malmö: SAF, 1907.

24 a. Myrdal, Alva. "Education for Democracy in Sweden," in *Education for Democracy.* The Proceedings of the Congress on Education for Democracy Held at Teachers College, Columbia University, August 15–17, 1939. New York: Bureau of Publications, Teachers College, Columbia University, 1939.

24 b. ———. *Efterkrigsplanering.* Para Pacem 32. Stockholm: Informationsbyrån Mellanfolkligt Samarbete för Fred och Världssamling för Fred, 1944.

24 c. ———, and Myrdal, Gunnar. *Kris i befolkningsfrågan.* Stockholm: Albert Bonniers, 1934.

25. Myrdal, Gunnar. "Population Problems and Policies," *The Annals of the American Academy of Political and Social Science,* Vol. 197 (May 1938).

26. *När jag gick i skolan: skol och ungdomsminnen från 1800-talets senare hälft.* Berättade av 34 svenska män och kvinnor. Uppsala: Äppelbergs Förlag, 1934.

27 a. Rudenschöld, Torsten. *Den svenska folkskolans praktiska ordnande.* Lund: Pedagogiska Skrifter, 1921.

27 b. ———. *Tankar om folkskolan.* Lund: Pedagogiska Skrifter, 1921.

27 c. ———. *Tankar om ståndscirkulation.* Stockholm: P. A. Norstedt & Söner, 1845.

27 d. ———. *Tankar om ståndscirkulations verkställighet.* Stockholm: P. A. Norstedt & Söner, 1846.

27 e. ———. *Tankar om vår tids samhällsfrågor.* Lund: Pedagogiska Skrifter, 1920.

28. Rydén, Värner. "Grundläggande synpunkter på enhetsskoleproblemet," *Tiden* (May 1927).

29 a. Siljeström, Per Adam. *Folkbildning: något om emigrationen samt ett ord till herrskapsklassen.* Stockholm: Dagens Häfder, 1853.

29 b. ———. *Handlingar och skrifter rörande undervisningsväsendet.* Stockholm: Fritzes, 1884.

29 c. ———. *Lärjungen—eller om individualitetens betydelse för uppfostran.* Smärre Skrifter, No. 1. Stockholm: P. A. Norstedt & Söner, 1884.

29 d. ———. *Om skolhusen och skolmaterialen.* Föredrag i Pedagogiska Föreningen, 1853. Handlingar och Skrifter. Stockholm, 1853.

29 e. ———. "Om utsikterna och hindren för en högre folkskolebildning," *Framtiden,* No. 2 (1877).

29 f. ———. "Promemoria av 1858 till folkskolestyrelsen i Göteborg," in *Göteborgs folkskoleväsen i gamla dagar och i våra* (S. Ohlander, ed.). Lund: C. W. K. Gleerups Förlag, 1923.

29 g. ————. *Resa i Förenta Staterna.* Stockholm: P. A. Norstedt & Söner, 1852.

29 h. ————. "Tankar om uppfostran," in *Årsböcker i svensk undervisningshistoria* (B. R. Hall, ed.). Lund: C. W. K. Gleerups Förlag, 1929.

29 i. ————. *The Educational Institutions of the United States: Their Character and Organisation* (F. Rowan, trans.). London: John Chapman, 1853.

30. Socialdemokratiska Partistyrelsen. *Berättelse för år 1945.* Stockholm: Tidens Förlag, 1946.

31. Socialdemokratiska Ungdomsförbund. *Skolan och folket.* Stockholm: Tidens Förlag, 1941.

32. Stålfelt, Edvin. *Vår förening och dess program.* Stockholm: SAF, 1931.

33 a. Sveriges Folkskollärarförbund. *Skolkommissionens principbetänkande.* En redogörelse sammanställd av Bengt Hillman. Trelleborg, 1948.

33 b. ————. *Sveriges folkskollärarförbund om skolreformen: remissyttrande över 1946 års skolkommissionens principbetänkande.* Stockholm, 1948.

34. Sveriges Konservativa Studentförbund. *Grundskola: ett alternativ.* Stockholm: Studentförlaget Horisont, 1962.

35 a. Sveriges Socialdemokratiska Arbetareparti. *Kongressmotioner.* Stockholm: A. B. Arbetarnas; Tiden, 1918–1948.

35 b. ————. *Protokoll.* Stockholm: A. B. Arbetarnas; Tiden, 1918–1948.

36 a. Sweden. *Bidrag till Sveriges officiella statistik: folkundervisningen. December 31, 1868.* Stockholm, 1869.

36 b. ————. Statens Offentliga Utredningar [2] 1938:7. *Betänkande angående barnbeklädnadsbidrag.* Stockholm, 1938.

36 c. ————. SOU 1946:68. *Betänkande om det fria och frivilliga folkbildningsarbetet.* Stockholm, 1946.

36 d. ————. SOU 1923:56. *Sammanfattning av utlåtanden och yttranden i anledning av Skolkommissionens betänkande afgivna den 28 april 1922, I & II.* Stockholm, 1923.

36 e. ————. SOU 1963:53. Stockholm, 1963.

36 f. ————. SOU 1948:45. *Svensk långtidsprogram 1947–1952/3.* Stockholm, 1948.

36 g. ————. SOU 1944:7 & 12. *Utredningar angående ekonomisk efterkrigsplanering, I & II.* Stockholm, 1944.

37 a. ————. Arbetsmarknadsstyrelsen. *Att välja yrke.* Stockholm, 1949.

[2] Hereinafter referred to as SOU.

37 b. ———, ———. *Gymnasisternas ämnesval*. Stockholm, 1948.

37 c. ———, ———. *Skolor för yrkesutbildning*. Stockholm, 1949.

38 a. ———, Ecklesiastikdepartementet. *1946 års Skolkommissionens betänkande med förslag till riktlinjer för det svenska skolväsendets utveckling*. SOU 1948:27. Stockholm, 1948.

38 b. ———, ———. *Den psykologiska forskningens nuvarande ståndpunkt i fråga om den psykiska utvecklingen hos barn och ungdom*. Utlåtanden avgivna till 1940 års skolutredning av Professorna G. A. R. Anderberg, J. K. G. Elmgren, D. Katz, och J. Landquist. Bilaga II. SOU 1943:19. Stockholm, 1943.

38 c. ———, ———. *Sammanfattning av allmän organisationsplan*. Bilaga VI. SOU 1945:62. Stockholm, 1945.

38 d. ———, ———. *Tillkallade sakkunniga: utredning angående det svenska skolväsendets organisation*. SOU 1926:5. Stockholm, 1926.

38 e. ———, ———. *Sambandet mellan folkskola och högre skola*. SOU 1944:21. Stockholm, 1944.

38 f. ———, ———. *Skolan i samhällets tjänst; frågeställningar och problemläge*. SOU 1944:20. Stockholm, 1944.

38 g. ———, ———. *Skolöverstyrelsens utlåtande över vissa av 1940 års skolutrednings betänkanden och 1946 års skolkommissionens principbetänkande jämte sammanfattning av avgivna yttranden*. SOU 1949:35. Stockholm, 1949.

38 h. ———, ———. *Skolpolitikstidens skolformer: I. Allmän organisationsplan*. SOU 1945:60. IV. Stockholm, 1945.

38 i. ———, ———. *Utredning och förslag angående vidgade möjligheter till högre undervisning för landsbygdens ungdom*. SOU 1944:22. Stockholm, 1944.

38 j. ———, ———. *Vissa frågor rörande tillämpning av 1927 års skol-organisation*. SOU 1929:32. Stockholm, 1929.

39 a. ———, Riksdagen. *Bondeståndets protokoller vid riksdagarne 1828–1830*. II. Stockholm, 1831.

39 b. ———, ———. *Kommittee berättelse 1918*. Vol. 3, No. 50. Stockholm, 1919.

39 c. ———, ———. *Kungl. Maj:ts proposition 1950:70: angående riktlinjer för det svenska skolväsendets utveckling*. Stockholm, 1950.

39 d. ———, ———. *Kungl. Maj:ts proposition No. 116: bihang till riksdagens protokoll*. Vol. 1. Stockholm, 1927.

39 e. ———, ———. *Motioner i Andra Kammaren 1867*. No. 137. Stockholm, 1867.

39 f. ———, ———. *Motioner i Andra Kammaren 1894*. No. 87, 88. Stockholm, 1894.

39 g. ———, ———. *Motioner i Första Kammaren 1927. Förhandlingar onsdagen den 18 maj angående omorganisation av det högre skolväsendet.* No. 31. Stockholm, 1927.

39 h. ———, ———. *Presteståndets protokoller vid riksdagarne 1837.* II. Stockholm, 1838.

39 i. ———, ———. *Protokoll vid lagtima riksmötet 1918, Andra Kammaren.* Vol. 6, No. 4. Stockholm, 1919.

39 j. ———, ———. *Riksdagens protokoll. Andra Kammaren 1935.* No. 1. Stockholm, 1935.

39 k. ———, ———. *Riksdagens protokoll. Andra Kammaren 1936.* No. 2. Stockholm, 1936.

39 l. ———, ———. *Riksdagens protokoll. Andra Kammaren 1944.* No. 4. Stockholm, 1945.

39 m. ———, ———. *Riksdagens protokoll. Andra Kammaren.* No. 2. Stockholm, 1950.

39 n. ———, ———. *Riksdagens protokoll. Andra Kammaren. Förhandlingarna fredagen den 20 maj angående skolarbetets inre gestaltning.* No. 33, 34. Stockholm, 1927.

39 o. ———, ———. *Riksdagens protokoll. Andra Kammaren. Förhandlingarna onsdagen den 18 maj angående omorganisation av det högre skolväsendet.* No. 32. Stockholm, 1927.

39 p. ———, ———. *Riksdagens protokoll. Första Kammaren 1940.* No. 3. Stockholm, 1940.

39 q. ———, ———. *Riksdagens protokoll. Första Kammaren 1950.* No. 41, Bilaga 1. Stockholm, 1950.

39 r. ———, ———. *Riksdagens riksstat.* Stockholm, 1870, 1880, 1890, 1900.

39 s. ———, ———. *Riksdagens skrivelse.* No. 262. Stockholm, 1927.

39 t. ———, ———. *Riksdagens skrivelse angående inrättande av kommunala flickskolor, den 5 juni 1928.* No. 356. Stockholm, 1928.

39 u. ———, ———. *Särskilda utskottets utlåtande.* No. 1. Stockholm, 1950.

40 a. ———, Skolkommissionen. *Skolkommissionens betänkande: I. Grunder för en ny läroverksorganisation; II. Historiska översikter och särskilda utredningar; III. Statistiska utredningar; IV. Det högre skolväsendet i utlandet.* Stockholm, 1922.

40 b. ———, Skolöverstyrelsen. *Försöksverksamhet med nioårig enhetsskola: sammanfattande redogörelse, 1949/50–58/59.* Stockholm, 1959.

41 a. ———, Social Welfare Board. *Social Sweden.* Stockholm: The Board, 1952.

41 b. ———, ———. *Social Work and Legislation in Sweden.* Stockholm: The Board, 1928.

42. ———, Statistiska Centralbyrån. *Statistisk årsbok*. Stockholm, 1914–.

43. ———, *Svenska statsrådets protokoll, juni 1924*. Stockholm.

44. Swedish Institute. *Facts about Sweden*. Stockholm: Bokförlaget Forum, 1964.

45. Swedish State Institute for Race Biology. *The Racial Characteristics of the Swedish Nation* (H. Lundborg and F. J. Linders, eds.). Uppsala: Almqvist & Wiksell, 1926.

46. Tegnér, Esaias. *Om fattigvården i Vexiö stift*. Vol. 4. Stockholm: Nordiska Bokförlag, 1848.

47. Ullsten, Ola. *Folkpartiet och reformerna: liberala riksdagsinitiativ 1902–1960*. Stockholm: Folk och Samhälle, 1960.

48. Utrikespolitiska Institut. *Svensk utrikespolitik under andra världskriget*. Stockholm: Kooperativa Förlaget, 1946.

49. Wellander, Erik. "Bottenskolelogik," *Svenska Dagbladet*, May 6, 1927.

50 a. Wigforss, Ernst. *Ekonomisk demokrati*. Stockholm: Natur och Kultur, 1948.

50 b. ———. "The Financial Policy during Depression and Boom," *Annals of the American Academy of Political and Social Science*, Vol. 197 (May 1938).

SECONDARY SOURCES

51. Anderson, Perry. "Sweden: Mr. Crossland's Dreamland," *New Left Review*, No. 9 (May–June 1961).

52. Andrén, Nils. *Modern Swedish Government*. Stockholm: Almqvist & Wiksell, 1961.

53. Aquilonius, Klas. "Det svenska folkundervisningsväsendet 1809–1860," in *Svenska folkskolans historia* (V. Fredriksson, ed.). Stockholm: Albert Bonniers, 1942.

54. *Arbetet*. 1930–1938.

55 a. Arvidson, Stellan. "Education for Democracy," in *Scandinavian Democracy* (J. A. Lauwerys, ed.). Copenhagen: The Danish Institute, 1958.

55 b. ———; Blomberg, Ivan; and Stenholm, Britta. *Enhetsskolan växer fram*. Malmö: C. W. K. Gleerups Förlag, 1953.

56. Banks, Olive. *Parity and Prestige in English Secondary Education: A Study in Educational Sociology*. London: Routledge and Kegan Paul, 1955.

57. Berg, Hjalmar. *Anders Berg, en föregångsman i den svenska folkskolan*. Stockholm: Svenska Bokförlaget, 1940.

58. Bergevin, Paul. *Adult Education in Sweden: An Introduction*. Indiana University Monograph Series in Adult Education, No. 1. Bloomington: Bureau of Studies in Adult Education, Indiana University, 1961.

59 a. Bergqvist, B. J. *Sveriges ungdomsskolor.* Stockholm: P. A. Norstedt & Söner, 1931.

59 b. ———. *Våra skolor: en granskning i anledning av Skolkommissionens reformförslag.* Stockholm: P. A. Norstedt & Söner, 1923.

59 c. ———. "Sweden," in *Educational Yearbook of the International Institute of Teachers College, Columbia University: The Expansion of Secondary Education.* New York: Bureau of Publications, Teachers College, Columbia University, 1931.

60. Bergstrand, Anna B. *Demokrati och skolväsen i England.* Göteborg: SAF, 1940.

61. Berlin, Isaiah. *Historical Inevitability.* Auguste Comte Memorial Trust Lecture, No. 1. London: Oxford University Press, 1954.

62. Björck, Wilhelm. *Skolreformen: en orienterande redogörelse för Skolkommissionens förslag till enhetsskoleorganisation.* Stockholm: P. A. Norstedt & Söner, 1922.

63. Björklof, Sune. "Fridtjuv Berg: pedagog och provokatör," *Lärartidningen,* Vol. 2 (March 13, 1965).

64. Bogoslovsky, Christina S. von H. *Educational Crisis in Sweden in the Light of American Experience.* New York: Columbia University Press, 1932.

65. Bolén, B. "Organisation och riksdagen," *Tiden,* Vol. 46 (1954).

66. Bolton, I. M. "Social Services," in *Democratic Sweden: A Volume of Studies Prepared by Members of the New Fabian Research Bureau* (M. Cole and C. Smith, eds.). New York: Greystone Press, 1939.

67. Börjeson, Gösta. *Folkskolläraröverflödet.* Uppsala: Äppelbergs, 1926.

68. Braatöy, Bjarne. *The New Sweden: A Vindication of Democracy.* London: Thomas Nelson, 1939.

69. Broms, Klas. *Fridtjuv Bergs pedagogik: med tyngdpunkt på tiden före hans första statsrådsperiod.* Årsböcker i svensk undervisningshistoria, Vol. 112. Stockholm: Föreningen för Svensk Undervisningshistoria, 1964.

70. Carlsson, Ingvar (ed.). *Ung mening.* Stockholm: Tidens Förlag, 1964.

71 a. Carlsson, Sten. *Bonde-präst-ämbetsman: svensk ståndscirkulation från 1680 till våra dagar.* Stockholm: Bokförlaget Prisma, 1962.

71 b. ———. "From the Estates to the Educational Society," in *The Intellectual Face of Sweden.* (Special issue of *Ergo International.*) Uppsala: Uppsala Student Union, 1964.

72. Cederblad, Carl. *Kamratskap.* 3 vols. 1: *Skolkamrat;* 2: *Kamratskapets väg genom hem och "ny skola";* 3: *Kamratskapet mognar till demokrati.* Stockholm: Kooperativa Förbundets Bokförlag, 1951.

73. Cederschiöld, Wilhelm. *Skolfrågan ur samhällets synpunkt.* Stockholm: Wahlström & Widstrand, 1927.

74. Childs, Marquis W. *Sweden: The Middle Way*. New Haven: Yale University Press, rev. ed., 1947.

75. Counts, George C. *The Challenge of Soviet Education*. New York: McGraw Hill Book Company, 1957.

76. *Dagens Nyheter*. 1927–1950.

77. Dahlbom, Fredrik. *Den svenska folkskolans kristendomsundervisning 1842–1919*. Stockholm: Svenska Kyrkans Diakoniststyrelsens Bokförlag, 1927.

78. Danell, Gideon. *Svenska Dagbladet*, November 20, 1940.

79. Edenman, Ragnar. "Brantings första riksdagar (1897–1902)," *Statsvetenskapliga studier*. Uppsala: Almqvist & Wiksell, 1944.

80. Edin, Karl Arvid, and Hutchinson, Edward P. *Studies of Differential Fertility in Sweden*. Stockholm Economic Studies, No. 4. London: P. S. King and Son, Ltd., 1935.

81. Elder, Glen H., Jr. "Life Opportunities and Personality: Some Consequences of Stratified Secondary Education in Great Britain," *Sociology of Education*, Vol. 38, No. 3 (Spring 1965).

82 a. Elmér, Åke. *Från fattigsverige till välfärdsstaten: socialförhållanden och socialpolitik i Sverige under 1900-talet*. Stockholm: Bokförlaget Aldus, 1963.

82 b. ———. *Svensk socialpolitik*. Lund: C. W. K. Gleerups Förlag, 3d ed., 1948.

83. Elvander, Nils. *Role of the State in Sweden's Cultural Life*. Stockholm: The Swedish Institute, 1965.

84. "Enhetsskolan: ett bristfälligt och helt illusoriskt förslag," *Nya Dagligt Allehanda*, May 13, 1922.

85. Fraser, W. R. *Education and Society in Modern France*. London: Routledge and Kegan Paul, 1963.

86. Fredlund, G. J. *Konturer till en enhällig skolorganisation: huvudsakligen i vad den rör anknytningen mellan barna och ungdomsskolan*. Stockholm: C. E. Fritzes Bokförlag, 1926.

87. Friis, Henning (ed.). *Scandinavia between East and West*. Ithaca: Cornell University Press, 1950.

88. Gardiner, Patrick. *The Nature of Historical Explanation*. London: Oxford University Press, 1952.

89. Gerdner, Gunnar. *Det svenska regeringsproblemet 1917–1920*. Uppsala: Almqvist & Wiksell, 1946.

90. *Göteborgs Handelstidning*. 1935–1947.

91. Gottschalk, Louis (ed.). *Generalization in the Writing of History*. Chicago: University of Chicago Press, 1963.

92. Hall, Bror R. (ed.). "Tidiga enhetsskoletankar," *Föreningen för Svensk Undervisningshistoria*, Vol. 18 (1926).

93. Hallendorf, Carl, and Schück, Adolf. *History of Sweden.* Stockholm: C. E. Fritzes Bokförlag, 1929.

94 a. Hänninger, Nils. *Den amerikanska uppfostringsvärlden: studier och strövtåg.* Stockholm: P. A. Norstedt & Söner, 1922.

94 b. ———, and Falk, Dagn. "Sweden," in *Education Yearbook of the International Institute of Teachers College, Columbia University, 1936* (I. L. Kandel, ed.). New York: Bureau of Publications, Teachers College, Columbia University, 1936.

95. Hanson, Sigfrid (ed.). *Svenska folkrörelser.* Stockholm: Lindfors Bokförlag, 1936–1937.

96. Harlock, Walter E. *Svensk-engelsk ordbok.* Stockholm: Svenska Bokförlaget, 1949.

97 a. Håstad, Elis. *Det moderna partiväsendets organisation* (2d ed.). Stockholm: Albert Bonniers, 1949.

97 b. ———. *Partierna i regering och riksdag* (2d ed.). Stockholm: Albert Bonniers, 1949.

97 c. ———. *Sveriges historia under 1900-talet.* Stockholm: Albert Bonniers, 1958.

98. Heckscher, Eli F. *An Economic History of Sweden.* Cambridge: Harvard University Press, 1954.

99 a. Heckscher, Gunnar. "Interest Groups in Sweden," in *Interest Groups in Four Continents* (Henry W. Ehrman, ed.). Pittsburgh: University of Pittsburgh Press, 1958.

99 b.* ———. "Pluralist Democracy," *Social Research,* Vol. 15 (1948).

99 c. ———. *Staten och organisationerna* (2d ed.). Stockholm: Kooperativa Förbundets Bokförlag, 1951.

99 d. ———, and Helti, Verner. *De politiska åskådningar och partierna.* Stockholm: Studieförbundet Medborgarskolan, 1950.

100. Hedlund, Karl V. (ed.). *Svensk folkhögskola under 75 år.* Stockholm: L. Hökerberg, 1943.

101. Helén, Gunnar. "Present Trends and Political Issues," in *Differentiation and Guidance in the Comprehensive School* (T. Husén and S. Henrysson, eds.). Stockholm: Almqvist & Wiksell, 1959.

102. Helger, Nils. *Barnens rätt: några synpunkter i ett par aktuella skolfrågor.* Uppsala: J. A. Lindblads Förlag, 1927.

103 a. Hermansson, Ester. *I amerikanska skolor.* Pedagogiska Skrifter, No. 167–169. Stockholm: Svensk Lärartidnings Förlag, 1940.

103 b. ———. "Swedish Education during the 1940's" (J. Mjöberg, trans.), *Harvard Educational Review,* Vol. 21 (Fall 1951).

104. Hildebrand, Karl. *Gustav V som människa och regent.* Stockholm: Almqvist & Wiksell, 1948.

105. Hirdman, Gunnar. *Adult Education in Sweden*. Stockholm: Kooperativa Förbundet, 1947.

106. Höijer, Ernst. *Sveriges befolkningsutveckling genom tiderna*. Verdandis Skriftserie, No. 11. Stockholm: Svenska Bokförlaget, 1959.

107 a. Höijer, Karl J. *Social Welfare in Sweden*. Stockholm: The Swedish Institute, 1949.

107 b. ———. *Svensk socialpolitisk historia*. Stockholm: P. A. Norstedt & Söner, 1952.

108. Holmberg, Åke. *Sverige efter 1809: politisk historia under 150 år*. Verdandis Skriftserie, No. 9. Stockholm: Svenska Bokförlaget, 1961.

109. Hovde, B. J. *The Scandinavian Countries, 1720–1865: The Rise of the Middle Classes*. Ithaca: Cornell University Press, 1948.

110. Hultqvist, K. A. *Om Tegnér och folkskolan*. Lund: C. W. K. Gleerups Förlag, 1925.

111 a. Husén, Torsten. *Begåvning och miljö: studier i begåvningsutvecklingens och begåvningsurvalets psykologisk-pedagogiska och sociala problem*. Psykologisk-Pedagogiska Bibliotek, No. 6. Stockholm: Hugo Gebers Förlag, 1948.

111 b. ———. *Fridtjuv Berg, folkskollärarkåren och stavningsreformerna*. Göteborg: Pedagogiska Skrifter, 1946.

111 c. ———. *Fridtjuv Berg och enhetsskolan*. Göteborg: Pedagogiska Skrifter, 1948.

111 d. ———. "Loss of Talent in Selective School Systems: The Case of Sweden," *Comparative Education Review*, Vol. 4, No. 2 (October 1960).

111 e. ———. *Problems of Differentiation in Swedish Compulsory Schooling*. Stockholm: Svenska Bokförlaget, 1962.

111 f. ———. "Social Determinants of the Comprehensive School," *International Review of Education*, Vol. 9, No. 2 (1963–1964).

111 g. ———. "The Educational Explosion in Sweden," in *The World Yearbook in Education 1965: The Education Explosion* (George Z. F. Bereday and Joseph A. Lauwerys, eds.). London: Evans Brothers, 1965.

112. Jägerskiöld, Stig. *Från prästskola till enhetsskola*. Stockholm: Almqvist & Wiksell, 1959.

113. Kälvesten, Anna Lisa. *The Social Structure of Sweden*. Stockholm: The Swedish Institute, 1961.

114. Kandel, I. L. "The End of an Era," in *Educational Yearbook of the International Institute of Teachers College, Columbia University, 1941*. New York: Bureau of Publications, Teachers College, Columbia University, 1941.

115. Key, Ellen. *The Younger Generation* (Arthur G. Chater, trans.). New York: G. P. Putnam's Sons, 1914.

116. King, Margaret L., and Male, George A. *Sweden: Educational Data.* Washington, D. C.: U. S. Department of Health, Education and Welfare, 1965.

117. Koht, Halvdan. *The American Spirit in Europe: A Survey of Transatlantic Influences.* Philadelphia: University of Pennsylvania Press, 1949.

118. Kunn, Elfred. "Vem var Per Albins farfars far?" *Tiden,* Vol. 37 (1945).

119. Landauer, Carl. *European Socialism: A History of Ideas and Movements from the Industrial Revolution to Hitler's Seizure of Power.* Berkeley: University of California Press, 1959.

120. Landquist, John. "Sweden's Educational System," in *Scandinavia Past and Present: Five Modern Democracies.* Copenhagen: Arnkrone, 1959.

121. Lind, Albin. *Popular Movements in Sweden.* Stockholm: Arbetarnas Bildningsförbund, 1940.

122. Lindberg, John S. *The Background of Swedish Emigration to the United States: An Economic and Sociological Study of the Dynamics of Migration.* Minneapolis: University of Minnesota Press, 1930.

123. Lindbom, Tage. *Den nya fronten.* Stockholm: Kooperativa Förbundets Bokförlag, 1949.

124 a. Lindgren, John. *Per Albin Hansson i svensk demokrati, 1885–1920.* Vol. 1. Stockholm: Tidens Förlag, 1950.

124 b. ———. *Varför Sverige icke är republik.* Stockholm: Tidens Förlag, 1955.

125. Lipset, Seymour. *The First New Nation: The United States in Historical and Comparative Perspective.* New York: Basic Books, 1963.

126. Lorwin, Lewis. *National Planning in Selected Countries.* National Resources Planning Board Technical Paper No. 2. Washington, D. C.: U. S. Government Printing Office, 1941.

127. Malmqvist, Eve. "Enhetsskoletanken i Sverige: en historisk överblick," *Skola och Samhälle,* Vol. 6 (1952).

128. Michanek, Ernst. *For and Against the Welfare State: Swedish Experiences.* Stockholm: The Swedish Institute, 1964.

129. Moberg, Vilhelm. *The Emigrants* (G. Lannestock, trans.). New York: Simon and Schuster, 1951.

130 a. Montgomery, G. Arthur. *How Sweden Overcame the Depression, 1930–1933.* Stockholm: Albert Bonniers, 1938.

130 b. ———. *Industrialismens genombrott i Sverige.* Stockholm: Skoglunds Bokförlag, 1947.

130 c. ———. *Svensk socialpolitik under 1800-talet.* Stockholm: Skoglunds Bokförlag, 1934.

130 d. ———. *The Rise of Modern Industry in Sweden.* Stockholm Economic Studies, No. 8. London: P. S. King and Son, Ltd., 1939.

131. *Morgontidningen.* 1948–1950.

132. Myrdal, Alva. *Nation and Family: The Swedish Experiment in Democratic Family and Population Policy.* New York: Harper & Brothers, 1941.

133 a. Myrdal, Gunnar. "Kontant eller *in natura* i socialpolitiken," *Nationalekonomisk Tidskrift,* April 1938.

133 b. ———. *Population: A Problem for Democracy.* The Godkin Lectures, 1938. Gloucester, Massachusetts: Peter Smith, 1962.

133 c. ———, and Myrdal, Alva. *Kontakt med Amerika.* Stockholm: Albert Bonniers, 1941.

134. Nordland, Eva. *Verdier i gammel og ny skole; fra debatten om reform i skolen i svenske aviser, 1920–1956.* Oslo: Aschehough, 1958.

135. Nordstrom, G. Hilding. *Sveriges socialdemokratiska arbetareparti under genombrottsåren 1889–1894.* Stockholm: Kooperativa Förbundet, 1938.

136. Nordström, Simon. *Kort öfversikt öfver det svenska folkskoleväsendets utveckling till år 1842.* Stockholm: Bonniers Förlag, 1887.

137. Nylund, Sven. *Våra folkskolor.* Stockholm: A. V. Carlsons Bokförlag, 1924.

138. Ohlson, Nils G. *Det pedagogiska problemet i Sverige under frihetstiden och gustavianska tiden till omkring år 1805.* Stockholm: Westerbergs, 1939.

139 a. Oldberg, Ragnar. "Idéalisten och skolreformen," *Perspektiv,* No. 2 (1953).

139 b. ———, and Söderlund, Adolf. "Skolkris och—krisskola?" *Pedagogisk Tidskrift,* Vol. 9 (1952).

140 a. Olsson, Oskar. *Demokratiens skolväsen: iakttagelser i amerikanska skolor.* Stockholm: P. A. Norstedt & Söner, 1926.

140 b. ———. *Skolreformen: tal och uppsatser.* Stockholm: Oskar Eklunds, 1945.

141. Östergren, David L. "The Folk High Schools of Sweden." (Unpublished doctoral dissertation) Teachers College, Columbia University, 1949.

142. Papenek, Ernst. "Political and Educational Interaction within the Austrian School." (Unpublished doctoral dissertation) Teachers College, Columbia University, 1960.

143. Paulston, Rolland G. "The Swedish Comprehensive School Reform: A Selected Annotated Bibliography," *Comparative Education Review,* Vol. 10, No. 1 (February 1966).

144. Richardson, Gunnar. *Kulturkamp och klasskamp: ideologiska och sociala motsättningar i svensk skol och kulturpolitik under 1880-talet.* Göteborg: Akademiförlaget Gumperts, 1963.

145. Robbins, James J. *The Government of Labor Relations in Sweden.* Chapel Hill: University of North Carolina Press, 1942.

146. Rodhe, Edvard. "Den svenska folkskolans förhistoria särskilt under medeltiden," in *Svenska folkskolans historia* (V. Fredriksson, ed.). Stockholm: Albert Bonniers, 1940.

147. Rönnblom, Hans-Krister. *Frisinnade landsföreningen, 1902–1927.* Stockholm: Saxon och Lindström, 1929.

148. Rostow, Walt W. *The Stages of Economic Growth: A Non-Communist Manifesto.* London: Cambridge University Press, 1962.

149. Russell, Bertrand. *Education and the Good Life.* New York: Boni and Liveright, 1926.

150. Rustow, Dankwart A. *The Politics of Compromise: A Study of Parties and Cabinet Government in Sweden.* Princeton: Princeton University Press, 1955.

151. Salqvist, B. "Torsten Rudenschöld och Fridtjuv Berg," *Skola och Samhälle,* Vol. 75 (June 1942).

152. Schumpeter, Joseph. *Capitalism, Socialism, and Democracy* (3d ed.). New York: Harper & Brothers, 1950.

153 a. Segerstedt, Torgny. "An Investigation of Class Consciousness among Office Employees and Workers in Swedish Factories," in *Transactions of the Second World Congress of Sociology,* Vol. 2. London: International Sociological Association, 1954.

153 b. ———, and Lundquist, Agne. *Man in Industrial Society.* Stockholm: The Industrial Council for Social and Economic Studies, 1956.

154. Severin, Frans. *The Ideological Development of Swedish Social Democracy.* Stockholm: The Swedish Social Democratic Labour Party, 1956.

155. Sjöstrand, Wilhelm. *Pedagogikens historia, från antiken till första världskriget.* Malmö: C. W. K. Gleerups Förlag, 1954.

156. Skäringer-Larson, Elsa. *Demokratisk fostran i U. S. A.* Pedagogiska Skrifter, No. 171–172. Stockholm: Svensk Lärartidnings Förlag, 1941.

157 a. Sorenson, Anna. "Det svenska folkundervisningsväsendet, 1860–1900," in *Svenska folkskolans historia* (V. Fredriksson, ed.). Stockholm: Albert Bonniers, 1942.

157 b. ———. *Pedagoger och pedagogiska problem: Pedagogiska Sällskapet i Stockholm, 1892–1942.* Pedagogiska Skrifter, No. 176–177. Stockholm: Svensk Lärartidnings Förlag, 1942.

158. Springer, Ursula K. "West German School Reform in Social-Political Context." (Unpublished doctoral dissertation) Teachers College, Columbia University, 1964.

159. Stensland, Per G. "Adult Education," in *Scandinavia between East and West* (H. Friis, ed.). Ithaca: Cornell University Press, 1950.

160. *Stockholms Tidningen.* 1927–1950.

161. Stolpe, Herman. *Ungdomen och folkrörelserna.* Stockholm: Kooperativa Förbundets Bokförlag, 1944.

162. Sturmthal, Adolf. *The Tragedy of European Labor.* New York: Columbia University Press, 1943.

163. Svalastoga, Karre. *Prestige, Class and Mobility.* Copenhagen: Gyldendal, 1959.

164. Svanström, Ragnar, and Palmstierna, C. Fredrik. *A Short History of Sweden* (J. Bulman, trans.). London: Oxford University Press, 1934.

165. *Svensk Lärartidning.* 1918–1950.

166. *Svensk Skoltidning.* 1948–1950.

167. *Svenska Dagbladet.* 1927–1950; 1956.

168. *Svenska Morgonbladet.* 1948–1949.

169. "Sweden Clears Bills in Secret: Closed-Door Investigations Pave Path to Compromise," *The New York Times*, May 10, 1964.

170. *Sydsvenska Dagbladet.* 1947–1950.

171. Thermenius, Edvard. *Sveriges politiska partier.* Stockholm: Hugo Gerbers Förlag, 1933.

172. Thunander, G. *Fattigskola-medborgarskola.* Malmö: C. A. Anderson, 1946.

173. *Tiden.* 1918–1950.

174. Tingsten, Herbert. *Den svenska socialdemokratiens idéutveckling.* Stockholm: Tiden, 1941.

175. Verney, Douglas. *Parliamentary Reform in Sweden, 1866–1921.* Oxford: Clarendon Press, 1957.

176. Wagnsson, Ruben. *ABC: vår folkundervisning från medeltid till enhetsskola.* Malmö: Förlaget Svenska Folkrörelser, 1955.

177. Wahlund, S. "Utbildningens demokratisering," in *Ungdomen bygger framtiden.* Stockholm: Kooperativa Förbundet, 1944.

178. Warne, Albin. *Till folkskolans förhistoria i Sverige.* Stockholm: Svenska Kyrkans Diakonistyrelsens Bokförlag, 1929.

179. Westerlind, Erik, and Beckman, Rune. *Sweden's Economy: Structure and Trends.* Stockholm: Bokförlaget Prisma, 1965.

180. Westling, K. A. "C. A. Agardh, F. F. Carlson och undervisningensfri-

het," in *Till Bengt J. Bergqvist*. Lund: C. W. K. Gleerups Förlag, 1920.

181. Wikström, Nils. "Anmälan," *Svensk Skoltidning*, Vol. 1, No. 1–2 (January 8, 1944).

182 a. Wohlin, Nils. *Den jordbruksidkande befolkningen i Sverige, 1751–1900*. Emigrationsutredningen, bilaga 9. Stockholm: Almqvist & Wiksell, 1909.

182 b. ————. *Svenska jordstyckningspolitiken*. Stockholm: Almqvist & Wiksell, 1936.

Personal interviews were held in Stockholm with the following:

Stellan Arvidson, Rektor, Stockholms Folkskolaseminarium. August 31, 1965.

Folke Haldén, Chief of Training, Swedish Employers Confederation. August 26, 1965.

Matts B. Larsson, member, 1957 School Commission. July 26, 1965.

Jonas Orring, Vice-Director, Royal Board of Education. September 13, 1965.

Nils Ramsten, Ombudsman, Swedish Trade Union Council. July 2, 1965.

Pierre Schori, Secretary, Social Democratic Labor Party. June 28, 1965.

APPENDIX A

THE PERIOD OF IMPLEMENTATION, 1950–1968:
A SELECTED ANNOTATED BIBLIOGRAPHY [1]

Arvidson, Stellan. "Education for Democracy." *Scandinavian Democracy* (Joseph A. Lauwerys, ed.), pp. 294–315. Copenhagen: The Danish Institute, 1958.

Faults teacher-centered selective schooling as ideologically incompatible with the Swedish welfare state philosophy and individual needs for "self realization." Believes the new comprehensive school will remedy this situation by training pupils for independence, responsibility, and readiness to cooperate.

Arvidson, Stellan. *Education in Sweden.* Stockholm: The Swedish Institute, 1955. 106 pp.

Describes the over-all organization of education and outlines the 1946 School Commission's major criticisms of Swedish education. Summarizes proposals for its complete reordering into a comprehensive, nonselective system.

Björklund, Eskil, and Svensson, Nils-Eric. "Educational Research in Sweden." *International Review of Education,* Vol. 13, No. 2, 1967, pp. 194–197.

Reviews changes in Swedish educational research from a "committee research" emphasis to "production" oriented types of projects.

Carlsson, Gösta, and Gesser, Bengt. "Universities as Selecting and Socializing Agents: Some Recent Swedish Data." *Acta Sociologica,* Vol. 9, 1965, pp. 25–37.

With the implementation of *grundskolan* and the progressive change-over in secondary schooling from an elite to an egalitarian orientation, Swedish universities have been forced' to modify their traditional functions. The authors document these changes and discuss trends in the development of a new Swedish higher education.

Central Bureau of Statistics. "Sweden: Educational Statistics." *Paedagogica Europaea. The Yearbook of Educational Research 1965,* pp. 272–275. Council for Cultural Cooperation of the Council of Europe. Amsterdam and Brussels: Elsevier, 1965.

[1] Many of the entries in this appendix are reprinted, by permission of *Comparative Education Review,* from a work published in its February 1966 issue: Rolland G. Paulston, "The Swedish Comprehensive School Reform: A Selected Annotated Bibliography," *Comparative Education Reveiw,* Vol. 10, No. 1, pp. 87–94.

With the comprehensive school replacing all Swedish elementary and lower secondary school types after 1962, parallel agencies for the collection and organization of educational statistics have also been replaced by the Central Bureau. This article describes categories used by the Bureau and scope of its activities.

Dixon, Willis. *Society, Schools and Progress in Scandinavia*. Long Island City, N. Y.: Pergamon Press, 1965. 193 pp.

Chapter 8 presents a succinct, well-researched survey of the committee work and legislation leading to the *grundskola* reform: "social and political considerations provided the main impetus for the reform, backed by the fact that every inquiry confirmed that the school system reflected the class divisions of society." Bibliography.

Düring, Ingemar (ed.). *The Swedish School Reform: A Summary of the Government Bill at the Request of the 1946 School Commission*. Uppsala: Appelbergs, 1951. 171 pp.

Summarizes 1950 school legislation establishing, in principle, a new nine-year, examination-free comprehensive school to replace all previous schools. Presents guidelines for experimentation and implementation. Creates an egalitarian "bottom school" in a complete rejection of traditional selective practice.

Edenman, Ragnar. *Utbildning och politik i ett progressivt samhälle*. Stockholm: Socialdemokratiska Arbetarepartiet, 1960. 24 pp.

The Labor government's position on "education and politics in a progressive society" by the Minister of Education and past chairman of the 1957 School Commission. Outlines the Socialist party's goals on questions of supply and demand in education, the right to individual election of study paths, vocational training, and the "democratization of education." Stresses the role of long-term planning based on research.

Elmgren, John. *School and Psychology: A Report of the Research Work of the 1946 School Commission*. Stockholm: Ministry of Education, 1952. 342 pp.

The author, who was attached to the Commission as a psychological expert, summarizes the extensive empirical evidence used by the Commission and others to support the decision in favor of an undifferentiated nine-year comprehensive school.

Erickson, H. "Adult Education and Swedish Political Leadership." *International Review of Education*, Vol. 12, No. 2, 1966, pp. 129–143. Describes the formative and compensatory role of adult education vis à vis inadequate primary and secondary schooling before comprehensive school reforms equalized and extended educational opportunity, especially in rural areas.

Grundskolan och näringslivet. Stockholm: Studieförbundet Näringsliv och Samhället, 1961. 91 pp.

Reviews a detailed study of interrelationships between the comprehensive school and the national economy. Conducted by a private, industry supported research group, the study exemplifies the close planning and co-operation between politicians, educators and economists that has led to *grundskolan's* successful implementation.

Haldén, Folke. "Swedish Industry and the School Reforms." *The Anglo-Swedish Review,* November 1963, pp. 9–12.

The writer, Chief of Training for the Swedish Employers' Confederation, expects the comprehensive school to benefit industry through a broadening of recruitment to secondary education. "The great problem of the Swedish economy today is the shortage of manpower. The present education policy is expected to meet the demand for more skill and higher education, while the demand for numbers will have to be met by further mechanization and automation. Thus the reform seems to be closely linked to contemporary economic developments."

Härnqvist, Kjell. "Recent Educational Research in Connection with the Swedish School Reform." *International Review of Education,* Vol. 7, No. 1, 1961, pp. 85–90.

Evaluates a selection of curriculum and grouping studies conducted during the 1950–1960 decade of educational experimentation. Concludes that "research studies like those reported here cannot be directly translated in terms of school organization." Rather, they should "suggest new approaches" and "challenge some prevailing conceptions."

Helén, Gunnar (ed.). *Sju år av skolreformer.* Stockholm: Studieförbundet Näringsliv och Samhället, 1957. 144 pp.

The editor, a leader in the Liberal party and school reform, has here assembled material describing the period of exprimentation from 1949 to 1956, the first seven years of selected partial implementation. Special attention is devoted to problems of vocational training. An excellent bibliography of Swedish works on all aspects of the reform is included.

Henrysson, Sten. "Equalization of School Marks in Sweden." *College Board Review,* No. 52, Winter 1964, pp. 21–23.

Explains the Swedish practice stimulated by school reorganization to establish uniformity of marking through the use of standardized tests for national achievement and marking norms.

Henrysson, Sten. "Swedish System for Equalizing Marks." *Educational Research,* No. 6, February 1964, pp. 156–160.

Explains the new rationale for evaluating student performance in the comprehensive school, which stresses social over academic learning and at the same time streams students for differentiated postsecondary study.

Hermansson, Ester. "Swedish Education During the 1940's." *The Harvard Educational Review,* Vol. 21, No. 4, Fall 1951, pp. 233–242.

Discusses dysfunctional aspects of primary and secondary education in post-World War II Sweden. Emphasizes focal role of politicians to initiate reform, establish goals, and direct research.

Hildeman, Nils-Gustav. "Democratic Teamwork or Intellectual Elite?" *The American Swedish Monthly,* April 1965, pp. 12–14.

The writer, Cultural Attaché at the Swedish Embassy in Washington, observes that although the principle of "late streaming" is now law, the current reforms are "not a final definite action which will establish a permanent unchangeable system for decades to come." Rather, changing social and technological demands will necessitate a constant remoulding of education through partial reforms.

Holmberg, Börje. "Correspondence Instruction and the Use of Self-Instructional Media in Schools." *Comparative Education* (Oxford), Vol. 3, No. 3, June 1967, pp. 225–230.

Describes development of self-instructional media in Sweden "to make it equally possible for the son or daughter of a poor family in the forests north of the Arctic Circle as for the child of a Stockholm businessman or civil servant to get the type of schooling that prepares him or her for a university career." See the author's earlier work on supplementary correspondence education in *The Parents' Review*, No. 5, 1959.

Huntford, Roland. "Education in the Outback." *Industrial International*, 1964, pp. 117 ff.

Examines the variety of problems encountered in implementing the new nine-year comprehensive school in vast and sparsely settled northern Sweden. Discusses the need for educational and occupational opportunities in rural areas as a corrective for excessive internal migration. Cites impressive evidence of the government's efforts to provide equal educational facilities for all Swedish students.

Husén, Torsten. "Case Study in Policy-Oriented Research: The Swedish School Reforms." *The School Review*, Vol. 73, Autumn 1965, pp. 206–225.

Emphasizes central role of applied educational research in directed educational change, and the leading position that Sweden has come to occupy in this activity. Bibliography.

Husén, Torsten. "Current Trends in Swedish Teacher-Training." *International Review of Education*, Vol. 10, No. 2, 1964, pp. 206–211.

Analyzes the impact of new comprehensive school teacher requirements on Sweden's traditional teacher training system and its resulting reorganization. Explains why subject and higher-form teachers strongly opposed the nine-year comprehensive school at the expense of selective schools. Suggests a redefinition of the teacher's social role from one of merely transmitting knowledge to one of educator, counsellor and youth leader.

Husén, Torsten. "Curriculum Research in Sweden." *International Review of Education*, Vol. 11, No. 2, 1965, pp. 189–208.

Presents a detailed and well-illustrated account of the use of empirical techniques in developing new curricula necessitated by the change from selective to elective secondary education.

Husén, Torsten. "Detection of Ability and Selection for Educational Purposes in Sweden." *Year Book of Education 1962: The Gifted Child*

(George Z. F. Bereday and Joseph A. Lauwerys, eds.), pp. 295–314. New York: Harcourt, Brace & World, Inc., 1962.

A thorough review of Swedish educational research on problems of identification of talent, development of intellectual potential, and efficiency of talent utilizatio.. Findings are summarized as follows: (1) early selection into separate schools is not mutually beneficial for bright and less able students; (2) results from the fifth up to the eighth year indicate it matters little if bright pupils are in a comprehensive or selective milieu; (3) less able students gain more in an undifferentiated milieu "where the whole range of interests and abilities are represented."

Husén, Torsten. "Educational Change in Sweden." *Comparative Education*, Vol. 1, No. 3, June 1965, pp. 181–191.

Describes sequence of educational reform before and after 1950 and the final comprehensive school pattern legislated by Parliament in 1962.

Husén, Torsten. "Educational Structure and the Development of Ability." *Ability and Educational Opportunity, 1961* (A. H. Halsey, ed.), pp. 113–134. Paris: O.E.C.D.

A paper presented at the conference organized by the Office of Scientific and Technical Personnel in collaboration with the Swedish Ministry of Education at Kungälv, Sweden, June 11–16, 1961. Examines the arguments for and against selective and comprehensive school systems using the example•of Sweden. Concludes that comparison must take into account wastage rates and needs for highly trained second-level personnel.

Husén, Torsten. "Loss of Talent in Selective School Systems: The Case of Sweden." *Comparative Education Reveiw*, Vol. 4, No. 2, October 1960, pp. 70–74.

Evaluates the relative influence of ability, status and social class background for success in the selective lower secondary *realskola*. Finds such systems are accompanied by high failure rates and loss of talent. Concludes that high wastage rates in selective systems must be questioned in terms of modern social and educational needs.

Husén, Torsten. *Problems of Differentiation in Swedish Compulsory Schooling*. Stockholm: Svenska Bokförlaget, 1962. 64 pp.

Traces discussion of the differentiation problem during the 1940's and 1950's and evaluates its influence on the Comprehensive School Act of 1950. The social, psychological, and educational arguments in favor of an early and a late "creaming off" of academically talented children are reviewed and appraised.

Husén, Torsten. "School Reform in Sweden: A Liberal Democracy Adopts the Comprehensive School System." *Phi Delta Kappan*, Vol. 53, No. 2, November, 1961, pp. 86–91.

Discusses the ideological, political and pedagogical motives behind Sweden's "planned and controlled shift from the European-type dual system of schools, representing old class divisions, to the comprehensive, class-less public school, so characteristic of the United States." Summarizes proposals of the 1950 and 1957 committee reports.

Husén, Torsten. "Social Determinants of the Comprehensive School." *Comparative Education Research and the Determinants of Educational Policy* (Proceedings of the Comparative Education Society in Europe), pp. 71–86. Amsterdam: The Society, 1963.

Examines the sequence or "rank order" of educational reform in Sweden: (1) establishment of the welfare state; (2) political initiative and parliamentary legislation; and (3) new curricula and the reform of teacher training. The writer stresses that school reform, like all other social reforms, ultimately rests on political evaluations.

Husén, Torsten. "The Educational Explosion in Sweden." *The World Yearbook in Education 1965: The Education Explosion* (George Z. F. Bereday and Joseph A. Lauwerys, eds.), pp. 297–301. London: Evans Brothers.

Explains increased demand for education in Sweden as a consequence of rapid social change and expansion of educational opportunity. Questions ability of current educational planning techniques to forecast properly future demand for secondary and university places, and for teacher requirements.

Husén, Torsten. *The Role of Educational Research and Planning in Connection with the Swedish School Reform.* Berlin: Deutsche Stiftung für Entwicklungsländer, 1963. 19 pp. Processed.

The author describes the research needs and consequent development of research facilities and skills that followed Parliament's 1950 decision to implement a nine-year common school on an experimental basis during the 1950's.

Husén, Torsten; Dahllöf, Urban; and Bromsjö, B. "Curriculum Research in Sweden." *Educational Research*, Vol. 7, No. 3, June 1965, pp. 165–185.

The writers analyze findings from a series of curriculum research and design studies. The problem—to coordinate curriculum in the comprehensive school with upper secondary *gymnasia* and continuation schools—is organized in four parts: (1) appraisal of the empirical approach; (2) mathematics and communication skills; (3) social studies; and (4) curriculum needs of the *gymnasium* and pre-university education.

Husén, Torsten, and Henrysson, Sten (eds.). *Differentiation and Guidance in the Comprehensive School: Report on the Sigtuna Course, 1958.* Stockholm: Almqvist & Wiksell, 1959. 196 pp.

Report of the course organized by the Swedish government under the auspices of the Council of Europe at Sigtuna, Sweden, in August 1958. Theoretical and practical aspects of the Swedish reform experience are compared with (1) more general problems of secondary education in modern European society; (2) psychological foundation for differentiation; and (3) guidance and counselling as related to various school systems.

Reports from group discussions agree only on the fact that "it is impossible to state in a definite way the age at which organizational differentiation should take place."

Husén, Torsten, and Svensson, Nils-Eric. "Educational Research in Countries Other than the United States: Sweden." *Review of Educational Research,* Vol. 32, No. 3, June 1962, pp. 327–331.

Categorizes and examines Swedish activities in educational research after 1956 in four problem areas: differentiation; content of curriculum and methods of instruction; achievement testing and marking practices; and teacher selection and training. A bibliography of works in Swedish and English is included.

Husén, Torsten, and Svensson, Nils-Eric. "Pedagogic Milieu and Development of Intellectual Skills." *The School Review,* Vol. 68, No. 1, Spring 1960, pp. 36–51.

Reviews the authors' research on achievement in relation to grouping and social background. A tentative conclusion offered is that "children from the culturally less privileged homes respond most strongly to selective academic-type teaching. Children from homes of higher status apparently are receiving full intellectual stimulation outside the school."

Johnson, Roy. " 'Middle Way' Education." *The American-Scandinavian Review,* Spring 1964, pp. 39–48.

Contrasts differences in comprehensive school origins and functions in Sweden and the United States. Points out that subject teachers fear loss of status and "that the social development of the child will replace the concept of basic education in the skills."

Kerr, Anthony. *Schools of Europe.* Westminster: The Canterbury Press, 1961. Pp. 33–41, 248–250.

Provides selected factual data on old and new Swedish school-types in a period of transition. Also includes a description of basic aims and problems in establishing the comprehensive and continuation schools.

King, Margaret L., and Male, George A. *Sweden: Educational Data.* U.S. Office of Education (OE 14034–78), Washington, D. C.: Government Printing Office, 1965. 35 pp.

Presents a useful compendium of basic descriptive and statistical data on the Swedish public school system.

Koerner, James D. "Swedish Education: Paradise for Planners." *Saturday Review,* July 16, 1966, pp. 59–61, 69–71.

A popular presentation of Swedish national educational planning during the 1960's. Underscores the social and political rationale for the creation of a unified school system, and the unique conditions in Sweden facilitating rapid and thoroughgoing educational change. Other reform-minded nations should view the successful Swedish reforms in "the context of Swedish culture and society."

Kutschinsky, Berl. "Law and Education: Some Aspects of Scandinavian Studies into 'The General Sense of Justice.'" *Acta Sociologica,* Vol. 10, 1966, pp. 21–41.

Presents a detailed examination of how popular attitudes toward public education have changed in Scandinavia, and of how group consensus has been brought to bear in bringing about educational change through legal means.

Landquist, John. "Sweden's Educational System." *Scandinavia Past and Present,* Vol. 3. Copenhagen: Arnkrone, 1959.

Chapter 23 provides a historical survey of Swedish education from the medieval period to the sweeping reforms of the 1950's.

Lindegren, Alina Marie. *Education in Sweden.* Washington: Federal Security Agency, Office of Education. Bulletin, 1952, No. 17. 90 pp.

A descriptive account of the Swedish educational system during the period of widespread experimentation with the comprehensive school. A bibliography of sources in English on Swedish education is included.

Malmquist, E. "Recent Developments in Reading in Sweden." *Conference on Reading, University of Chicago,* Vol. 27, 1965, pp. 102–111.

Relates reading achievement gains and problems to various functional changes introduced with the nationwide implementation of *grundskolan* in the 1960's.

Marklund, Sixten. "Educational Reform and Research in Sweden." *Educational Research,* Vol. 9, November 1966, pp. 16–21.

Describes the growth of applied educational research and the important role it has come to play in the formulation and implementation of Swedish educational change. Discusses related problems and future plans.

Marklund, Sixten. "Scholastic Attainments as Related to Size and Homogeneity of Classes." *Educational Research,* November 1963, pp. 63–67.

Presents data that support the egalitarian organization and aims of the comprehensive school in contrast to earlier highly selective and discriminatory compulsory schools.

Marklund, Sixten. "The Attitudes of Intending Teachers to School Reform in Sweden." *The Yearbook of Education 1963: The Education and Training of Teachers* (George Z. F. Bereday and Joseph A. Lauwerys, eds.), pp. 432–442. New York: Harcourt, Brace and World, Inc., 1963.

Reports on a study carried out at Swedish teacher training establishments in 1959. Finds that higher-form teachers are "decidedly more negative to the reform than those in the intermediate grades" and that graduates from schools of education are more favorably disposed toward the reform than are university graduates. Concludes that a strong positive correlation exists between high information level and positive attitudes, and that the school reform has essentially "proved to be a teacher problem."

McCreary, Anne Phillips. "The Swedish School Reform Observed by a Foreigner." *International Review of Education,* Vol. 9, No. 1, 1963–64, pp. 82–89.

Compares theory as legislated by Parliament in 1962 with practice in the comprehensive school and finds numerous shortcomings: (1) pupil-centered instruction has not replaced teacher-centered instruction; (2) desired social skills of group interaction, cooperation, and ability to adapt rapidly are not suitably cultivated: (3) study skills, objective evaluation and critical thinking are inhibited by authoritarian attitudes in instruction and society; and (4) "the desire for equality has led to a uniformity at the cost of creativity and imagination."

Moberg, Sven. "Sweden." *The Planning of Education in Relation to Economic Growth* (O.E.C.D. Policy Conference on Economic Growth and Investment in Education, Washington, October 16–20, 1961), pp. 33–40.

A succinct account of theory and practice in Swedish educational planning. Problems of content, organizing, and relating educational planning to economic planning are summarized. Moberg concludes that economic planning cannot be sufficiently long-term to give the ideal basis for educational planning. "The obvious corollary is that educational planning in Sweden must aim at making the educational system as flexible and adaptable as possible."

National Board of Education. *The New School in Sweden: Aims, Organization, Methods.* Stockholm: The Board, 1962. 47 pp.

An explanation of the government's 1962 decision and plan for *grundskolan*. Written for a popular audience, the pamphlet nevertheless provides an excellent general introduction to aims, organization, curriculum, and numerous other aspects of the new compulsory school.

"New Rules Suggested for Swedish Research Studies." *Sverige-Nytt.* Vol. 20, No. 1, January 3, 1967, p. 7.

Reports committee findings on current problems in Swedish graduate education. Recommends a shorter (i.e., four-year) doctoral program, a state salary for all candidates, more guidance, and a streamlining of doctoral programs.

Nordland, Eva. *Verdier i gammel og ny skole; fra debatten om reform i skolen o svenske aviser, 1920–1956.* Oslo: Aschehough, 1958. 132 pp.

An historical investigation of controversy and public debate accompanying attempts since 1920 to eliminate problems of parallelism between the *folkskola* and the *realskola*. Concludes chief anti-reform groups were conservatives, academicians, and higher form teachers.

Norinder, Yngve. "The Evolving Comprehensive School in Sweden." *International Review of Education,* Vol. 3, No. 3, 1957, pp. 257–271.

A descriptive survey of research, legislation, organization, and problems of guidance and teacher training during the experimental implementation of the comprehensive school. The writer is Director and Coordinator of Research and Experimentation at the Royal Board of Education in Stockholm.

Ögren, Gustaf. "Die schwedische Schulreform: Thema einer Studienwoche in Hamburg." *International Review of Education,* Vol. 11, No. 1, 1965, pp. 112–115.

A report on the international meeting in Hamburg, October 1964, devoted to foundations, problems, and relevance of the Swedish comprehensive school experience.

Organization for Economic Cooperation and Development. *La Politique et la planification de l'enseignement: Suède.* Paris: The Organization, 1967. 397 pp.

Presents a detailed survey of the present Swedish educational system (*l'école globale; secondaire; supérieure; des adultes*). Describes the economic planning innovation and rationalization aspects of the system. Three appendices, 110 figures and diagrams, and an introductory chapter by Sven Moberg are included.

Orring, Jonas. *Comprehensive School and Continuation Schools in Sweden: A Summary of the Principal Recommendations of the 1957 School Commission.* Albert Reed, trans. Stockholm: Kungl. Ecklesiastikdepartementet, 1962. 154 pp.

Summarizes essential points recommended by the 1957 School Commission on external and internal organization of the nine-year school. Also contains recommendations concerning *fackskolor,* the two-year continuation schools linked with comprehensive schools.

Orring, Jonas. *Die schwedische Schulreform.* Stockholm: The Royal Board of Education, 1959. 15 pp.

Provides an official description of administration, structure, and functions of the comprehensive school as of 1958.

Orring, Jonas. *The School System of General Education in Sweden.* Stockholm: The Swedish Institute, 1964. 14 pp.

Describes the socio-economic and pedagogical reasons for emphasis on general education in comprehensive and continuation schools. Contains a section on new regulations governing electives, streaming, and foreign language instruction in *grundskolan.*

Ostlund, Leonard A. "Recent Developments in Swedish Education." *School and Society,* Vol. 83, No. 2084, April 28, 1956, pp. 149–151.

A brief report on changes following the reorientation of a traditional, curriculum-centered philosophy of teaching to a student-centered one that "stresses actualization of individual potential in an educational milieu that strives to balance individual initiative with group experiences."

Paulston, Rolland G. "Educación secundaria para todos: un modelo de Europa." *Nueva Educación,* Vol. 40, No. 197, March 1967, pp. 17–22.

Examines relevance of the progressive unification of Swedish schooling to general problems of educational and socio-economic change in Europe and in Latin America.

Paulston, Rolland G. *Educational Change in Sweden: Planning and Accepting the Comprehensive School Reforms.* New York: Teachers College Press, Teachers College, Columbia University, 1968.

Provides a detailed historical study of the century-long movement in Sweden to unify compulsory schooling. Identifies forces and factors supporting and opposing the Swedish educational revolution, especially after the emergence of social democracy in 1932.

Paulston, Rolland G. "Reforma educativa y desarrollo nacional: el ejemplo de Suecia." *Nueva Educación,* Vol. 39, No. 196, December 1966, pp. 25–28.

Presents a short analysis of the four major periods of Swedish comprehensive school reform and nine underlying factors facilitating the movement toward unity in the educational system.

Paulston, Rolland G. Review of *Secondary Education in Sweden: A Survey of Reforms,* by Urban Dahllöf and others, in *Comparative Education Review,* Vol. 11, No. 2, June 1967, pp. 256–258.

Evaluates and relates the Swedish secondary school reforms of 1966 to the earlier *grundskola* reforms and the functional demands of an egalitarian society and a highly rationalized economy. Faults the absence of critical evaluation in the formulation and in the implementation stages of the reform discussed.

Postlethwaite, Neville. Review of *Övergång från textning till vanlig skrivstil,* by Eve Malmquist, in *International Review of Education,* Vol. 11, No. 3, 1965, pp. 372–373.

Favorably reviews the report of a small experimental study carried out in conjunction with the Board of Education's 1962 comprehensive school curriculum.

Ruge, Herman. *Educational Systems in Scandinavia.* Oslo: Norwegian University Press, 1962. 86 pp.

Surveys, in the section on Swedish education, transition in school structure and content. Sees research institutes set up at the universities of Stockholm, Uppsala, Lund and Göteborg as valuable centers for conducting nationwide "scientific pedagogical studies."

"School Reform in Sweden." *Foreign Education Digest,* Vol. 30, No. 1, July–September 1965, pp. 3–6.

Presents factual data on administration, organization, special school services, and research related to *grundskolan.* A digest of material drawn from secondary sources.

Sjöstedt, Carl Erik, and Sjöstrand, Wilhelm. *Skola och undervisning i Sverige och andra länder.* Rev. edition. Stockholm: Natur och Kultur, 1962. 398 pp.

Part one of this comparative education text traces (1) the historical development of Swedish academic, popular, and vocational education; (2) origins and practices in teacher training; and (3) school reform movements up to the 1962 Act.

Sjöstrand, Wilhelm. *För och mot den nya skolan.* Stockholm: Natur och Kultur, 1960. 221 pp.

A collection of critical articles written between 1955 and 1960 by the most outspoken opponent of the comprehensive school and professor of pedagogy at the University of Uppsala. Sjöstrand is concerned that lack of grouping and streaming in the nine-year school will penalize teachers and superior students, and result in lowering academic standards, initiative and discipline. Claims results of empirical studies do not justify elimination of the academic lower secondary school, nor was a satisfactory effort made to modernize this school.

Sjöstrand, Wilhelm. "Recent Trends and Developments in Primary and Secondary Education in Scandinavia." *International Review of Education* Vol. 13, No. 2, 1967, pp. 180–194.

Describes recent "unity school" trends in Sweden, Denmark, Norway, and Finland. Concludes that "the survival or collapse of the reform programme [in Sweden] more or less depends on the solution of this problem" [teacher training reforms].

Sjöstrand, Wilhelm; Pikas, A.; and Rudberg, B. "A Discussion about Authority-Authoritarianism and Equality-Quality as the Two Most Important Aspects of the Aims of Social Education in a Democracy," in J. Sandven and Torild Skard (eds.), *The Role of Educational Research in Social Education* (Papers of the Third International Congress for the University Study of Education), pp. 143–151. Oslo: Scandinavian University Books, 1963. Summary in German.

Reports on the partial results of a research study of children's attitudes toward two different kinds of authority: the "rational" and the "restrictive." Seeks to ascertain if early streaming after the sixth grade of the comprehensive school makes better use of the child's aptitudes—"necessary in a small democratic country"—and is as beneficial in the development of character in so far as the school can develop the foundations laid by the home and other social background.

Statistiska Centralbyrån. *Statistisk årsbok för Sverige.* Vol. 55. Stockholm: The Bureau, 1968.

This yearly publication in both Swedish and English has since 1914 presented summaries and surveys of the economic, social, political, and cultural statistics of Sweden. Very thorough. See especially the chapters on social welfare and education.

Stenhouse, Lawrence. "Comprehensive Education in Norway: A Developing System." *Comparative Education,* Vol. 2, No. 1, November 1965, pp. 37–42.

Presents a survey of the Norwegian comprehensive school reform experience which has been considerably influenced by the neighboring Swedish model. The new comprehensive school in Norway also covers nine years and has a marked egalitarian emphasis: "Parity is the key word . . . town and country, regions, social classes and individual pupils are to be treated equally."

Stenhouse, Lawrence. Review of *Society, Schools and Progress in Scandinavia,* by Willis Dixon, in *Comparative Education* (Oxford), Vol. 2, No. 3, June 1966, pp. 239–240.

The reviewer notes that European educators "are coming to realize that the Scandinavian experience may provide a better comparative base than the American."

Svensson, Nils-Eric. *Ability Grouping and Scholastic Achievement: Report of a Five-year Follow-up Study in Stockholm.* Acta Universitatis Stockholmiensis. Stockholm Studies in Educational Psychology 5. Stockholm: Almqvist & Wiksell, 1962. 236 pp.

This influential dissertation summarizes results of a five-year follow-up study of achievement in undifferentiated comprehensive and selective academic schools. The purpose was to see if any consistent relationship existed between intellectual achievement of pupils and the type of classes they attended. Findings support the argument for late differentiation.

Svensson, Nils-Eric, and Björklund, E. "Educational Research and Development in Sweden: Plans for 1966–67." *Sociology of Education,* Vol. 39, Winter 1966, pp. 86–98.

Stresses the role of research in planning Swedish educational change. Presents examples of educational programs under development and the new institutional structure supporting these activities.

Sveriges Konservativa Studentförbund. *Grundskola: ett alternativ.* Stockholm: Studentförlaget Horisont, 1962. 68 pp.

Published by the Association of Conservative Students prior to the 1962 legislative act on final comprehensive school form, content and methods. The booklet represents constructive opposition from the Swedish Right and makes four proposals: (1) streaming should begin in the seventh year and (2) consist of academic, technical, commercial and social streams that (3) should be adaptable to local conditions and (4) students who elect Swedish, foreign languages, mathematics, physics and chemistry should be grouped by ability and taught by separate methods.

Sweden. Ecklesiastikdepartementet. Statens Offentliga Utredningar (SOU) 1961:30. *Grundskolan. Betänkande avgivet av 1957 års skolberedning VI.* Stockholm, 1961. 881 pp.

Official report of the 1957 School Committee with recommendations for the final organization of the comprehensive school. Proposes a more flexible arrangement for electives and streaming than did the 1950 Commission. Condensed as *Comprehensive School and Continuation Schools in Sweden,* by Jonas Orring.

J Sweden. Social Welfare Board. *Social Sweden.* Stockholm: The Board, 1952.

Chapter 12 (pp. 349–389) explains the unification of elementary and secondary education into a common compulsory comprehensive school as the outgrowth of social, political and pedagogical pressures. The work in its entirety describes the background of social reform in which the comprehensive school reform was formulated and legislated.

The Industrial Council for Social and Economic Studies. *Mathematics and Communication Skills in School and Society* by Torsten Husén and Urban Dahllöf. Stockholm: The Council, 1960. 35 pp.

Report of an investigation carried out by the Stockholm Teachers College for the Council. Object of the study was to explore new approaches to designing curriculum and evaluating teaching methods. The writers' approach to curriculum development is sociological and attempts to determine "What qualifications in mathematics and the communication skills are required by a specific occupation?"

The Intellectual Face of Sweden. Special issue of *Ergo International.* Uppsala, Sweden: Uppsala Student Union, 1964. 150 pp.

This excellent survey of an emerging "educational society" provides an informative account of problems and progress in on-going reorganization at all levels of the Swedish educational system. A rich source for works on the historical, political and sociological background of educational change.

The Swedish Institute. "A General Survey of the Swedish School System and Higher Education in Sweden." Stockholm, 1963. 46 pp. (Mimeographed.)

A factual description of Swedish educational organization in the postwar decades and the impact of prolonged and altered secondary education on higher education. Contains a bibliography of works in Swedish.

Tomasson, R. F. "From Elitism to Egalitarianism in Swedish Education." *Sociology of Education,* Vol. 38, Spring 1965, pp. 203–223.

An examination of the interrelationships between social, political, and economic forces in shaping Swedish school reform policy. Attributes the new egalitarian orientation in education to the durability of Social-Democratic rule, the need for ideological congruence between social and educational philosophy, and a well established and prosperous social democracy. Includes an interesting discussion on the influence of the Swedish comprehensive school model in Norway and Denmark.

Tomasson, R. F. "Some Observations on Higher Education in Sweden." *Journal of Higher Education,* Vol. 37, December 1966, pp. 493–501.

Evaluates the comprehensive school reform and describes its implications for the ensuing reforms of secondary and higher education now in progress. Perceptive analysis.

UNESCO. *International Guide to Educational Documentation, 1955–1960.* Geneva: UNESCO, 1963.

Provides an annotated bibliography (pp. 378–387) on the following aspects of Swedish education: (1) reference works; (2) legislative and policy documentation; (3) administration; (4) structure and administration; (5) educational studies and research; (6) textbooks and instructional materials; and (7) educational associations, journals, statistics, biography, and libraries. The final section explains interavailability of educational resources. A very helpful reference source.

UNESCO. *World Survey of Education II: Primary Education.* Paris: UNESCO, 1958.

The section on Swedish primary education (pp. 936–948) describes *inter alia* new developments in policy, administration, control, finance, curriculum, and methods brought about by the change-over from 'selective to comprehensive schools.

UNESCO. *World Survey of Education III: Secondary Education.* Paris: UNESCO, 1961.

The section on Sweden (pp. 1039–1053) contains a description of aims, curricula, and organization of the comprehensive school's upper stage. A glossary of Swedish educational terms, a summary of school statistics, and a bibliography are included.

U.S. Office of Education. Division of International Education. *School Reform in Sweden.* By Torsten Husén. Washington: U.S. Department of Health, Education and Welfare, 1961. 45 pp.

Gives an historical summary of the growth of parallelism in Swedish schooling and reforms proposed in nineteenth and twentieth centuries to remedy the problem. Includes an extensive bibliography of Swedish and English sources.

Wallberg, K., and Cassel, P-G. *Demand for Higher Secondary School (Gymnasium) Education in Sweden.* Paris: Organization for Economic Cooperation and Development, November 22, 1963. 41 pp.; tables, figures. Processed.

Presents a study of factors influencing intensified demand for *gymnasium* studies in Sweden. Stresses importance of structural reforms at the presecondary level in this development as well as other factors. Discusses a theoretical basis for predicting future needs for educational facilities at the postprimary level.

Wiskari, Werner. "Swedish Students Help Run Schools." *The New York Times,* January 12, 1968.

Describes the rationale of the Swedish School Board's decision to grant secondary school students the right to participate directly in the administration of their schools: ". . . training in democracy is not possible merely through lectures. It must be made a part of the pedagogical process." Students are active in two areas of administration: (1) in disciplinary measures, where two representatives each of the students and the teachers join with the school principal and a member of the school board to settle all discipline problems; and (2) in curriculum planning, where student representatives participate and express their opinions but have no vote. Swedish university students have had the right for at least 25 years to help decide on the kinds of courses to be offered.

POPULATION DISTRIBUTION IN SWEDEN IN 1950

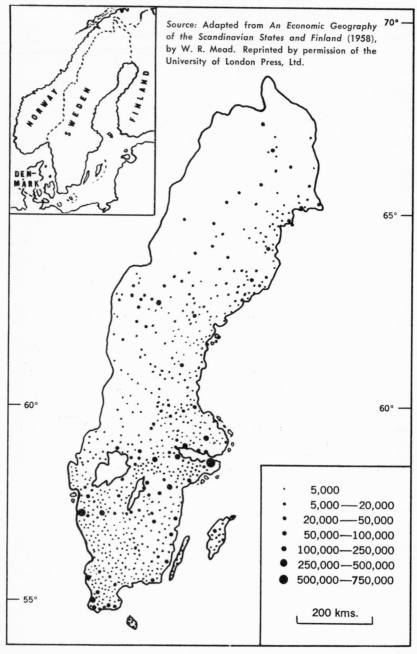

Source: Adapted from *An Economic Geography of the Scandinavian States and Finland* (1958), by W. R. Mead. Reprinted by permission of the University of London Press, Ltd.

. 5,000
. 5,000—20,000
. 20,000—50,000
. 50,000—100,000
. 100,000—250,000
. 250,000—500,000
. 500,000—750,000

200 kms.

POLITICAL PARTY STRENGTHS IN THE FIRST AND SECOND CHAMBERS OF THE RIKSDAG, 1905–1952 [a]

	Conservative	Liberal	Farmers Assn.	Social Democrat	Left Soc. Dem.	Communist	Other
			First Chamber:				
1908	130 [b]	15		2			
1912	85	51		12			2
1915	89	47		14			
1918	88	45		16	1		
1921	37	40	19	50	4		
1922	41	38	18	51	1	1	
1925	44	35	18	52		1	
1929	49	31	17	52		1	
1933	50	23	18	58		1	
1937	45	16	22	66			1
1941	35	15	24	75		1	
1945	30	14	21	83		2	
1947	26	14	21	86		3	
1949	23	18	21	84		3	1
			Second Chamber:				
1905	90	106		13			
1908	98	98		34			
1911	64	102		64			
1914	86	70		74			
1915	86	57		87			
1917	57	62	14	86	11		
1920	72	46	30	75	7		
1921	62	41	21	93	6	7	
1924	65	33	23	104		5	
1928	73	32	27	90		8	
1932	58	24	36	104		2	6 [c]
1936	44	27	36	112		5	6 [c]
1940	42	23	28	134		3	
1944	39	26	35	115		15	
1948	23	57	30	112		8	
1952	30	59	27	109		5	

Note: Figures are not available for the years before 1905. Elections are held in the autumn of the year preceding the meeting of a new Parliament, and, until the 1918–21 reform, were held triennially.

[a] *Source:* Adapted from Douglas Verney, *Parliamentary Reform in Sweden, 1866–1921*, p. 246. By permission of the Clarendon Press, Oxford.

[b] Approximate.

[c] Independent Socialist.

APPENDIX D

THE SWEDISH SCHOOL SYSTEM IN 1940 AND PROPOSALS OF THE 1940 SCHOOL COMMITTEE FOR STRUCTURAL CHANGES

School Year					Age
10	Vocational and higher *folkskola*				16
9		Higher *folkskola*	Academic *realskola*		15
8	Continuation school				14
7				Academic *realskola*	13
6					12
5					11
4	*FOLKSKOLA*				10
3					9
2					8
1					7

1. The School System in 1940

180

School Year		Age
10	Vocational and practical *realskola* (higher division)	16
9		15
8	Higher *folkskola* — Academic and technical *realskola*	14
7		13
6	Practical *realskola* with possibility for differentiated instruction	12
5		11
4	FOLKSKOLA	10
3		9
2		8
1		7

2. Reorganization Proposed by the Secondary School Group

School Year		Age
10	Vocational and practical *realskola* (higher division)	16
9	Vocational *folkskola* — Academic *realskola*	15
8	Practical *realskola*	14
7		13
6	FOLKSKOLA	12
5		11
4		10
3		9
2		8
1		7

3. Reorganization Proposed by the *Folkskola* Group

APPENDIX E

EMIGRATION FROM SWEDEN, 1851–1926

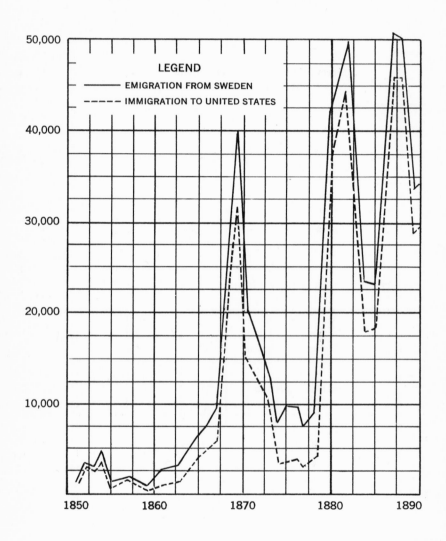

Source: Reprinted from *The Background of Swedish Immigration, 1840–1930* (Social Service Monographs, No. Fifteen), by Florence E. Janson, by permission of The University of Chicago Press. Copyright 1931 by The University of Chicago.

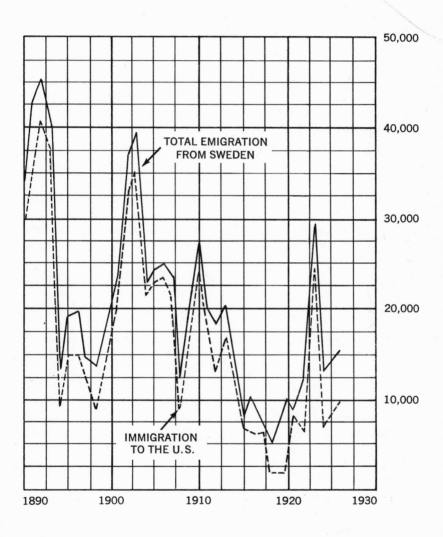

183

GLOSSARY

GENERAL AND TECHNICAL TERMS

allmänbildande. Providing general education.

arbetsskolan. Activity school (from the German *Arbeitsschule*).

bottenskola. Basic elementary school common to all children.

enhetsskola. Comprehensive foundation school for all children in a given area (literally, unity school). See also *bottenskola, grundskola.*

fattigskolor. Charity schools for children of the poor. Gradually replaced by *folkskolor* after 1842.

folkhemmet. The people's home (i.e., a democratic nation with equality of opportunity for all). Chief slogan for the welfare state of the Social Democratic Party.

folkhögskolor. The people's high schools (public and private boarding schools providing continuing general education with no set curriculum, usually in a one-year course; founded for the common people in the nineteenth century and typical for Scandinavia).

folkrörelser. Folk (popular) movements (e.g., cooperatives, nonconformist churches, temperance organizations, labor movement). Adult education in Sweden is administered mainly by the folk movements.

folkskola. State elementary school (six or more years), until the 1920's generally for the lower social classes. Founded in 1842; being replaced by *grundskolan* after 1950.

grundskola. Basic or foundation school; the final name of the nine-year comprehensive school legislated in 1950. See also *bottenskola, enhetsskola.*

gymnasium. The three- or four-year higher secondary school that prepares for university studies.

husförhör. Examinations in the Scriptures, administered in private homes by parish clergy before 1842.

kommunala mellanskolorna. Municipal middle or lower secondary academic schools, parallel to the *realskola*; being replaced by the *grundskola* after 1950.

lektor. Teacher (often, head teacher) in an upper secondary school (*gymnasium*).

184

lyceum. The seven-year combined secondary school proposed in the 1918 School Commission report.

lärare. Teacher.

lärarutbildning. Teacher education, teacher training.

lärda. The learned (i.e., the educated).

läroverk. From the beginning: any educational institution. Specifically, since 1904: a secondary academic school combining the *realskola* and the *gymnasium*.

medborgerlighetskola. Citizenship school.

ny skola. New school.

praktiska ungdomsskolor. Vocational schools.

prästskolor. Academic schools taught by the clergy to prepare for the professions.

realexamen. The lower secondary school-leaving examination that qualified for the three-year *gymnasium*.

realskola. Lower secondary school that prepares for the *gymnasium*. Being replaced by *grundskolan* after 1950.

remiss. Evaluation of work of government committees.

riksdag. Parliament.

skolväsendet. The general educational system.

småskola. Primary school (first two grades, now the first three grades).

studentexamen. The *gymnasium*-leaving examination that until 1968 qualified for university entrance.

studiecirklar. Study circles (i.e., informal discussion or study groups, for adult education).

ståndscirkulation. Social mobility.

universitet och högskolor. Institutions of higher education.

yrkesundervisning. Vocational education.

ORGANIZATIONS

Arbetarnas bildningsforbund (ABF). Workers Educational Association.

Arbetssmarknadsstyrelsen. The Labor Market Board.

Bondeförbundet. The Agrarian Party; Farmers Party; recently changed its name to *Centerpartiet*.

Centerpartiet. See *Bondeförbundet*.

Ecklesiastikdepartementet. The Ministry of Education and Ecclesiastical Affairs; since 1967 called *Utbildningsdepartementet*.

Folkpartiet. The Liberal Party (literally, Folk Party, People's Party).

Föreningen for svensk undervisningshistoria. The Association for the Study of the History of Swedish Education.

Högerpartiet. The Conservative Party (literally, The Party of the Right).

Kommerskollegium. The Board of Trade.

Konjunkturinstitutet. The National Institute for the Study of Economic Trends.

Landsorganisationen (LO). The Central Federation of Trade Unions.

Skolöverstyrelsen. The National Boaard of Education. (An agency under the Ministry of Education.)

Socialdemokratiska partistyrelsen. The Social Democratic Party Central Committee.

Socialdemokratiska ungdomsförbundet. The Social Democratic Youth Association.

Socialstyrelsen. The Social Welfare Board.

Statens offentliga utredningar (SOU). Official Reports by Government Committees.

Statistiska centralbyrån. The Central Bureau of Statistics.

Sveriges allmänna folkskollärarförening (SAF). The Elementary School Teachers Association.

Sveriges folkskollärarförbundet (SFF). The Elementary School Teachers Association.

Sveriges socialdemokratiska arbetarepartiet. The Swedish Social Democratic Party; also called Labor Party or Social Democratic Labor Party.

INDEX

Academic education, vi, 10, 11, 14, 17, 18, 27, 29, 32, 34, 40, 42, 44, 56, 62, 71, 73, 78, 79, 81, 84, 91, 97, 100, 105, 110, 113, 117, 121, 122, 123, 132, 139, 144, 146. *See also* Education Acts
Academy, Royal, 26
Achievement, 80–1, 112, 117
Activity method, 17, 29, 43, 55, 100, 115, 122, 123
Adeler, Gösta, 124
Adult education: *see* Worker education
Agardh, K. A., 16, 17, 18, 21, 30, 111
Agrarian party (Agrarians), 7, 8, 31, 50, 52, 54, 59, 64, 67, 71, 95, 96, 98, 128, 130, 135, 140
Agriculture, 5, 7, 8, 9, 13, 14, 20, 24, 39, 40–1, 47, 89, 97, 129
Aliens, 5
Alm, Harald, 124
Almqvist, N. J. F., 51, 54, 55
Ambulatory school: *see* Mobile school
Anderberg, G. A. R., 85
Andrén, Georg, 139
Andrews, C. C., 25
"Apologist" school; *see* Town school
Aptitudes, 84, 85, 112, 117, 122. *See also* Psychology
Arvidson, Stellan, 89, 90, 109, 110, 117, 118, 120, 124, 125, 141

Bagge, Gösta, 78, 79, 87, 95, 135
Barnard, Henry, 30
Bell–Lancaster system, 19
Bengtsson, Frans, 84–5
Berg, Anders, 31

Berg, Fridtjuv, vi, 12, 27, 31–4, 39, 42, 61, 69, 94, 99, 111
Bergqvist, B. J., 40–1, 46, 56
Berlin, Isaiah, 3
Biology, "race," 85
Birth rate, declining, 64–6, 69, 90; rising, 107, 125
Board of Education, National (formerly, "Royal"), v, 7, 40, 54, 71, 118, 122, 134, 140
Bottenskola; see Comprehensive school; Elementary education
Branting, Hjalmar, 47, 66, 131, 136
Budget: school, 19, 22, 25–6, 54–5, 64, 74, 134–35; social welfare, 6, 71, 106. *See also* Welfare state
Bureaucracy, 7, 14, 15, 19, 45, 129, 143
Burghers, 5, 14, 15, 32, 33, 52–3, 67, 98, 143, 144, 146

Capitalist culture, 6, 106, 128. *See also* Public ownership
Carlson, F. F., 23, 26
Central Federation of Trade Unions, 119
Charity schools, 18, 20, 23, 25, 30, 33
Children: aid to, 63, 65, 67–8, 70, 106 (*see also* Social benefits); rural, 55, 67, 70, 71–2, 75, 89, 135 (*see also* Peasant); working, 19, 41, 62, 63, 73, 86, 89 (*see also* Working class)
Christian socialism, 19
Chronology, 3, 4–5
Church: dissenting, 5, 129, 130; state Lutheran, 5, 15, 16, 19, 21–2,

187